Strange MICHIGAN

MORE Wolverine Weirdness

by Linda S. Godfrey
and Lisa A. Shiel

TRAILS BOOKS
Madison, Wisconsin

D0763264

Library of Congress Control Number: 2008933094
ISBN 13: 978-1-931599-84-9

Editor: Mark Knickelbine
Designer: Cheryl Smallwood Roberts

Printed in China.
13 12 11 10 09 08   6 5 4 3 2 1

Trails Books, a division of Big Earth Publishing
923 Williamson Street • Madison, WI 53703
(800) 258-5830 • www.trailsbooks.com

Evergreen Cemetery, Ontonagon

Dedication

To all who have seen the Michigan Dogman, Bigfoot, Pressie or
other unknown creatures or phenomena and somehow gathered
the courage to come forward and give us their accounts.
It is to them that we owe our legends.

—Linda S. Godfrey and Lisa A. Shiel

Fire hydrant, Ironwood

Table of Contents

Yooper Tourist Trap, Ishpeming

Nunica cemetery

Acknowledgments

Our deepest appreciation goes to the many folks who helped make *Strange Michigan* a reality. First on the list are the great mass of good-humored people who allowed us to interview them, contributed stories and art, or shared personal experiences. Special thanks to Michigan MUFON; Linda Last and the Northville Historical Society, Dorsch Memorial Library, Monroe; Rosemary Oliver at the Comstock Township Library; Dawn Triplett and the Kalkaska Genealogical Society; Ralph Haugen; Nick Redfern; Stephen Wiggins; Bill Konkolesky; and Bill Kingsley; John Hogan of the *Grand Rapids Press*; Jarrod Showers; Susan Blum; Amy Williamson; Justin Wendzel; Rick Griswold; Bobby Glenn Brown; Maryanne of the UP Paranormal Society; University of Michigan Special Collections, and the generous ladies at the Marquette Area Chamber of Commerce.

Personal debts of gratitude are owed to the Media Maven's Breakfast Association, Steven Godfrey, Grendel the Lhasa apso for being a patient pup, the folks at Unknown Creature Spot for excellent reports and feedback, Walt and Kerry Shiel, Suzy and Tom Zuro, and Tyler Tichelaar.

Introduction

A giant white rabbit inhabiting Michigan woods, maverick artists, ancient earthworks, the Dogman, blue rain, spook lights, bat-eating lumberjacks, fairy rings and, naturally, Bigfoot…all of these things and more are why Strange Michigan had to be written. There is simply too much going on in the Wolverine State that would otherwise slip by the day-to-day consciousness of the ordinary citizen. And the strange tableau that makes Michigan unique deserves preservation alongside the more mundane texts cramming our bookstore and library shelves.

First, of course, there was Linda Godfrey's *Weird Michigan*, published by Barnes & Noble in 2006. Because of space limitations, much was left out of that book that still needed to see the light—or twilight—of day. Besides, the stories and weird things just kept coming. People were determined to share their own sagas of the strange. Tips and tales poured in via e-mail, and sometimes even handwritten letters laced with diagrams and maps arrived via the postman.

Many generous professionals also contributed to this pastiche of oddness, researchers, artists, and writers who wanted to add their own bits of state legend. Still others sent e-mails to tell of their brushes with spooks, unknown beasts, UFOs, and other things we had never dreamed of. We offer these sometimes anonymous stories as fascinating but unverifiable tidbits of Michigania, the sorts of things that are usually whispered among friends rather than shared with the public.

We found ourselves, finally, with a multifaceted jumble of home-grown eccentricity to arrange. Since people always seem to ask, "What's near my hometown?" we decided to assemble it alphabetically by city. Of course, we could not fit everyone's hometown into the book, but we did our level best to include a representative sampling. To put the various stories in some sort of context, each is identified with an icon representing one of nine categories:

• **Bizarre Byways:** Whoa! What was that? Anything spotted along the road, day or night, from highway spooks to giant fiberglass road guardians, is fair game here. Sometimes the roadside treasures hardest to recognize are those in our own neighborhoods. And while a few favorites in our ever-changing landscape may have disappeared by the time this book hits the stands, that's all the more reason to remember them here

• **Campfire Tales:** Legends, lore, things that can't be proven but survive by word of mouth will all be found in this neck of the dark, rustling woods. Good for the retelling…but don't let the campfire go out or "they" will come and get you for sure.

• **Graveyard Gate:** Cemetery lore, strange tombstones, spectral figures that cannot seem to leave the living alone all clamor from behind this icon's rusty spikes. *Strange Michigan* urges graveyard visitors to treat these places with the special respect they deserve; follow the posted rules and remember that the memorials are each sacred to someone, somewhere.

• **Freaky Fauna:** Michigan is particularly rich in unexplained creature reports, everything from Bigfoot to "werewolves," and some that must simply remain, "whatzits." It's a freakish zoo, all right, and one without fences, boundaries, or keepers. These entities have been reported by sober, credible citizens from Detroit to Ontonagon, and the sheer volume of sightings is enough to make the most die-hard skeptic wonder.

• **Haunted Habitats:** Just what is a ghost? Very few people can agree on that question and *Strange Michigan* offers no final definition, either. Most folks, though, will tell you they know one when they see one. And an astounding number of Michiganders claim some type of encounter with a spirit, spook, or whatever term you prefer. Old inns, taverns, and theaters seem especially rife with ghostly activity, and every town has more than one haunted house. We offer these stories of "haints" and the people who see them as a mere smattering of the stories that make our knees knock and the hair stand up on our cold, sweaty necks.

• **Unconventional People:** Who knows what makes people do the things they do? And yet, those who follow their own inner bagpiper are always fascinating to the rest of us. Michigan seems to produce them in droves, for reasons yet undiscovered. All we can do is shake our heads at them in wonder, and perhaps secretly think about where that faint melody inside each of us might have led, had we followed its siren song.

Lisa A. Shiel

• Art and Architecture Amok: There is a great swell of creativity in Michigan, much of it untutored. The state bursts at the seams with visionary art such as houses shingled with old mannequins, Paul Bunyans assembled from scrap heap items, even tiny buildings made to accommodate Lilliputian-sized inhabitants. Many painters and sculptors turn their art loose on their immediate environments, intriguing the neighbors and manifesting their own mindscapes. Some have already been survived by their art. Gazing awestruck at their rollicking output, we hope to glimpse in their work something beyond the ordinary pale of existence; something only those possessing second sight—and the talent to express it—can bestow upon us.

• Puzzles of the Past: The land was here long before our forebears roped it off and named its confines "Michigan." For millennia, people have lived here, creating their own cultures and leaving artifacts we still ponder. Some of our more recent buried past also fits this category. These mysteries may never be solved, but they will ever be scrutinized. Pull out your magnifying glasses and marvel away.

• Eerie Enigmas: Unexplained things like unidentified flying objects, strange atmospheric phenomena, or incidents that simply boggle the mind with their impossibility; we have collected these as your own private sideshow. Read 'em and freak!

A few final caveats. As noted earlier, the landscape of our state is a shifting shadow; what stands before us today may not be there tomorrow. While much of this book comprises a diverse touring resource that can be tossed into your vehicle of choice for travel reference, some places, people, and things may be gone before you get there. We simply have no way to know which treasures will be preserved and which will fall prey to the ravages of nature and man. Others may be closed to public trespass. *Strange Michigan* takes no responsibility for travelers who defy either the law or standards of responsible exploration. They must plead their own cases either to the local authorities or to the ancient, vigilant, and vengeful gods of legend-tripping.

And, of course, most of the unexplained creatures profiled in this book are choosy about where, when, and to whom they appear. The Michigan Dogman will not be found standing around like some character at Disney World, lounging at the North Bar in Luther and waiting for visitors to hand it a chunk of maggoty roadkill. Cryptozoological encounters are available not by appointment but whim of chance.

Also, while stories are fact-checked as well as possible, please remember that legends and ghost tales are often things alive in their own right; one telling may be different than another. Addresses, phone numbers, and even road names may weave and bobble. Writing a book like this one is much like shooting at the proverbial moving target. All we can do is hope that most of it will stand still long enough for everyone to take a good gander at the scenic, persistently offbeat land that is our own *Strange Michigan*.

Linda S. Godfrey

Alba
Antrim County
Dead Man's Hill

The woods of Michigan buzzed with saws of lumberjacks in the early 20th Century, with particularly intense activity in the lush Jordan River valley near Alba. Although most tree-fellers toiled in obscurity, working until either the wood or their backs gave out, one Jordan River valley teamster known as "Big Sam" became a legend; But his fame was not of the type anyone would desire.

Big Sam, born Stanley Graczyk, was only 21 in May 1910. He labored willingly in the valley, hoping to earn money for his upcoming wedding to a longtime sweetheart. On the 20th day of that month, a routine drive down the steep hill with a big-wheeled wagon full of logs went terribly wrong and Sam was crushed to death. He was buried at St. Charles Cemetery in Elmira. The slope has been known ever since as "Dead Man's Hill," and the state forest management still posts a warning sign for people to stay off the lethal incline. Look for a small sign a few miles north of Kalkaska on M-66 for the turnoff to the breathtaking scenic overlook.

PLEASE STAY OFF HILL

Albion
Calhoun County
The Father of Sliced Bread

We all know the expression "the best thing since sliced bread." Ever wonder where it came from? So do we. But while we can't answer that question, we can tell you where sliced bread came from—the mind of Otto Frederick Rohwedder, who invented the bread-slicer. Born and raised in Iowa, Rohwedder moved to Albion in the southern part of Michigan in 1951, where he lived until two years before his death. He spent his final years in a nursing home in Concord, not far from Albion.

If you've ever wanted to thank the man who brought pre-sliced bread into our homes, then drive to Albion and pay a visit to the Riverside Cemetery, Lot 1 of Block 11. This is one sight you don't have to lay out a lot of dough to see.

Allouez
Keweenaw County
The Healing Vortex

Prospector's Paradise. The name calls to mind scruffy men panning for gold in a river. The village of Allouez, on the Keweenaw Peninsula, contains a different kind of Prospector's Paradise—a store with an associated museum and, best of all, a healing vortex in back.

The rock shop displays every variety of stone, ancient sharks' teeth, and numerous fossils. Walk up the stairs beside the checkout counter to view the larger fossils and rocks, some enclosed in glass cases, others sitting on shelves. Prospector's Paradise also features an Ancient Copper Culture Museum. And behind the store lies something even more mysterious…an alleged healing vortex. Not a healing tornado or maelstrom, this gentle vortex reportedly consists of energy that relieves arthritis and other ailments. Visitors must decide for themselves whether the vortex lives up to its rep.

The shop, on US Highway 41 in Allouez, also hosts an annual metaphysical get-together called the People's Fair.

Alpena
Alpena County
The Kaiser Lumberjack

Ever heard of the Kaiser automobile? If you say no, you're not alone. Kaiser stopped producing automobiles more than 30 years ago, yet the legacy of the Kaiser car lives on in Alpena, in an unusual monument to recycling.

Back in the '60s, William Woelk, owner of the Paul Bunyan Gas Station in Gaylord, commissioned a statue to make his business stand out from the other gas stations in the area. He hired artist Betty Conn and architect Edward X. Tuttle to design and construct a lumberjack statue befitting the station's namesake. You'll find Paul Bunyans all over Michigan, but this statue stands apart from all others.

The 30-foot "Kaiser lumberjack" consists primarily of fenders and hoods from Kaiser automobiles.

The lumberjack guarded the Paul Bunyan Gas Station for many years, then was moved to the office of Gaylord realtor Bernard Hamilton. Finally, in 1998, Hamilton arranged to donate the statue to Alpena Community College, where the behemoth has stood since 2001.

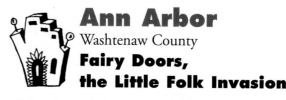

Ann Arbor
Washtenaw County
Fairy Doors,
the Little Folk Invasion

Like all good things, eccentric phenomena can come in small packages. In 2005, rumors began circulating around downtown Ann Arbor that fairies were moving into many businesses. The main clues were the miniature doors that began appearing in places such as the Selo/Shevel Gallery, Sweetwater's Café, The Peaceable Kingdom, The Ark Bookstore, Red Shoes Gifts, and Dickens Elementary.

Since then, a few of the six-inch doors have popped up inside the buildings, too. At Sweetwater's, a teensy orange entrance near the floor on an outside wall betrays the presence of coffee-sipping wee folk, and in The Peaceable Kingdom, a glass window reveals dollhouselike fairy lodgings ensconced under the front window platform. The fairies evidently crave feedback, because they have left journals for people to record their reactions at many of their new homes. Entries in The Peaceable Kingdom's journal say things like, "Dear Fairy, I saw that people only left you pennies and I felt sorry for you so I left you 15 cents. Rosie, age 12." Or, "Dear Farirs, I like your house I thought fariys houseis were made of nature things." Or, the pragmatic note, "What will they do with all this money? Perhaps a fund for disabled fairies?"

A local artist, Jonathan Wright, has proven strangely knowledgeable about the fairy explosion, spinning theories about fairies pushed out of their woodland environments into the concrete jungle to compete with humans for urban space. Incriminating evidence includes the fact that at least four fairy doors have appeared in Wright's own house, with one in the fireplace and another that opens onto its own tiny stairs that lead to another tiny, possibly enchanted door the humans have not been able to access.

Wright explained, "Well, they've got tiny hands, and they

might use some magic as well. It's a really peculiar phenomenon, but I can tell it's more of a mimicking of human architecture and conventions. And I've noticed lately that while at first all the doors were at ground level, they seem to have gone beyond the mimicry now and placed some of them higher up. It's as if they suddenly got a clue and said, 'Hey, we can fly, so why not.'"

Wright also noted that the interior fairy room in The Peaceable Kingdom imitates the idea of a human shop. "But as far as I can tell, the fairies have little or no business sense," he noted. "Their business hours are slim to nonexistent." The "merchandise" that seems to keep piling up inside the tiny room (which includes several rows of baby teeth, possibly left by the Tooth Fairy) consists largely of articles people have left for the fairies. The presents include acorn caps, coins, costume jewelry, marbles, and even polished stones.

Wright, who studied architecture before becoming a graphic artist and designer of children's products, took a year's leave to study the fairy invasion. He is working on three books: a coffee table pictorial on the doors, a fairy field journal, and a storybook. He has also used his artistic skills to draw some of the fairies. Wright believes there are so many fairies that it will be an enormous task to document them all. And in the meantime, the increasing number of fairy doors indicates a fay (an Old English word for fairy) population explosion. Ann Arbor business owners can only hope that banshees and leprechauns don't follow.

RIVERBANK STADIUM

"Home of the River Rats"

Haunted Huron High

Theaters and auditoriums are probably the most consistently haunted type of building. This holds true even when the theater is located in a public high school, such as Huron High in Ann Arbor. The story there goes that a girl working on a school production as a stagehand lost her balance in the rafters and fell. Students have claimed they can still sometimes hear her screaming at night. Others say that her name, Mary, was found written upside down on a wall behind the stage area, and that her wandering figure can still be glimpsed around the auditorium when lights are low.

Atlanta
Montmorency County
Elk in a Box

As you drive down State Highway 32 into the hamlet of Atlanta in the northeastern part of the state, a sign welcomes you and at the same time proclaims Atlanta the elk capital of Michigan. Passersby may wonder at the sign's meaning, given that no elk roam the streets.

Drive a little farther and you'll see. On the north side of the highway, in front of the post office, stands an elk in a box.

The elk, stuffed and displayed in a large glass enclosure, gazes out at the highway. The proud animal stands tall, as he did in life, neck stretched, mouth open, as if uttering a welcoming cry. A plaque mounted on a rock next to the box explains Atlanta's claim to fame concerning elk.

Around 1877, the native elk of Michigan became extinct. Then in 1917, somebody decided Rocky Mountain elk might like Michigan, so they released seven of them in the area now known as Atlanta, in Pigeon River country. In nearly a century since the release of the original seven elk, Michigan's herd has grown into the largest bunch of wild elk east of the Mississippi. When oil and gas drilling threatened the elk's habitat, folks rallied all the way to the Supreme Court to save it. Not only did the so-called little people save the elk and the Pigeon River country, they helped clean up Michigan's oil and gas industry to boot.

Atlanta's elk-in-a-box memorial commemorates more than the reintroduction of elk; it reminds us of what people can do when they band together for a cause. Maybe the elk has his mouth open to shout "Hooray!"

Lisa Shiel shows the lilliputian proportions of the Wayside Chapel

Atwood
Antrim County
The Church for Lilliputians

Tired of cathedrals that feel as big and impersonal as shopping malls? Do you crave an intimate space in which to worship? The tiny burg of Atwood, south of Charlevoix, has the church for you. Welcome to the Wayside Chapel.

At just 12 feet by 8 feet, the chapel serves as the antidote to megachurches. It would be hard to fit a small choir in here, much less a congregation of thousands. The Atwood Christian Reformed Church maintains the chapel as a rest stop for travelers, most of whom likely zoom right past on adjacent US Highway 31. Occasionally used for weddings, the chapel stands silent and peaceful on a dirt drive called Blue Heaven Lane just off the highway. The itty-bitty church remains lit and open 24 hours a day.

Baldwin
Lake County
Shrine of the Pines

Shrine of the Pines bills itself as "The World's Largest Display of Rustic Pine Furniture," but it's weirder than that. The lifetime work of Raymond W. Overholzer, a hunting and fishing guide turned white pine artist, is a preserved cabin that features oddities such as a table made from a 700-pound stump, strange lozenge-shaped windows, and all manner of twisty-legged chairs, lamps, and other north woods necessities. Mounted deer heads occupy any space not filled by carved pine.

All of the pieces were made from stumps or found wood so as not to disturb living trees. Overholzer was known as a very patient man, creating handmade pegs to use as nails and waiting until he was out of school to marry his third-grade teacher, who was twenty-four years older. Visitors are encouraged to enjoy the woodsy surroundings, including a platform by the Pere Marquette River built specially for watching trout frolic and splash. Found just off South M-37 outside of Baldwin, the place closes from mid-October to mid-May, in deference to northern Michigan winters.

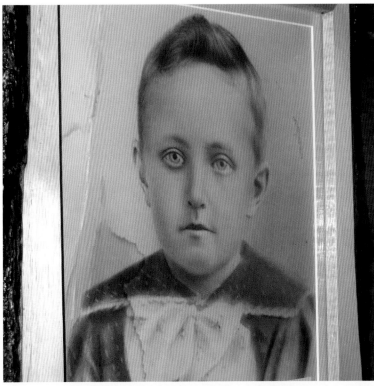

Raymond W. Overholzer, the builder of the Shrine of the Pines, as a child

Paul Bunyan Antique Mall Statue

There is no mistaking the Paul Bunyan Antique Mall at 3253 South M-37 in Baldwin. The aging, giant plywood cutout sign of the legendary lumberjack has stood there as a local landmark for well over 30 years, according to the current owners, and was already attracting motorists when they bought the place several decades ago. *Strange Michigan* appreciates its homespun style as an antidote to mass-produced signage everywhere, and wishes more shop owners would haul out their jigsaws and create their own original tourist attractions.

Beaver Island

Keweenaw County

Stone Circles and Religious Zealots

Strange things can be found almost everywhere, but certain places on this earth seem to attract more than their share of strangeness. Beaver Island, a 32-mile ferry hop from Charlevoix, is Michigan's mecca of religious oddities. Although famous for hosting two of the country's strangest religious sect leaders in the mid-1800s and early 1900s, it wasn't until late in the 20th century that many realized the 55-square mile island was also home to ancient and enigmatic stone pillars that reminded some of the prehistoric Stonehenge circle in Great Britain.

Europeans were early visitors; French explorers probably stopped at Beaver Island in the early 1600s. In 1832, the island's Native American inhabitants became the subject of missionary efforts by the famed "Snow-shoe Priest," Father Frederic Baraga. Only 15 years later, in 1847, a Mormon breakaway sect led by charismatic James Strang debarked on the Beaver Island shores to build their own town, St. James.

Strang became nationally known after he donned a crown and red velvet robe in 1850 to proclaim himself emperor of the island. His brave new kingdom ended after he was gunned down in 1856 by a disgruntled follower, and he died soon after in his original, also failed settlement of Voree near Burlington, Wisconsin. The village of St. James still exists, and is home to the Old Mormon Print Shop Museum and another museum dedicated to the island's fishing industry (open only in summer).

Another offbeat group was drawn to the area in 1912 when Brother Benjamin Purnell and his commune, the Israelite House of David, purchased land on nearby High Island, part of the Beaver Island chain. Celibate vegetarians who never cut their hair, House of David members were known in the lower part of the state for their bearded baseball teams and a popular amusement park near Grand Haven.

The group established an island lumber operation and set up a colony that included an eight-sided building called the "House of Virgins" where young, unmarried females lived. Local tongue-waggers claimed the octagonal building served as Purnell's private "harem house," even though he only journeyed twice to the island. And since one of the commune's basic tenets was that its members would live eternally on earth, the group's thriving enterprises went into permanent decline when their supposedly immortal leader died in 1927.

Of course, area native people had their own long history here. Mounds excavated in 1871 yielded archaic axes, chisels, grinding stones, arrowheads and other articles made from a wide variety of stone. The "mounds" may have been fossilized sand dunes rather than specially constructed earthworks, but they continued to yield stone treasures for many years. One major cache of implements was dug out of the present yard of the Mormon Print Shop Museum. Hand-made gunflints dating from before 1670, manufactured by local tribes to use in their European flintlock muskets, turned up near St. James harbor.

But in 1985, the *Detroit News* revealed that a part-Ojibwe teacher named Terri Bussey, who was also director of the *Michigan Indian Press*, had discovered a 397-foot circle of 39 roundish, half-buried stones on the west side of Beaver Island. The circle appeared to be directly oriented toward sunrise on the mid-summer equinox.

The boulders ranged from a couple of feet in diameter to ten feet across. The central stone bore a hand-hewn hole that observers guessed was either intended to hold a a sundial pole or offerings.

Most experts believe the circle, now known as "The Circle of the Sun" or "The Sleeping Sisters," was used as a calendar marker and observatory, but the identity of its builders remains controversial. Some think a mysterious and sophisticated group of Native Americans, the far-ranging Mississippian culture, constructed it to guide their travels. Others believe sea-faring Vikings managed to reach these shores and leave stone monuments behind. Both groups would have been attracted to the region for its abundant copper. Either way, traditions of the present-day tribal occupants, Chippewa (Ojibwe) and Ottawa (Odawa), indicate the stones were already in place when their own ancestors arrived several hundred years ago.

A view of Beaver Island, the central boulder of the stone circle (inset)

The precisely placed stones would be amazing enough by themselves, but other monumental arrangements—over a half dozen eight-spoked medicine wheels up to 200 feet in diameter—have been found not far from the main circle. They are similar to "medicine wheels" usually seen in the Western Plains states, and may have had both ceremonial and astronomical uses.

Another possibility is that the stones were used as a navigation station. Researchers Betty Sodders (*Michigan Prehistory Mysteries*) and Archie Eschborn ("The Great Beaver Island," *The Best of Astraea*) have both noted that the center rock features a carving of a map of Lakes Michigan, Superior, and Huron and their surrounding land masses as they would have appeared thousands of years ago. Depressions representing the lakes are obvious when water is poured onto the rock. But perhaps the truth about the circle's origin is stranger than anyone suspects.

In 1998, an area resident named Lee Olsen told a gathering of the Beaver Island Historical Society that Native American folk legends about the island included visits by "aliens" who came in craft that resembled modern-day UFOs. The visitors took some ancient tribal members on a vacation to their home planet near Arcturus, he said, and the stone circles were star maps to that place. Also, the aliens left behind small spirit people that Olsen had personally observed. Olsen noted that a snowplow had recently cracked the big circle's main stone. He warned this meant islanders should not let commercial development obscure the island's stone treasures.

Whether the circles were built by ancient Celts, Mississippians, or aliens from Arcturus, they testify to the fact that Beaver Island seems to be a magnet for those seeking sacred soil. And it's a pilgrimage that will probably continue for as long as people can ferry or fly their way across the choppy waters of Lake Michigan.

Bessemer
Gogebic County
The World's Largest Ski Flying Hill

Ever dream of flying like Superman? While you may never fly quite like the Man of Steel, you can come awfully close on Copper Peak near Bessemer. Copper Peak features the only ski flying hill in the Western Hemisphere, an artificial ski jump that also stands as the largest such structure in the world.

Ski flying could be thought of as ski jumping for the extreme adrenaline junkie. Ski flying hills rise higher, let the skier achieve higher speeds, and hurl the human missile farther through the air. Copper Peak's ski flying hill tops out at 170 meters, 50 meters higher than the tallest ski hills used in Olympic skiing, hurtling skiers over 600 feet through the air. Flying really may be the best way to describe the way skiers descend this 360-foot peak.

Big Bay Point
Marquette County
A Ghostly Six-Pack

The old 1896 lighthouse that stands on the promontory 25 miles north of Marquette, Michigan, is reported by its owners to be haunted by no fewer than six ghosts. Now converted into a modern bed and breakfast, its half-dozen revenants range from a young woman with an ax to grind to former light keeper William Prior. Prior hanged himself nearby after disappearing into the woods carrying a rope, a shotgun, and a bottle of strychnine. He's identified by his beard and keeper uniform, and has been seen by a guest or two, standing at the foot of their beds and staring at them with a baleful expression and dark, hollow eyes.

Birmingham
Oakland County
Red UFOS

I was seven years old at the time, but there was a healthy amount of adult corroboration on this, so, you know, whatever that's worth.

I was staying with my aunt, uncle, and four cousins, who lived on Cedar Hill Drive, in Birmingham, Michigan, in July or August 1980. Cedar Hill Drive is just a few blocks west of Lincoln Hills golf course. My aunt and uncle had a mobile home, which I was really impressed with, so one of the nights that I was staying there my cousins and I decided to sleep in the mobile home, which was parked in the driveway. The mobile home had a portable TV installed, and we were sort of half-attentively watching that night's TV 50 movie, which was (strangely enough) the film adaptation of Whitley Streiber's Wolfen .

It was probably around 10 p.m. when the neighbors across the street came

over and started pounding on the side of the mobile home. They were friends of my cousins, and this was an attempt to start some kind of play rumble. My cousins and I obligingly piled out of the mobile home and some shoving and yelling ensued. My aunt and uncle came outside to tell us to quiet down. At some point shortly after that, I became aware that everyone was looking up at the sky. I've taken a look at some maps, and as near as I can tell they were probably looking out towards the southwest, towards 14 and 13 Mile roads. Hovering in the sky were two red star or planelike lights, but each was singular, in other words there were no accompanying lights to make either one resemble an airplane. There was a lower light, and then an upper light positioned quite a good distance diagonally above.

Because I have no idea how far away these lights were, it's difficult for me to estimate their relative distance from one another. It is highly unlikely, though, that they were two lights on the same craft; there appeared to be a lot of empty space between them. What I know for certain is that they rigidly maintained their relative diagonal positions, without any variation, as they moved horizontally across the sky. They moved slowly, but at an even, steady pace. They moved from one end of that side of the horizon to another, from the southwest to the southeast.

At this point I became aware that other people all up and down Cedar Hill were on their driveways watching the lights. So however quickly they moved, it was slow enough for people to come out of their houses and take note of what was happening. It was a summer night, so I don't know, maybe some people were already outside, in their backyards or something. Eventually the lights glided to a standstill, holding still in their relative positions. After a while they rotated, smoothly, so that they were in perfect horizontal alignment. Their relative distance to one another remained constant. They held this position for some time, then suddenly dropped, with incredible speed, down behind the treeline of our horizon. Just after they vanished from view, a low rumble rolled towards us across the landscape. And that was it.

There was a fair amount of discussion about what we'd just seen; the neighbor kids went back home and my aunt and uncle (who I kind of hoped could explain everything) were no more enlightened than my cousins and I. This distressed me, and I suddenly had visions of the lizard guy from Star Trek breaking into the mobile home while we slept. My aunt and uncle assured me that everything was going to be fine, but we decided to sleep in the house anyway.

The next day, I went into the kitchen to talk to my aunt and she told me to shush. She was listening to local AM talk radio, and sure enough they were discussing the sighting from the previous night. A number of people had called in, wanting to know what the hell they had seen. The radio announcer stated that area airports and government officials were saying they had no knowledge of or explanation for the sighting. Every few years I run into my cousins, or talk to my aunt, and I always bring it up. They're still just as in-the-dark as I am, but I always run through the facts of the sighting, if for no other reason than to make sure I've got them straight in my head.

–J., by permission of writer

Black Lake

Cheboygan County
Spreading a Legacy

When a loved one is cremated, what do you do with the ashes? For one labor leader, the answer was simple: Spread his ashes over Black Lake.

Why would someone want his ashes spread over a lake, particularly a lake in the northern reaches of the Lower Peninsula of Michigan? During his 62 years on Earth, Walter Reuther became a heavyweight in the United Auto Workers, leading the union through several major strikes and surviving two assassination attempts before becoming active in the civil rights movement. Reuther died in a plane crash near Pellston, Michigan, on May 9, 1970, along with his wife, May, and four others, while en route to the UAW's Family Education Center on Black Lake. After purchasing the property in 1967, the UAW had transformed it into a 1200-acre recreation center complete with golf course and campground. The center sits on Hangore Bay, on the western side of Black Lake.

In a ceremony conducted atop a hill, across from the main lobby of the center, mourners cast the ashes of both Walter and May Reuther to the winds over the lake. The labor leader and his spouse now rest in peace with the walleye, perch, pike, and sturgeon in the 10,100-acre lake.

It puts a different slant on the phrase "sleeping with the fishes."

The shores of Walloon Lake and Hemingway's Windemere (inset)

Boyne City

Charlevoix County
The Maiden Ghost of Walloon Lake

Ernest Hemingway loved Michigan. Often during his lifetime, he returned to his childhood home in the deep woods on Walloon Lake to a cottage called Windemere, which still sits in its original place on the lakefront. It was here as a teenager that he met Prudence, a young Native American girl with whom he fell in love. Prudence later became pregnant. Speculation exists that her baby was Hemingway's. But their love was not to be.

Hemingway's obligations separated the lovers and tragically, three months into her pregnancy, Prudence committed a painful suicide, drinking strychnine in the woods surrounding Walloon. As the story is told, her dying screams were heard for hours, echoing among the trees like wandering spirits. Some say the ghost of Prudence still walks the periphery of Walloon Lake through the Michigania Campgrounds, wailing, searching for Ernest, howling for his return to Windemere and their love.

—*Cheri L. R. Taylor, contributor*

Boyne Falls
Charlevoix County
The Highway Triangle

A sighting found on the National UFO Reporting Center Website describes a triangular object floating low in the sky over M-75 on October 4, 2007, moving down to cross over US 131. The witness estimated the triangle hovered slightly higher than the hill at the local ski resort. Boyne Mountain, the ski hill adjacent to US 131, rises 1190 feet. The witness also stated that the lights from vehicles and buildings reflected on the craft's underside.

Brown City
Sanilac County
Creature of the Corn

In the year 2000, I was seven and staying at a friend's house in Brown City in the thumb of Michigan. I was waiting outside for my friend, sitting on the steps of his porch when the dogs just freaked out and started barking madly at a dark figure about a 100 yards away. It was coming out of a cornfield in front of what may have been an abandoned slaughterhouse because there were cow skulls all over the place.

The creature stood about 6 or 7 feet tall, was black, and very furry. It walked out of the cornfield on two feet, then got down on all fours and walked out onto the road. The dogs stayed over by me and growled and barked. When it noticed them it stood up on two feet again, looked at us, and took off into the cornfield.

This is the most interesting part. My friend said his dog killed a lot of animals. I believed him because it is a big Samoyed and has a lot of wolf in it. I think his dog was dragging in what that thing killed. He told me both before this incident and after it that he has seen a werewolf around his house many times. He said him and his two older sisters were home alone when the dogs sparked up and started barking. They pulled back the curtains to see what it was and a wolf's face was looking right in the window. They said it was on two feet and was crouched over level with them. They say it was probably 6 or 7 feet tall with black fur.

They immediately ran upstairs and locked a door, as they were home alone, and they didn't come back out till morning. After a while the dogs stopped barking and everything seemed to be normal again.

A similar account happened when I was there. This was a couple of months after I had seen it by the cornfield. The dogs were inside and in the basement. Once again they started barking. A big two-legged animal was running across the yard towards where I had seen it before. We thought it was some kind of burglar so we ran upstairs and hid in a bedroom.

Similar accounts happened by the abandoned building. My friend kept telling me stories about a werewolf running around out by where I had seen that thing. Up until I had heard about Dogman, I thought the thing I saw was an alien or something. He told me about a werewolf jumping out of a tree and injuring its leg.

Now I live in Caro, Michigan, which is also in the thumb about 50 miles west of Brown City. Back in the '80s or '60s there was a Bigfoot hunt for a big furry bipedal animal in the woods. Everyone said it was Bigfoot but I think it might have been Dogman. About a year ago I told some friends about the thing I saw in Brown City and they told me they had seen something very similar walking around our fort that we had back in the woods. They slept out there a lot and had seen a big black animal lurking around in the year 2002.

—Joe

Illustration by Linda S. Godfrey

Cadillac
Wexford County
Look! Up in the Sky!

Photos of UFOs, like photos of Bigfoot, tend to flunk the clarity exam, showing up as blurry images of something in the sky or woods—a photographic Rorschach test. Some photos are hoaxed, others taken by sincere folks who honestly believe they've snapped a picture that will change the world.

In August 2006, the *Cadillac News* reported on photos taken by a local man which may or may not show UFOs in the skies over Wexford County. On August 27, at about 8:30 p.m., Dave Dunford went outside to take snapshots of the sky near his home when he noticed a disk-shaped object in the heavens. With his camera handy, he tried to photograph the object. His photos came out rather blurry, to Dunford's dismay. But he still felt he had photos of a genuine UFO—and when he examined the images on his computer, he picked out other "slender rectangular" objects in the frame as well.

The newspaper contacted Peter Davenport at the National UFO Reporting Center, who felt the photos did not show a genuine UFO, and remarked that the blurriness and the great distance between the photographer and the object made the image less than convincing. No one else reported a UFO sighting to the police or the FAA on August 27.

Does all of this mean Dunford didn't see a UFO? Since no one can tell from the photos whether the object is a bird or a plane, whatever Dunford saw must go down in history as an unknown. As Dunford told the *Cadillac News*, if aliens did visit the area that night, he hoped they would get his message, "Come closer, I want a better shot of you!"

Abandoned buildings left over from the preserve's mining heyday

One of the many sinks at the preserve

Caffey
Mackinac County
Michigan's Longest Cave

For those who wish to go underground, the Fiborn Karst Preserve can take a person deeper than anyplace else in Michigan. The preserve's Hendrie River Water Cave stretches far enough into the depths—over 2000 feet—to satisfy even a vampire. Water from a swamp balanced atop an escarpment runs as a stream into the cave, flowing against the slope of the ground, over a waterfall nearly 10 feet tall, and down through a sump into the earth, essentially vanishing.

The preserve began as a limestone quarry, named Fiborn after William Fitch and Chase Osborn, the men who founded the quarry in 1905. The quarry shut down in 1936, though some of the buildings remain as ruins, including the giant machine shop. Today the Michigan Karst Conservancy owns and manages the property.

Spelunk through the longest cave in the state, see a swamp balanced on an escarpment, or spy streams that disappear underground, but beware—that sinking feeling you get may be a real sinkhole!

Close-up of the sign at Joe's Pasty Shop in Ironwood, another renowned source of the Michigan delicacy

Calumet
Houghton County
PastyFest

When immigrants arrived in the Keweenaw, many of the men took jobs as copper miners. They toiled by candlelight deep underground, in mine shafts both cramped and stiflingly hot, hacking bits of red metal from the earth. The large population of miners who had come over from Cornwall, in England, brought with them a Cornish dietary staple—a meat pie called a pasty. The pasties the men ate for lunch kept them nourished on those long, dark days in the mines. Eventually the mines closed, leaving the pasty in need of a new niche in life. Thus was born PastyFest.

A word of caution: Don't walk into a UP bakery and ask for "paste-eez," which sounds like the risqué ornaments worn by exotic dancers. The word is pronounced "past-ee."

But leave it to Yoopers to celebrate a meat pie with all the excitement usually reserved for a champion athlete or a teen pop diva. Every year in late June, Calumet turns its downtown into pasty heaven, with a cornucopia of events, music, and (of course!) pasties…chopped meat and rutabaga smothered in gravy and enveloped in pastry.

What does a festival for meat pies offer visitors? Contestants vie for the titles of Pasty King and Queen, while everyone can participate in the PastyWalk and watch the PastyParade down Fifth Street. You surely will see Toivo the Pasty, the world's only meat pie that walks and talks—the only one we know of, at least. And would-be pasty chefs may enter the Pasty Bake-Off for a chance to win the coveted Copper Pasty.

For kids, PastyFest includes an array of specialty games, including the Rutabaga Shot Put, the Onion Pass, the Egg Toss, potato sack races, and the PastyPull. If gazing upon a pasty inspires you to wax poetic, write down your ramblings and enter the PastyPoetry contest. You could become the next Pasty Laureate! Visit MainStreetCalumet.com for photos of past years' events.

The Statue Harvard Didn't Want

Monuments to the heyday of copper mining in the Keweenaw Peninsula abound and are easily recognizable—ruins of mine buildings, great hunks of copper on display, the towering silhouette of the Quincy hoist building—yet some reminders of the past sit in cryptic silence. Why, for instance, does a huge bronze statue of a professorial-looking man adorn a parking lot in Calumet?

The man in question was Alexander Agassiz, president of the Calumet & Hecla Mining Company. Agassiz presided over the company from 1871 until his death in 1910. The statue depicts Agassiz as a professor clad in academic robes, watching over his students with detached solemnity. The inscription on the statue's base describes him as "a man of science who developed a great mine and wrought the welfare of its people."

The statue originally sat up the road at Agassiz Park. In 1974, it was moved to its present location in front of Calumet & Hecla's old library. Fittingly, the man of science now resides not far from the Calumet schools and public library. Agassiz's father had promised that when mining operations ceased the statue would go to Harvard University in Cambridge, Massachusetts, where the elder Agassiz had taught. But in the 1960s, after much debate via correspondence, Harvard relinquished its claim to the statue. Calumet & Hecla had asked Harvard to pay the moving expenses, which amounted to $1,250—more than the university wished to pay, even for a man of science. So Agassiz, all one and a quarter ton of him, stayed in Calumet. Now he guards a copper boulder, which sits across the parking lot from him, right along US Highway 41.

Canandaigua
Lenawee County
Running Bigfoot

One day in 1996, as dusk approached, Karen and her husband drove home along M-156. A figure ran into the road in front of their car, dashed across the highway, and vanished into the foliage on the other side. Karen described the figure as 6' to 6'5" tall, dark in color, and upright.

At the time of the sighting, Karen noticed another car, coming from the opposite direction, which ground to a full stop when the creature ran into the road. Several days later, Karen was listening to a local radio show when someone called in to talk about the possible Bigfoot they had seen on Highway 156 on the same evening as Karen and her husband. She figured the caller must have been from the other car. The sighting had left Karen dumbfounded, and she did not try to call the radio station herself. Today, she wishes she had.

Illustration by Linda S. Godfrey

Capac
St. Claire County
The Capac Porch Entity

Fugitive from a UFO? Follicle-challenged Bigfoot looking to abduct some Rogaine? "Entity," the usual code word for something of undetermined weirdness, really is the best descriptive word in this odd case involving an anonymous man from the Michiganufos.com Web site (which credits *Filer's Files #18*, April 30, 2003).

The man, who lived in the little town of Capac about 20 miles north of Detroit, was having a hard time sleeping the night of March 28, 2003. He finally got up to take a pain reliever about midnight, and settled onto the living room sofa to watch a little TV. He had barely seated himself, however, when he heard something…or someone…running across his porch. He jumped up immediately and looked out the front door just in time to see the intruder disappear around the house, still on the wrap-around porch that extended around the corner.

He said it was "of average height, but had abnormally long arms. Its arms and legs were somewhat spiny and it had a larger than normal bald head. I did not get a good look at the face but I could tell that it was not human."

Within seconds after the creature left the man's field of vision, the electricity suddenly winked out in the man's house, and he could see two large, blue spotlights in a nearby field, about 800 yards away. The lights moved as if they were searching for something, he said. When they finally moved into the distance, his house lights came back on. A neighbor confirmed the next day that her lights also went out at that time, and that she saw the blue lights in the field, as well. And, according to the story, she admonished the enquiring witness, "people around here don't talk about these things."

illustration
by B.M.
Nunnelly

Caseville
Huron County
Serpent of Saginaw Bay

Steve M., now a science teacher in Michigan, was only 16 when he and a 30-something friend decided to participate in a carp shoot held on Saginaw Bay near Heisterman Island. The water, at a maximum of five feet, afforded a clear view of the lakebed, and they could see carp swimming busily below, earning their reputation as bottom feeders. Steve sat on the bow of a 16-foot fishing boat as his friend piloted the craft. Suddenly, to the pair's amazement, the carp completely disappeared from view.

Confounded, they glanced around the center of the bay and noticed what appeared to be two dark, inflated garbage bags floating on the water's surface. The men decided to be good citizens and fish the trash out of the lake, so they headed toward it. But as they approached, a great splash arose around the two "bags" and they sank quickly from view. As the men continued to watch, a large wake proceeded from that point, heading rapidly out of the small bay. As Steve reported in a post on the Cryptozoology.com Web site, "We were left speechless during this event and could not believe what we had witnessed in a place that was so familiar to us." He added that his best guess at the creature's form would be some type of serpent. Whatever it was, it sure knew how to put the damper on a carp shoot.

Cedar

Leelanau County

Blue Moon Bears

A trio of cool polar bears enlivened The Blue Moon Ice Cream Shop in Cedar when *Strange Michigan* passed through town in the summer of 2006. Since then, we've learned the place has changed hands and the bears may not still grace the front parking lot, but we offer their photo just in case they somehow wander back from the North Pole.

Charlevoix
Charlevoix County
Stone Hobbit Houses

Rounded little stone houses with mushroom-cap roofs plunked around the lake neighborhood of Charlevoix might make any visitor think he had somehow wandered into a village from *The Hobbit*. But these houses are inhabited by normal-sized humans, and were built by local realtor and amateur architect Earl Young in the mid-20th Century.

Young was a rock hound, and made a hobby of hunting for boulders that appealed to him, then burying or hiding them until he was ready to build a home. Standing only five feet tall, Young was close to hobbit stature and he sized the houses to fit himself, with some bathrooms so tiny that most adults must stoop to get in and out of the tub. Interiors of many of the homes are cavelike, with chains of small rooms; some feature the distinctive boulders Young loved set into entryways or other prominent places. He shingled the cedar shake roofs in curving patterns to emphasize the roundness of each building's design.

The first house he built was for his own family in 1921. The charming place still stands at 304 Park Avenue, next door to a retirement house he built two decades later. Other Young homes stand at 301 Clinton Street, and at 1 Lakeshore Drive off Boulder Avenue. Young also designed a massive stone fireplace in Stafford's Weathervane Restaurant that includes a meteor rock and a giant boulder shaped like the State of Michigan. Young died in 1975, leaving his stone fairy-tale buildings to endure as his legacy.

Funky Yard Art

For yard art that puts the "fun" in funky, drive south from Charlevoix on US Highway 31. A few miles outside of town, on the east side of the highway, you'll spot your target: A wooden wagon parked along the highway in someone's front yard. Beyond the wagon, a tin man lumberjack perches atop a log holding chain reins, urging his blue ox to pull that log onward. Next to the ox sits a wooden cannon. Go a few yards farther and you'll see a little farmer statue, complete with denim overalls, holding the reins on another wagon, this one pulled by a gray ox. A sign on the wagon reads "Smith's Little Acre." When *Strange Michigan* happened upon the display in the autumn of 2007, a rusted-out flatbed trailer loaded with pumpkins completed the tableau.

Atlas's Hands

As you drive south from Charlevoix on US Highway 31, watch on the right side of the road for a gravel parking area in front of an unassuming wooden shack. Now look closer. Several enormous hands protrude from the ground surrounding the parking lot. One hand makes a thumbs-up sign; another crosses its fingers; while a third tilts one finger toward the wooden shack that houses the Cycling Salamander Fine Art Gallery.

The hands are the work of Ogi, an artist originally from Bulgaria who now resides in West Michigan. Ogi creates the sculptures using a wire armature, which he overlays with concrete.

Truly the "handiwork" of another inspired Michigan folk art artist.

Clare
Clare County
The Clare Deer Man

Even though I have personally never set eyes on the Deer Man of Clare Michigan, the idea of such a creature still sticks in my mind after 37 years.

During that time, I was a field investigator for APRO (Aerial Phenomena Research Organization), a leading UFO organization in the 1960s. I had read in the *Lansing State Journal* of numerous sightings of UFOs in Clare, Michigan. It just so happened that some friends of mine owned a cabin a little west of Clare, and they invited me up for Memorial Day weekend. They felt a little adventure was in order and I was sure I could serve that up for them.

The year was 1971 and UFO sightings were still being reported in the newspapers near, if not on, the front page. The public attitude toward UFOs at that time was that anyone who saw a UFO had to be drunk or smoking the local weed. Worse yet, anyone who investigated UFOs was crazy. Many ufologists were in the closet in those days.

This UFO event in Clare had been going on for several weeks. I could only hope that it was still going on. I had read in the newspaper that there was a lot of UFO activity in an area that was a local lovers lane, on Herrick Road just out US Highway 10.

My friend and I were now well on our way to Clare. We were traveling up North 127 in my 1963 VW bug. The plan was to meet my friend's brother at the cabin. As luck would have it, just as we entered the Clare area a Michigan State Trooper pulled me over for some vehicle equipment issues. While we had the trooper's attention, I mentioned the reason we were up there and wanted to know what he knew about the sightings. At first I thought he was going to laugh at us and then impound the car. Instead, he grew very serious, told us what he knew, and confirmed the location of the sightings. The reports involved strange lights that ran up and down the county road named Herrick, harassing the local lovers who on occasion gave chase to the lights

In the middle of our discussion, the Trooper paused and then asked if we had heard of what the locals called the Deer Man. That took me by surprise; I was speechless but managed to get a "no" out. I do not remember all the details of the sightings, but I believe hunters and local residents made the reports in the 1950s. The Deer Man was reported to be between four and five feet in stature, and was a biped. The lower half of the body was like that of a deer's hindquarters. The upper half was very humanlike. It had arms, hands, fingers, and a normal-looking head. The eyes, though, were a bit odd. They were brown and deerlike, yet seemed to have a human structure. The body hair was short and nappy; however, the lower half of the body hair was more like deer hide: brownish in color, similar to what a deer's color would be in October in Michigan.

It was also reported that the Deer Man moved about in a leaping motion like a deer on the run. It was very agile and maneuvered well in the woods. It was also reported that the Deer Man would emit sounds similar to a deer's.

At first, I thought it might be one of those strange kangaroo sightings we had in the East Lansing area. This happened on the southern part of Michigan State University's land holdings in the late 1960s. After listening to the Deer Man description, I thought differently.

The officer thought that I might be interested in researching the Deer Man sightings. He was right on target, but I was hunting UFOs at the time so I had to file the Deer Man away for a future cryptid investigation. It seems to me that the Deer Man is very similar to the satyr known as Pan, from Greek Mythology, who is half man and half human. Maybe there is something to the Pan myth. It appears his American cousin, the Deer Man of Clare, Michigan, is alive and well and perhaps still out there somewhere.

—*Joseph Stewart, contributor*

Coldwater
Branch County
Michigan's First (and Biggest) Earthquake

Most of us think of the West Coast as the only place where quakes occur but, while the Pacific states live with the greatest threat of seismic danger, Michigan has had its share of temblors. Settlers reported strange shakings as early as 1793, although those tremors may have stemmed from unnatural causes such as mine collapses or explosions. The first recorded, definitely natural earthquake in Michigan occurred on August 10, 1947. The quake measured 4.7 on the Richter scale. While Californians might harrumph at anything less than a six pointer, Michiganders certainly noticed the ground heaving beneath them.

The Coldwater quake also holds the record as the largest natural quake in the state's history. Centered just north of Coldwater, the quake rattled the communities of Athens, Colon, Sherwood, Bronson, and Union City. The rumble damaged chimneys, broke windows, cracked plaster, and tumbled brick cornices. Residents of Wisconsin, Illinois, Indiana, Ohio, and Ontario in Canada felt the quake too.

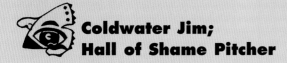

Coldwater Jim; Hall of Shame Pitcher

Some might call Jim Hughey the worst baseball player in history. Others might call him a victim of fate. In any event, after a promising start in the minor leagues, "Coldwater Jim" Hughey ended his career in the majors by becoming the last pitcher to lose 30 games in one season.

Born in 1869 in Wakeshma Township in Kalamazoo County, Hughey grew up mostly in the Coldwater area. He started his athletic career in Coldwater, gradually working his way up through the minors and into the major leagues. After earning praise early in his career, in 1899 Hughey wound up on the worst team in major league history, the Cleveland Spiders, who accumulated a 20-134 record that year. Hughey finished the season with 4-30 record, earning his place in infamy.

Hughey died in 1945 and was buried in Lester Cemetery southeast of Coldwater.

Colon
St. Joseph County
Deep In the Bowels of Magic Town

People in Colon love to ask visitors if they are just passing through. And bumps in the city streets are called "polyps." Don't even ask about what happens when traffic gets, um, backed up.

It wasn't as if the town even had any good reason to forever make itself the butt of digestion jokes. In 1831, its founders simply decided to open a dictionary and point at random to a word, and whatever that word was would be chosen as the city's official moniker. The dictionary fell open in the "Cs" and the selector's finger landed on "colon." It must have taken a little intestinal fortitude to retain that choice, but Colon became the town's name.

Thankfully, the town has another big draw, its reputation as a mecca for magicians with an annual magic festival. In fact, the town greeting reads, "Come and experience the magic of Colon." Every year professional magicians pop in at festival time to perform, compete, learn new feats of legerdemain, and shop at the historic Abbott's Magic Store, started by Percy Abbott and Recil Bordner in 1934. Abbott's 470-page catalog of magic tricks is the holy grail of stage magicians worldwide.

The company is now run by Greg Bordner, son of Recil and a skilled magician in his own right who told *Strange Michigan*, "Dogs do tricks, I do miracles." The company's main building is part store, part showroom, part museum of magic. Magic memorabilia, photos, and old magic show posters plaster the walls. There's a stage where local professional magicians put on a show every Saturday at

Above left: Greg Bordner performs acts of legerdemain on his in-store stage; above right: portrait of Harry Blackstone; above, lower right: sign outside Abbott's Magic Store

1:00 p.m. in the summer, while paintings of Percy Abbott and the world-famous magician Harry Blackstone keep lifelike eyes on the customers.

Blackstone was Colon's original connection to the magic business. His show troupe used to spend summers near Kalamazoo, and Blackstone and his wife found the little community of Colon while out driving one day. They bought 208 acres fronted by Sturgeon Lake on one side and a series of streams on the other. Soon their magician friends began visiting, and many of them also became entranced with Colon and bought their own places.

Colon's cemetery reflects its magic heritage with the graves of the Harry Blackstones, Sr. and Jr., along with others such as Ricki Dunn, "America's Greatest Pickpocket," and Bill Baird, "The Magnificent Fraud."

The famous names in magic still flock to Colon for what is now called the Annual Magic Get-Together, and Bordner has sold illu-

sion equipment to the likes of Penn and Teller, David Copperfield, and Arsenio Hall. The rest of the town has taken advantage of the magic connection too, with businesses such as Illusions Hair Care, the Magic Café, and even the town's Internet service provider, Magic.net.

Bordner told us his company's most popular trick is a $5 illusion called "Changing Nickels to Dimes." But one of his favorites is the $375 "Mutilated Parasol," which starts out pristine, becomes ripped and shredded, then returns to its pre-mutilated position. Standards like the Magic Top Hat and Sawing a Woman in Halves are always good sellers.

The town naturally hopes Bordner's company will continue to wave its magic wand over the local economy. But whatever the magic factory's future, magicians are sure to remain a regular tradition in this town. Besides, in Colon, everything always seems to come out all right.

Comins
Oscoda County
Heads Up...Giant Stone Indian

An oversize stone head representing an unknown Native American can be spotted on the grounds of the *Michigan Magazine* Museum, in northeastern Lower Michigan between the rural communities of Fairview and Comins on M-33. The museum, housed in a pristine new log building, also features a casting of a Bigfoot footprint found by the Mayville's Bigfoot Investigation Association. Another museum highlight features the original notes of Houghton Lake songwriters Tommy Durden and Mae Axton, who penned *Heartbreak Hotel*, Elvis Presley's first gold record. Other artifacts from the *Michigan Magazine* print and TV versions round out the collection. The oversized head sculpture was created and donated by Onaway sculptor Tom Moran. Moran, who usually works in scrap metal, departed from his usual medium by using native Onaway stone to create this tribute to Native Americans everywhere.

According to Dell Vaughn, *Michigan Magazine* co-creator, the head consists of thirty-six tons of Onaway stone, and stands fourteen feet high and twelve feet wide at the base. Moran gave the statue to the *Michigan Magazine* Museum in May 2004 after the magazine published an article about his work.

1949 Kalamazoo Gazette photo of Comstock Township resident Tom Ford with the bell that once hung in the belfry of the Alphadelphian's two-story activity center, courtesy of the Comstock Township Library

Comstock Township
Kalamazoo County
A Doomed Michigan Utopia: Alphadelphia

Swept up in a national craze for fresh spirituality in the 1800s, Michigan became a fertile hotbed of new cults and religious movements. One of the most memorable was a group of Christian communists called the Alphadelphians, started in 1843 with 56 persons in Comstock Township, Kalamazoo County. The group followed the teachings of Charles Fourier, a French Utopian socialist who believed families should live and work in farm communes to practice the teachings of the earliest Christian church as shown in the Bible's New Testament.

The Alphadelphians attracted as many as 300 followers, and published a newspaper called the *Alphadelphian Tocsin*, which was mocked by no less than Edgar Allen Poe in New York's *The Weekly Mirror*. Poe made fun of both the *Tocsin's* claim to eight editors and its ponderous name when he asked incredulously, "What on earth is the meaning of Alphadelphia?" (*Strange Michigan* doesn't know either.) Poe concluded testily that the "double A's in Alphadelphia were "too easily slipped into 'A-double-S."

Other testimonials to the fledgling group were even less compelling. The first couple married in the Alphadelphian community was P.H. Whitford and Emeline Wheelock, who were promptly immortalized by the group's resident poet in a sizzling verse entitled, "The Socialist's Bride."

Alas, the idealism that propelled the community soon fizzled, and as the *Kalamazoo Gazette* explained in 1937, "Then hope began to wane and the serpent entered the garden. Chiselers and shirkers appeared. A few absconded with unearned increment." After only four years, Alphadelphia disbanded and the site west of Galesburg was eventually purchased for a county "poor farm." It is ironic that the outcasts of capitalism became the final occupants of the socialist group's fields.

Coopersville

Ottawa County

The Coopersville Hitchhiker

There are numerous, and I mean numerous, strange sightings in Coopersville, Michigan. If you are on I-96 and you need to take the Coopersville Exit late at night, you just might see a male hitchhiker. Everyone described this hitchhiker as a man, early mid-30s in age. If you pick him up, he will ask you if you believe in God. After you have answered this question, he will disappear. Through the years, I have received many emails about this mysterious hitchhiker, and my former father-in-law was one of the "fortunate people" that picked him up about 10 years ago.

—*Nicole Bray, contributor*

Coopersville hitchhiker; photo illustration; photo from collection of Linda Godfrey

Cross Village
Emmet County
The Fairy Ring of Halloween

During Samhain (known as Halloween to most people) the Fairy Ring of Halloween appears in the Cross Village area called Larks Lake Haunts. This ring, over 25 feet in diameter, is right off Larks Lake Road. Smaller rings appear about 10 miles north of this parent one, also off Larks Lake Road. All the rings in the area follow the "yellow brick road" of Larks Lake.

Little is ever written about our fairy rings. Fairy rings show up throughout the United States and elsewhere with little mention. Fairy rings are normally located in a field of tall grasses. They are indented in a circle by (supposedly) a fungus—or is it stardust? In the far distance a lone tree can be seen standing by itself. The Fairy Ring of Halloween has its own tree.

Another ring farther south on Larks Lake Road is the Snow White Mushroom Ring. This ring is composed of a circle of beautiful, white-capped mushrooms. Mushroom rings usually appear in forested areas and not in fields of grasses like fairy rings. This ring is about 30 feet in diameter.

Are fairy rings supernatural landing sites, or interdimensional stargates? I believe that these rings connect with that which is above and below: the stars and the aquifer. The aquifer is part of Michigan's best kept secret—the underground tunnel system which exists in the Larks Lake area. Fresh springs from the aquifer, 27 feet below, provide us with our water.

Some believe spirit beings tend the rings. The Ipswich are brownish "invisibles" that are full-bodied Keepers of the Stargate. They can easily be seen with the naked eye throughout the area. Usually, no head, feet, or hands are seen on them. They are the fairies' friends and companions. Also, the Ipswich are the tenders of the Larks Lake Haunts.

The fairy kingdom is a part of a much larger group known to some as the interstellars of the fifth dimension.

The fairies and the interstellars' bodies are clear and often times see-through.

Some of these beings can travel etherically, without feet nor body, beyond the speed of sound and light. Fairies can be seen small or human-sized. With a trained eye, the fairies and interstellars are easily seen in nature.

—*Jennifer Cupples, contributor*

Legs Inn; Legs, Wood and Polish Sausage

Do not imagine human gams on display when you hear the name of this restaurant. The legendary Emmet County establishment is named for legs that have nothing to do with human limbs or the tangle of carved wooden artifacts and décor that fills the interior. The name "Legs Inn" comes from the row of old cast iron stove legs that accent the log restaurant's roof jutting into the sky like strange spikes on some ancient fortress.

Indoors, Legs Inn is a marvel of wood sculpture, starting with the bulbous wooden figure called "Struggle," which may be named for the viewer's problem in determining what the artwork depicts. It appears to be a fleshy creature in some sort of torment…fanged mouth gasping, eyes popping.

Antler collections and more weird carvings, such as a snake made from a length of driftwood, cover the rest of the walls. The art show continues in the outside gardens with totem poles and other rustic pieces. Many customers are taken with the choice of 100 Polish beers, intended to wash down such delicacies as *pierogi* and *golabki*.

The restaurant's builder and wood artist was a Polish immigrant named Stanley Smolak. Smolak arrived in 1921 after working in Detroit and Chicago auto factories for a few years, and made such good friends with the resident Ottawa tribe that they adopted him.

Inspired by northern Michigan's abundance of wood and stone, he began to put together his lodge in the late 1920s, starting with a curio shop where Native American handiwork could be sold. The tavern and dining room followed, with bars made from huge trees cut into great slabs, and tables with legs made by tying tree branches together until they grew into the right shape to support a table top. He added four massive fireplaces built from the native stone.

Stanley Smolak passed away in 1968, but the restaurant is still run by the Smolak family. The Legs Inn is a State of Michigan Historical Monument, and with its strange blend of Old World food and New World architecture gives the phrase "Polish-American" a whole new spin.

Crystal Falls Township
Iron County
The Ice Wheel

It was almost noon on November 30, 2006, when retired cabinetmaker Ralph Haugen heard a knock on his front door in the township of Crystal Falls. An area resident, Mark Navarre, was standing there wide-eyed, and told Haugen he needed to come and see something in the river close to the Haugen's house. Navarre explained he had just been crossing the Hemlock River, heading east over the Kivimaki Bridge, when he happened to spy something extremely unusual in the river just to his right. Haugen and his wife, Monica, pulled on their jackets and ran to the riverbank with Navarre.

There, the three of them gaped in astonishment at a floating circle of ice 55 feet in diameter. The half-inch-thick circle lay spinning in the flowing river as a strong current rotated it clockwise. The circle was so perfect and its edges so clean, Haugen told *Strange Michigan*, it appeared to have been cut by a laser. And yet, cut from what? The water around it was not frozen.

The *Iron County Reporter* ran a story featuring one of Ralph Haugen's photos of the phenomenon, and agreed that the circle appeared cut out by some type of machine or laser. But as the newspaper noted, the ice circle was not the only strange thing to happen on the Hemlock on November 30.

Earlier, at about 12:45 a.m., Navarre had been driving home from his job as a mechanic and night watchman at a flooring manufacturer in Amasa, tooling along Townline Road and approaching Bates-Amasa Road, when he spotted a pulsing white light over the normally dark Hemlock River. He could not think of any rational explanation for the light. The *Iron County Reporter* offered its opinion that

the pulsing light and circle of ice were related, but could not come up with any other possible origin for the frozen, spinning platter. And the ice, of course, soon melted, leaving Ralph Haugen's photos as the only remaining evidence.

Strange Michigan did a little digging and discovered that an area ski resort about 15 miles from Amasa had reported in its online "snow blog" on November 29 that temperatures were expected to drop very rapidly that night, ending up in the low teens (Fahrenheit) on November 30th. Could it be that the temperature dip fast-froze an area of the top layer of river water, which was then rotated and "machine edged" to circular perfection by the river currents? Makes sense to us, and yet…what were the pulsating lights Navarre saw over the same spot 11 hours earlier?

Ralph Haugen wondered in a phone conversation with *Strange Michigan* whether UFOs might have caused the circle. He cited a story told to him by a retired police officer who was fishing on Muskellenge Lake near Eagle River, Wisconsin, with his son 25 years ago when a round object flew silently overhead and then just hung there over the men's boat. The object had lights all around its rim, the man told Haugen. To the pair's astonishment, a second, identical object then flew up next to the first one and the two craft hovered ten minutes before flying away in different directions, neither object having made any audible sound. Eagle River is not far over the Wisconsin-Michigan border.

Was the ice circle a gift from Mother Nature or a covert, nighttime operation by visitors from some other world?

Ralph Haugen

Daggett

Menominee County

Flashing Cow and Cutout Cheerleader

Michigan does have cows, true, but it isn't known as "the dairy state." So what is an excavation company just south of the little hamlet of Daggett on US Highway 41 doing with a giant, fiberglass cow sculpture next to its sign? The cow, it must be added, is no ordinary Holstein but a saucy Bossie joyfully exposing her udder. She is accompanied by a purple silo, a smaller bull, and plywood cheerleaders…a roadside statue party.

Owner Tom Wangerin told *Strange Michigan* the whole thing was planned and engineered by his girlfriend, Christine Jenkins. She decided that he needed a statue to attract attention to his roadside business, so she drove to Wisconsin and brought the big cow home on a flatbed trailer. The statue's creator told her it was one of only two like it; he was breaking the mold and not making any more. A week later, said Wangerin, he called Christine and asked if she would sell it back to him but she refused. The rest of the ensemble was added gradually, with Christine cutting and painting the plywood cheerleaders in honor of the pair's daughters.

Wangerin said that in the summer, 35 to 40 cars per week stop so people can pose for photos next to the cow. His favorite was a busload of nuns, each of whom posed smiling with an arm draped around the statue. The cow even made the front page of the Escanaba newspaper after he loaned it to the town for a float in the annual Escanaba Fun Run parade. And it has become a local landmark, with police relating their locations in proximity to the big cow.

The best look at the cow is probably from the air, though. Every August on the weekend closest to the 25th, Wangerin's birthday, he hosts a Power Parachute Fly-In. Directions to the fly-in are easy…just look for the flashing cow.

Detroit

Wayne County

The Mystic Intercessor of Detroit: Father Solanus Casey

From 1924 to 1957, Catholics of Detroit had a secret weapon in their prayer arsenal that provided miraculous results with fair regularity. When all else failed, desperate people sought out a mighty warrior of prayer known for his amazing intercessions. Lay people and church officials alike recognized Father Solanus Casey, ordained in the Capuchin order in 1904, as the man to see for "special favors" from God. Over the years, Father Solanus was said to have cured many hundreds of people from cancer and other diseases. He could also instantly solve the thorniest problems, and even saved Chevrolet Motors from bankruptcy in 1925 with a prayer that was believed to have brought in an order for 45,000 autos after worker John McKenna paid fifty cents to Father Solanus's prayer association.

Born in 1870 near Oak Grove, Wisconsin, Father Solanus decided to dedicate his life to God after witnessing an act of brutality by an inebriated sailor. He entered a seminary in Milwaukee. As he prayed, the Virgin Mary appeared to him and told him to go to Detroit. He obediently packed his bag and left. He entered a monastery there, and six years later left to minister in New York. It was here that people began to notice something strange. The good Father, forbidden to preach or hear confessions because of low marks on his seminary exams, had joined a prayer group called the Seraphic Mass Association. When people applied to join the group, Father Solanus was the person who took their application and first heard about their problems. Applicants soon began to realize that their prayers were often answered in quick and miraculous ways.

Father Solanus Casey

When Father Solanus returned to Detroit in 1924, he continued to take prayer applications from thousands of people. He worked as a simple doorman at St. Bonaventure Monastery, and enjoyed playing the violin and singing hymns (although most agreed his music was far from heavenly… listen to a sample at www.solanuscasey.org.)

He died in 1957 of skin cancer; but is remembered by many with the help of relic badges containing threads from his robes, and he has been proposed as a candidate for sainthood. Father Solanus' death at age 87 occurred 53 years to the day and *hour* from his first holy mass. In 1994, the TV show *Unsolved Mysteries* devoted a segment to Father Solanus and his favors, and Pope John Paul II gave him the posthumous title of "Venerable." The man who did so poorly in school ended up more than making the grade when it came to the mysteries of faith.

Above and below:
Scenes from the Solanus Casey Center, 1780 Mt. Elliott, Detroit

Burke's Nightmare on Heidelberg Street

As a boy, sculptor Tim Burke used to have a recurring nightmare that he was being chased by a bogeyman made of iron. But as an adult he repressed the scary Iron Man along with other memories of a troubled childhood, until he turned to art to heal his old problems and addictions. After taking a welding class, he began making a creature from scrap metal parts as an assignment. And when it was finished, Burke found himself staring at what he suddenly recognized as his childhood nemesis—he'd unwittingly resurrected the Iron Man!

That epiphany was a crucial step both in his healing process and in his art, Burke told *Strange Michigan*. "My work is my story," said Burke, now in his late 40s. "It took me a lifetime for it to bubble up out of me. Anyone else who has had trauma in their lives can relate to it." He still has the original Iron Man, but now he accepts commissions for similar figures for other people. Burke works as a treatment center counselor by day, but the rest of his time is spent scavenging for raw materials wherever old buildings are biting the dust in Detroit. He was headed for the remains of a demolished Motown Records building on the night *Strange Michigan* talked to him, hoping to pick up a few nice concrete flowers.

Despite concrete gardens and a house painted in the almost absurdly happy colors of tangerine and bright yellow, most of Burke's art is decidedly edgy. Rows of painted mannequin heads line the tops of two windows. The heads, which Burke scavenged from an abandoned storage garage, symbolize what happens to human bodies in war, he explained. He found the heads on a tip from another artist, who told Burke he had seen some "cool stuff" there one Easter Sunday. "I thought he had hidden them for me to find like an Easter egg hunt," said Burke, "except it was a head hunt." It turned out his friend hadn't even known the heads were in the garage.

Another sculpture in his yard is of a woman Burke calls the "Social Worker," in honor of an African American social worker he remembers from his childhood. The bright reds and yellows of the sculpture recall the innocent, literal mental image he had as a five-year-old when his mother told him a "colored lady" was

Born and raised in the Detroit area, Burke moved to his house on Heidelberg in 1987. It's just down the street from the famous Heidelberg Project founded by fellow artist Tyree Guyton, and fits well with the blossoming community art movement that has transformed the surrounding blocks over the past several decades. Burke and Guyton both profess to have been influenced by the other. But Burke's father, a blacksmith, created metal artworks, and Burke says that was also an early influence on his work.

Of course, his personal demons are what drive him to create such things as his "rabid bunny." The 18-inch rodents are made from plastic cylinders, and come complete with grisly, humanlike teeth made from old plaster dental molds Burke scavenged. And a trio of three burned timbers taken from a burned out Studebaker plant needed no embellishment. "I stood them up and they looked like totems," said Burke. They also reminded him of the skinny, charred forms of Italian sculptor Giacometti.

Burke's work has been increasingly accepted by galleries and various art shows, including the gift shop at the Detroit Institute of Art. His ultimate goal? "I see myself moving toward world domination," he said, laughing. "Where every home would have a piece of Tim Burke art. The rabid bunnies are coming!"

Hazen Pingree

Edward VII

Hazen Pingree, The King's Doppelganger

Newspaper editors and friends called Detroit shoemaker, mayor, and Michigan governor Hazen Pingree, "Ping." Those who didn't know better often called him King Edward VII.

Born in Denmark, Maine, in 1840, Pingree's destiny lay in Detroit where he became known as a great reform leader. But as his growing fame caused his picture to be published in Detroit newspapers, readers began to notice a great similarity between the features of Ping and those of Great Britain's top royal. Illustrators of the late 1890s had fun drawing Ping wearing a crown, and Ping even cut his whiskers to match Edward's.

Ping made several trips to Europe during his career, and on his first journey to England, the London newspapers also made much of the distinguished American's uncanny resemblance to their leader. On another trip in 1901, Ping fell ill with peritonitis in London. King Edward, perhaps not willing to watch someone who looked so much like himself die, sent his own physicians to Ping's bedside to see what could be done, but Ping died on June 18. His body was sent back to Detroit for a huge funeral and burial in Elmwood Cemetery.

Ping was much beloved by Detroiters for other reasons, especially his advocacy for the needy. Another of his nicknames was "Potato Patch Pingree." When the Money Panic of 1893 caused severe financial hardship for many Detroit families, Ping thought of using acres of idle land left over from the recent real estate bust as family garden plots. "Ping's Patches" were widely credited with helping the city avoid widespread starvation, and his idea was imitated all over the country. Poet Paul Laurence Dunbar even wrote a poem about Ping, and the final two lines read, "For Pingree's at the city's head, we'll vote for him and vote for bread."

Stuck underground where burrowing rodents and insects are their sole and undiscerning audience, strange coffins make one blowout appearance at the funeral and thereafter must be remembered by word and photo.

Detroit's most unforgettable vault was ordered by gangster "Maserati" Rick Carter, a drug dealer who met his maker in 1988. Only 29 years old, Carter was shot to death in Mount Carmel hospital as he lay recuperating from another gunshot wound. The auto-loving Carter's coffin was designed to resemble a Mercedes Benz with real parts added by the Lincoln Casket Company of Hamtramck. Costing his estate a hefty $16,000, it featured a gold-plated grille, headlights, and spinning wheels. Only the wheels were removed for interment in Detroit's Elmwood Cemetery.

On the law-abiding but still eccentric side, the *Detroit Free Press* told of a 58-year-old woman from Flint named Connie Scramlin who literally became a diehard Tigers fan. Knowing that she had terminal cancer, she ordered a special casket in the team colors, orange and blue, complete with the Tigers official emblem, and had it draped with a bouquet of tiger lilies. At her 1991 funeral, she was laid out in a full-fledged Tigers uniform and guests filed past the colorful coffin to the tune of, "Take Me Out to the Ball Game." The funeral director who assisted Scramlin in planning her own funeral said that the preparations made him feel as if he were "celebrating a pennant series."

How Herman Menz of Devil Statue Fame is Conducting an Aldermanic Campaign

The Stonecutter's Satan Shrine

The devil may be in the details, but in 1905 a Detroit stonecutter insisted the devil was in his frontyard. Not content with any of the usual holy statues erected by European immigrants, Menz declared that Satan was his true friend and promptly carved a huge, malicious-looking gargoyle to represent Beelzebub. To deepen the offense, Menz set the gargoyle on a stone altar in front of his house and chiseled Latin words that translated to, "Man is not created, but developed; God did not make man, but man made the gods."

Needless to say, the bold statement did not go down well with the neighbors. Menz was threatened and rocks and other debris were thrown at the gargoyle statue, to the point where police had to be called to control the crowd. Menz, grossly overestimating his popularity after the gargoyle incident, also tried unsuccessfully to run for 10th Ward Alderman. He died in 1919 at the age of 90.

MENZ IS MAKING MORE DEVILS

MENZ'S NEW DEVILS.

Herman Menz Will As Soon As He Can Erect More Gargoyles After Fashion of Notre Dame Cathedral.

"THE GARGOYLE."

This Monument, Erected to Satan By Herman Menz, Is Damaged By Angry Mob.

SPIRIT OF RIOT.

Continued From Page One.

with the strain on his overwrought nerves—for the old man seems to have some strange sort of affection for the queer stone thing that sits high up above his sidewalk and grins unutterable defiance on all below.

"You say you will knock its head off, hey? Well let them hurt my—my image," said the old German, drawing his coat closer about him, "and I will make the city pay for it."

Inside the house something of the anxiety that prevailed without seemed to have communicated itself. Even "Trilby," the fat little old fox terrier, ambled about in a forlorn way, as if scenting unusual and dire happenings in the air. Miss Menz, eldest daughter of the suddenly famous evolutionist, spoke hesitatingly of her own views on matters religious.

"Yes, I share my father's unorthodox opinions," she said. "It isn't that he forced me to them—no, indeed, long ago when I was a member of the Episcopalian church I became disgusted with much of what I saw and heard, but most of all with the picture that was painted for me of a—

UNVEILS MONUMENT OF HIS FRIEND THE DEVIL

Rich Detroit Infidel Shows His Contempt for Religion by a Stone Statue on His Front Lawn—Church People Scandalized.

1931

By LOUIS L. RICHARDS.

A STORY that went around the world and gave undying fame to a simple-minded old Detroiter in 1905 was the yarn which announced that Herman Menz had built a statue to the devil, and proposed to show his contempt for religion by placing his Satanic Majesty upon a pedestal in front of his home at 308 Stanton avenue.

Not only were the pious neighbors of old man Menz shocked, but religious - minded people all over the city rose in indignation and demanded that this disciple of Beelzebub be disciplined for his uncalled-for flouting of the Deity. So sensational was the incident that the story didn't die out for two or three years, the statue eventually being sold to a showman who placed it on exhibition in one of the amusement parks at the Belle Isle bridge approach, and ultimately it was lost in antiquity.

Mr. Menz

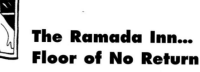

The Ramada Inn...
Floor of No Return

If *Strange Michigan* ever saw a hotel that looks as if it should be haunted, it's the Ramada Inn, downtown Detroit. The outside of the former brick apartment building on Bagley Street is ordinary enough, but inside, old brass elevator doors and unused vacuum tube mailboxes give the endless halls an ambience of days…and perhaps people…gone by. Adding to the mysterious atmosphere most evenings is the presence of many young Goth music fans dressed in black, their faces powdered white, who come to visit the popular Ramada basement club.

One Ramada employee who asked not to be identified told us that hotel personnel have been spooked by strange lights and noises over the entire building, but the main legend concerns the fourth floor. "People say that sometimes, if you go to the fourth floor, you can never leave it," she said. Shades of Hotel California! When *Strange Michigan* inquired at the desk about the possibility of staying in a fourth floor room, we were told only that the floor is closed. We did not press the matter.

Eagle Harbor

Keweenaw County

Is that George, George, or George?

The rocky point of Eagle Harbor has been home to three different lighthouse buildings since 1851, which were tended by (among others) three light keepers named George. Small wonder then that the spirit who befuddles modern Coast Guardsmen by turning off their radios when they play rock 'n' roll is named "George." George is also reportedly fond of pulling out dresser drawers to let them crash to the floor and rattle anyone nearby.

 ### The Scoofies

A quarter century ago, a group of monks relocated to the Keweenaw Peninsula, setting up a monastery at Jacob's Falls, on the shores of Lake Superior near Eagle Harbor. They chose the site for its remoteness and solitude, just as many others still do. As the brothers settled into their new home, they built themselves a beautiful and striking monastery situated alongside state highway M-26. Back when they first moved to the area, the brothers learned of a local legend that they have embraced, whether or not they take the tales literally.

A visitor to the monastery informed the brothers that, as a child, he heard folktales about little people who inhabited the ravine surrounding Jacob's Falls. Though the man who shared the story had never seen the wee folk himself, he couldn't help wondering whether such beings did reside in the mystical corners of the Keweenaw. Many places in the Keweenaw seem perfect for fairies—who, according to Celtic mythology, often lived in or near water. The Keweenaw's numerous waterfalls, big and small, and their associated gorges, overhangs, and caves offer dark and mysterious spots for the fairy folk to live. Why shouldn't Jacob's Falls host a population of magical creatures?

The possibility that fairies, elves, or leprechauns might dwell at Jacob's Falls has intrigued the brothers of the Holy Transfiguration Skete as well. They have named the magical, and heretofore unseen, inhabitants of the falls "Scoofies". Their website, SocietyStJohn.com, features Scoofy artwork and poetic musings on the possibility of the beings' existence, what they might be like, and how they might live. The brothers have even written a "Scoofy Song" about the little fellows.

The brothers operate a store called the Jampot, across the highway from the monastery. The Jampot sells many food items, including unique cookie combinations such as peanut butter, oatmeal, raisin, and chocolate chip—all in the same cookie! If you stop in to buy some jam or cookies, keep an eye on the woods. You never know when a Scoofy might pop into view.

The Mystery of Popeye Rock

Back in 1980, Eagle Harbor residents started an informal 10K run down Eagle Harbor Cutoff Road. It was an athletic event to honor a rock.

Years ago, so long in the past no one remembers exactly when, someone selected a boulder along Eagle Harbor Cutoff Road as his canvas. The anonymous artist painted the head of Popeye the Sailor on the rock, along with the phrase "strong to the finish." The artist's identity remains a mystery. So does the identity of the person who touches up the painting each year.

After years of looking at the rock, local residents got an idea. Why not have a 10K run in its honor? Later on they added a 5K run, and now every summer dozens of runners flock to Eagle Harbor to participate in the event. Perhaps downing a can of spinach would be the best preparation for the race.

Eagle River
Keweenaw County
Freak Drowning; Legendary Name

As you drive north through the Keweenaw Peninsula, you'll see two names crop up repeatedly—Douglass and Houghton. The city of Houghton, on Portage Lake. The Douglass House Saloon, in downtown Houghton. The county of Houghton, which encompasses the city and half of the Keweenaw. Behind the names lies the story of a man who made history.

In 1837 Douglass Houghton became Michigan's first state geologist. The state had recently acquired the Upper Peninsula, a myste-

rious outback with mineral resources, the extent of which was poorly understood. From 1838 until 1845, Houghton embarked on a mission to explore the UP and its geological resources. While he felt mining would prove more arduous than feasible, Houghton helped bring the Copper Country's resources to public attention. After Houghton's death, mines would pop up all over the Keweenaw.

In October 1845 Houghton drowned during a freak storm on Lake Superior, less than a mile from shore. The man who helped give the Copper Country its name would never taste the fruits of his endeavors, yet his memory lives on in the guise of a 15-ton hunk of greenstone, part of a memorial erected in 1914 in Eagle River. The boulder perches atop a base constructed from stones gathered from all over the UP, including rock from every mine in the Keweenaw. A metal plaque secured to the boulder memorializes Houghton, who died a mile from the spot where his monument hunkers.

Above and below:
Monument and plaque in memory of Douglass Houghton

East Tawas

 Iosca County

East Tawas Bar Hangs on... and on...to fave patron

If Chum's Bar in East Tawas ever gave a customer appreciation award for most faithful patron, Stan Humphrey, Sr., would be the shoo-in winner even though his award would have to be accepted posthumously. The used-car salesman started dropping by the bar at age eighteen and never missed a day thereafter for the rest of his life. After he retired, he would stop twice a day, first thing in the morning and then again at Happy Hour. A story in the East Tawas *Morning Sun* in 1989 quoted Stan as explaining, "I love it here or I wouldn't have been here 23 years. (Actually it had been longer than that.) My kids call it my second home." He was fond of saying that if he didn't show up one day, it would mean he was dead, and that is exactly how things went when Stan finally passed on in 1998 at the age of 83.

A former owner named Anna Busch had playfully told Stan one day that she was so used to having him around, he might as well leave his ashes with her when he died. Stan took her words to heart, and

instructed his family to give his cremains to Chum's Bar. They complied, and to stay even truer to Stan's habits, the ashes were not stashed in a normal funerary urn, but in an empty bottle of Stan's drink of choice, Imperial Whiskey. Not just any bottle of Imperial Whiskey, either. It's the last one Stan drank from before he died.

New owners Glenda and John Revord have remodeled the bar and adjacent eatery that together date back to 1920, but Stan's bottle remains in its place of honor on a shelf behind the bar, next to a little plaque that reads, "Past Patron, Forever Friend." His four sons return every summer for a little family reunion with their father at Chum's, where they all hoist a shot of Imperial to Dad. One waitress hinted to *Strange Michigan* that a few strange incidents in the place have made her think it's haunted, but no one knows whether that would be Stan or one of any number of owners or patrons from past years. As for Stan, his family and the bar owners are content knowing it's always Happy Hour as far as he's concerned.

Empire
Leelanau County
The Legend of Sleeping Bear Dune

Today, we know the shoreline along the northwestern edge of the Lower Peninsula as Sleeping Bear Dunes National Lakeshore. But do you know the mournful story that lies behind the name?

An Ojibwe legend tells the story of a mother bear and her two cubs who attempted to swim across Lake Michigan from Wisconsin. A forest fire drove them out of their home, into the water, where they had no choice but to swim for their lives. When the mother reached Michigan's shore, she turned to find her cubs gone. The twins, wiped out by the journey, had drowned.

North and South Manitou Islands—formed by the Great Spirit—memorialize the lost cubs, while the mother bear lies on a 400-foot-high plateau overlooking Lake Michigan, forever awaiting her cubs' arrival. Sleeping Bear Dune, perched atop that plateau north of Empire, symbolizes the mother bear. The park encompasses a 35-mile stretch of shoreline in Leelanau and Benzie counties, including both the dune and the Manitou Islands.

The lakeshore became a national park on October 21, 1970.

Escanaba
Delta County
The Snow Snake

In Michigan's Upper Peninsula, there are some winters when everything seems to be frozen white, even the animals. Legends of a monstrous, serpentine creature the color of snowdrifts circulate here when the days grow short. They tell of a beast that slithers through the avalanche of snow that falls every year in the UP. Never mind the fact that reptiles are cold-blooded creatures and don't function too well in freezing temperatures. Tales of the snow snake supposedly date back to ancient native lore, and local tribal nations once did indeed carve wooden snakelike figures to use in throwing games.

Contemporary witnesses are hard to find. Few people, it is said, who have seen a snow snake burst from beneath the crystalline surface to face its glassy stare have lived to tell the tale. Snow snakes are also accused of mischief; skiers who lose their balance or ice fishermen whose shanties shift on the ice will often blame the hoary-hued reptile for their problems. No snow snake body, living or dead, has yet been brought forth for examination, but some people claim to have seen its tracks winding through the pine forests, always ending mysteriously as if the creature had vanished into the ground below.

husband who died before the light was completed in 1867. In 1886, a fire ravaged the lighthouse. The next morning, the remains of 69-year-old Mary Terry turned up in the rubble. Later authorities determined that she died not from the fire but from unknown causes, with murder suspected. The case was never solved.

Fast forward to 1985, and Mary Terry becomes the requisite ghost for the lighthouse. Why not? Mary died of unnatural causes, with the circumstances surrounding her death still shrouded in mystery to this day. If anyone should roam the Sand Point Lighthouse for eternity, restless and searching for peace, that soul would surely be Mary Terry, who gave her life to and for the light.

The limestone cliffs at Fayette

 ## The Made-Up Ghost of Sand Point

Visit a lighthouse, in Michigan or anywhere in the U.S., and you will likely hear a tale about the ghost who inhabits the structure. Most lighthouses in Michigan date back a hundred years or more, which means that at some point someone probably died there—a light keeper or a member of his family. Ghost stories that speak of a tortured soul forever bound to the beacon he maintained in life can draw in tourists like iron flakes to a magnet. But what to do if your lighthouse has no ghost?

When the Delta County Historical Society took over the Sand Point Lighthouse in 1985, the place lacked a crucial element: It had no resident spook. The solution was simple—create one! Thus the spirit of Mary Terry became the specter-in-residence, blamed for any strange goings-on at the former coast guard facility. The real live Mary Terry served as the first keeper of the light, taking over for her

 # Fayette
Delta County
The Spider Man

The mysteries enshrouding the ancient people who inhabited Michigan thousands of years ago endure even today. Despite advances in technology, a veil still separates the ancients and our understanding of their society. While some monuments to ancient cultures—such as burial mounds bulging up in hay fields—stare us

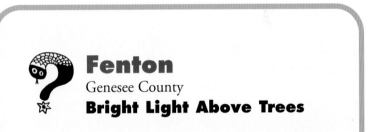

in the face, others reside hidden in our state. One of those hidden places sits on private property on the Garden Peninsula in Delta County.

Just south of Fayette State Park, nearly at the tip of the peninsula, lies a site of historic importance called Burnt Bluff. Here on the cliff face, and in caves that pockmark the 140-foot limestone precipice, lies one of only three rock art sites in the state recognized as genuinely ancient. The artwork consists of pictographs, figures painted onto the rock using red ocher. The site most likely dates to between 300 BC and 800 AD.

The pictographs at Burnt Bluff measure from six inches to as much as two feet in height. Some of the pictographs occupy wall space in the mouth of a cave which, depending on water levels, may sit either at the base of the cliffs or 10 to 15 feet up the face. This cave, known as Spider Cave, contains a pictograph nicknamed the Spider Man that shows a spider beneath a stout man, the two figures connected by a line that curves from the spider's body up and around the man, where it attaches to his abdomen. Beyond the cave, on the face of the cliff, a larger pictograph about two feet high depicts a humanoid figure called the Big Man. Other now-eroded figures scattered across the cliff face also suggest human forms.

While some caves near the pictographs housed human burials, projectile points litter other caves, including Spider Cave. The points have broken tips, as if ancient people hurled or shot the points into the cave from outside, probably from canoes on the lake. Archaeologists have posited that the arrows represent offerings to the *May-may-gway-shi*—humanoid spirit beings similar to the Celtic fairies—believed to live in caves and crevices near water. Modern Algonquian legends tell of the *May-may-gway-shi* inhabiting similar sites and also associate red ocher pictographs with the spirits. Sometimes the legends ascribe the pictographs to the *May-may-gway-shi* themselves.

Whatever their purpose, the Burnt Bluff pictographs still possess the power to enchant. Imagine fairylike beings cavorting in the caves, scaling the cliffs like our modern, cartoon version of Spider-Man. Perhaps the pictographs served as the ancient version of comic books!

Fenton
Genesee County
Bright Light Above Trees

On April 14, 2004, a mysterious object visited Lower Michigan. According to a report on the UFOINFO Website, a witness named Aaron was driving southbound on US 23 just north of Fenton at around 9:15 p.m. Suddenly he noticed a bright light hovering above the trees. The highway comes close to the treeline, which Aaron estimated at "a few feet" away from the road. The object resembled a low-flying plane. Aaron had the car's windows rolled down and the radio playing but, when he shut off the radio, he noted that the object made no sound. As he drove past the object, it remained visible in his rearview mirror, moving sideways now as if searching for something. Aaron continued on his way. He felt sure other motorists must have seen the same object.

Flint
Genesee County
The Giant Wolf of Flint

One consistently described feature of the Dogman, an upright-walking canine many witnesses claim stalks the woods and roadsides of Michigan, is its size…usually six to seven feet tall on its hind legs. It stands to reason, then, that massive, wolfen creatures should be glimpsed or even bagged by hunters now and then. That is exactly what happened to a deer hunter named Eastman around noon on November 18, 1935, on the third day of deerhunting season. Eastman was hunting near Flint around Rhody Creek Trail, and despite good weather and a great layer of tracking snow, there were absolutely no deer to be seen.

Eastman soon found out why. He suddenly heard what sounded like "horses running," and turned to see a massive timber wolf at a dead run. Eastman ended up shooting a wolf rather than a deer that day. He gutted it and dragged it into town to have it weighed and measured; it was 182 pounds even after gutting, and measured seven feet 11 inches tall when measured hanging vertically. The creature stood 39 inches at the shoulder! It was considered such a magnificent specimen that the carcass was sent to the Carnegie Institute in Pittsburgh where it was mounted and displayed. The entire story of the great Flint Wolf was told in the *Great Lakes Mariner*, Vol. 3, No. 6, 2005. And *Strange Michigan* found a copy of it displayed in the North Star Tavern in Luther, the town known for Dogman sightings and incidents.

Forester
Sanilac County
Minnie Quay, Fabled Lover from the Thumb

It's no wonder that something as deadly as the crashing waves of Lake Huron should produce ghosts by the sinking boatload. One of the most famous is no anonymous wraith, but the spirit of a particular resident of Michigan's Thumb.

Minnie Quay was a lovely young teenage girl who lived with her parents in the Lake Huron port of Forester in the mid-1800s. James and Mary Ann Quay had emigrated from New England to run a tavern, and Minnie was their oldest daughter. The bustling port of Forester catered to both shipping and the lumber business, and as a result was overrun with sailors and lumbermen.

The Quays looked upon these occupations as unsuitable for any future husband of their daughter, and they tried to keep Minnie from frequenting the massive pier that once extended onto the lake from Forester's shore.

Their efforts were to no avail. Minnie fell in love with a sailor, outraging James and Mary Ann. They told Minnie she could have nothing more to do with her suitor. Minnie was heartbroken, but the situation worsened when the young man's ship was lost in one of the frequent storms that plagued the Great Lakes. Despondent, Minnie jumped off the end of the Forester Pier and drowned herself, hoping to somehow join her lover in his watery grave. She is buried in the Forester Cemetery just off the shoreline, with a glistening view of the lake that brought her lover to Michigan.

Minnie might have been forgotten, except that people began to see her ghost. Some glimpsed the young girl trudging the rocky Forester beaches, wailing in search of her lost love. Others have sworn that she stands in the lapping waves along the shore and motions for them to follow her into the drink. Legend has it that at least one girl followed the ghost's invitation and also drowned. And just for good measure, ghosts of young boys, victims of a long-ago schoolhouse fire, are said to romp around the graves at midnight.

The great pier is long gone, but pilings are still visible in the water. The town of Forester is scarcely inhabited these days, but Minnie's house stands resolute across the street from a tavern on the main street through town. Tourists can have their photos taken standing behind a faded plywood cutout of an antique car, then walk to the cemetery where Minnie lies. And if some young girl should appear in the gray-blue waters, waving her arms as if to invite company, travelers should be warned: Lake Huron is cold and deep, and holds more secrets than any person should ever care to know.

The former home of Minnie Quay

The authorities in Fowlerville didn't know what to think the night Gary Browning phoned them to say he had just encountered "a grunting thing" that stood eight feet tall and had dark fur from head to foot. It was August 1978, and the *Livingston County Press* reported Browning took a rifle outside in the wee hours of the morning after he heard his livestock making distressed noises. He brought his dog along, and the hound took off into the brush to investigate. In a few moments, the dog came hightailing it back out as the grunting, huge creature appeared and began to walk toward Browning.

Browning fired three times at the behemoth, but rattled as he was, missed every time. He made the monster angry enough to chase the terrified Browning back to his farmhouse. Browning called the sheriff's department and vowed he would track it down with his 12-gauge. After a little target practice, presumably.

Tourist spot in Forester

Frankenmuth
Saginaw County
World's Largest Christmas Store

Imagine a Bavarian Disney World focused mainly on shopping, anchored by the World's Largest Christmas Store, and you begin to get the picture of the tourist haven that is the city of Frankenmuth. A snippet of Old Germany grafted onto a patch of Michigan soil, Frankenmuth's old-country atmosphere did not happen by accident. The theme was a calculated risk engineered by the city fathers half a century ago when the new freeway passed the town by.

In this gotta-have-a-gimmick world, the folks of Frankenmuth realized they could still draw crowds if only they had a place worth visiting. Taking stock of their assets, they shrewdly realized that their German heritage could be just the ticket. That heritage had been launched in 1847 when a group of 15 hardy Lutherans arrived from Bavaria to start a mission settlement. Local historians say they cobbled the name "Frankenmuth" together by combining *Franconia*, a duchy of Medieval Germany, and *muth,* which means "courage" in German.

Frankenmuth had stayed very German over the years and had developed crowd-pleasers like its signature German chicken dinner. The dish is a staple of several restaurants, including the renowned Zehnder's that has served chicken and cabbage to as many as 5,916 guests on a single day. (The first chicken dinner credit goes to an early hotel owner's wife who catered a Saginaw wedding in 1899.) The city's ploy has been an overwhelming success, with millions of tourists passing through its decked halls every year.

Bronner's CHRISTmas Wonderland (the capitalization is the intentional emphasis on the holiday's religious aspect by owner Wally Bronner) lies on the outskirts of Frankenmuth, but in the heart of the town's old-time Christmas spirit. In terms of Christmas paraphernalia,

if you can't find it at Bronner's, you can't find it anywhere. The massive parking lot is bordered by "hills" alive with giant statues of Santa, Frosty, and reindeer, with a 24-figure, life-size crèche and rows of angels parading in front of the store. Another oversized Santa hails shoppers from a rooftop perch.

Inside the store, Christmas dioramas of wacky elves, decked out animals, and every type of Christmas figurine imaginable…over 700 are animated…cram the rafters to the ceiling, to the point where shoppers may slam into each other because they are looking up, rather than where they are going. The sales floor alone is the size of 1.7 football fields. There is even a replica of the Oberndorf, Austria, *Silent Night* Memorial Chapel, with a verse from the hymn *Silent Night* written out in 300 languages.

In business since 1945, the store proudly notes on Bronners.com that it has been visited by such diverse luminaries as singer Marie Osmond, rocker Ted Nugent, First Lady Laura Bush, and race car driver Al Unser, Jr. And in December 1976, John Wayne himself ordered a Santa suit from Bronner's over the phone. It would be hard to imagine the Duke as St. Nick anywhere except Frankenmuth, but then, this is a place where it's rumored that anyone who stays too long risks turning into gingerbread.

Freeland
Saginaw County
Dice Road, a Dicey Ride

A long, north-south country road that alternates between rough pavement and gravel, Dice Road is the creepy site of choice for cruising teens in Freeland. A bridge at the corner of Dice and Graham is rumored to be haunted by the spirits of a warlock who hung three women from it as payback after he caught them stomping on his dead wife's grave. According to legend, people who dare arrive after dark say they can still hear the women screaming and choking as they gulp their last gasps of air. A man's voice, supposedly that of the warlock, sometimes chimes in. Travelers who linger too long are chased out of the area by a phantom white car that follows them and then vanishes.

One teen, an employee of a Freeland gas station, told *Strange Michigan* that she has had creepy experiences in Richland Lutheran Cemetery on Dice Road and has seen strange lights and orbs over the older graves. And of course, she told us, the road comes complete with an allegedly haunted farmhouse.

Gay
Keweenaw County
What's in a Name? The Gay Bar

Nope, this place has nothing to do with sexual orientation, but everything to do with beer choices. The Gay Bar is named after its little UP hometown of Gay, although it winks at the double-entendre by selling a line of jokesy T-shirts and other souvenirs arrayed on a wall near two giant, mounted bear heads that snarl down at bar patrons. *Strange Michigan* plopped ourselves down at the U-shaped bar to enjoy a couple of cold ones and sample the bar's specialties: cheeseburgers and foot-long hot dogs.

We found the locals very chatty and friendly. Since the population of Gay is only about 40, probably a third of the town was there that day. A couple of native-born brothers entertained us with little-known facts, such as their knowledge that timber wolves will stand on their hind legs when threatened, which, if true, almost explains the Michigan Dogman.

But we digress. Gay came about in 1896 when Ernest Koch discovered copper ore in the vicinity. Joseph Gay, director and later president of the Wolverine and Mohawk Mining Companies, started mining operations at the site and lent his name to the little community that sprang up. One remnant of the town's old manufacturing industry is a 265-foot concrete smokestack that once served the boiler plant here. The Gay Bar was once home to a prominent village resident, but was converted to a tavern after Prohibition and has remained essentially the same through a progression of owners ever since. The town hosts two very popular annual events: the Gay Fourth of July Parade and the Big Buck Balls contest during deer-hunting season.

Those who can't get to Gay but would like to order a Gay Bar koozie or black thong with pink Gay Bar logo may visit www.thegay-bar.com.

Gaylord
Otsego County
A Big Beer for a Big Buck

If you drive north or south on I-75, down the center of Michigan, your path will cross through the city of Gaylord. Speeding down the freeway at 70 miles per hour, you could miss the alpine-flavored buildings in downtown Gaylord, and even the water tower. But one sight will surely capture your attention.

A giant beer bottle.

The gargantuan brown bottle stands adjacent to the northbound lanes of I-75. The big beer dwarfs the restaurant behind it, the Big Buck Brewery & Steakhouse. At night spotlights on the ground, aimed upward, illuminate the intoxicating colossus. The label plastered across the bottle features a giant buck's head and the name of the brand: Big Buck Beer.

Grand Rapids
Kent County
The Weirdest Presidential Museum

Does any other state possess a weirder monument to a president than Michigan's Gerald R. Ford Presidential Museum? Perhaps...then

The .45 caliber pistol taken from Squeaky Fromme.

again, maybe not. The Ford museum features such freaky rarities as faceless mannequins bedecked in Betty Ford's gowns, a funky caricature statue of President Ford, a time travel airlock filled with anachronistic memorabilia, and out-of-place mementos to historic events that happened after Ford left office—such as chunks of the Berlin Wall and a partial I-beam from the World Trade Center.

Strangest of all, however, may be the gun mounted on the wall. The .45-caliber pistol commemorates a time that one would think Ford himself would've preferred to forget—the 17-day period during which he survived two assassination attempts by two different women who had both lost enough marbles to fill a goldfish bowl. The first would-be assassin, Squeaky Fromme, never got to use her .45—Secret Service agents jumped her first. The museum enshrines a letter written by the second assassin, Sara Jane Moore, in which she offers a tepid apology for her bungled attempt.

In spite of the attempts on his life, Ford still managed to accomplish one task for which we can all thank him. He signed the law that made ATM cash machines possible. And, yes, the museum has an ATM—though as a display only, not a cash outlet. So the next time an ATM spits a twenty at you, silently thank the man whose museum exemplifies the strange in Michigan.

The Apple of Godzilla's Eye

If you believe that an apple a day keeps the doctor away, then you must stop by Robinette's Apple Haus & Gift Barn. There you'll find a giant apple that will surely keep the doctor at bay for the rest of your life! The giant apple resides in a picnic area at Robinette's, on 4 Mile Road in Grand Rapids.

A Toothy Monument

For years a monument in Grand Rapids has celebrated the city's status as the first locale in Michigan to fluoridate its water. The original monument resembled teeth at a drinking fountain but, after 12 years, the city had to replace the monument. Why?

Tooth decay!

The original monument was hewn from marble. The harsh weather common to Michigan winters, plus a few vandals, ate away at the monumental teeth quicker than a diet of cotton candy and ice cream. Someone suggested a new monument consisting of an enormous tooth on a pole, but area dentists took offense at the notion—or perhaps they're just sick of looking at teeth. Whatever the rationale, the dentists wanted art. And, boy, did they get it! The new

Grand Rapids 53

monument, called "Steel Water," adopts a more abstract approach to teeth and fluoride, with a wavy steel structure 33 feet tall that weighs in at five tons. The monument resembles a tooth if you squint and tilt your head, or if you have a vivid imagination. But the monument succeeds as abstract art, and stands out in front of the Marriott Hotel like the old marble sculpture never could. Most importantly, the dentists are happy.

New Species Discovered: Cedar Sapiens

Many gardens boast topiaries—hedges sculpted into box shapes, for instance. But have you ever seen leafy green hula-hoop dancers, or a veggie version of the Loch Ness Monster? Georgia Donovan is a Grand Rapids artist and gardener who created both. You might also call her a garden anthropologist, for she has invented a new species. Georgia calls her creations *Cedar sapiens*. But you won't find this species in biology textbooks. Six years ago Georgia made her first specimens of the species for clients in the Fisk Lake area. The exact recipe remains a trade secret, though Georgia hints that it involves "bending and clipping" the bushes to achieve the right blend of human and vegetation qualities. So what would drive a woman to invent a new life-form?

One day as Georgia walked through the woods, she got that prickly feeling of being watched. The watcher turned out to be a tree with a humanlike shape, and inspired Georgia to create a new kind of topiary.

But the topiaries needed an ear-catching name to complement their eye-catching appearance. Taking the *sapiens* from *Homo sapiens*, and the cedar from...cedar, Georgia christened her topiaries *Cedar sapiens*. Sometimes she also calls them *Thuja wannadance*, marrying their predilection for hip-wiggling to the scientific name for cedar (*Thuja occidentalis*). The *Cedar sapiens* soon shimmied their way into yards throughout the Grand Rapids area.

Now pear-shaped cedar people with volcanic hairdos wave at onlookers from one backyard. Others seem to raise their arms in silent prayer to a lake—whoops, guess again! They're only hula-hooping. Georgia has dubbed the dancing folks *Cedar sapiens hula-hoopsii*. And these beings celebrate all the holidays, including Christmas, by wearing appropriate attire such as Santa hats and scarves. One cedar lady dons a bikini top in summertime, as she snags herself a cedar fish.

A colony of eight gregarious *Cedar sapiens* cavorts at the Breton Village Mall in Grand Rapids, on the corner of Breton and Burton. Georgia's creations also hang out in private gardens in St. Joseph, Grand Haven, and Grand Rapids. She has crafted *Cedar sapiens* in another state too—Montana.

Clockwise from upper left: *Cedar sapiens hula-hoopsii*; a dancing *Cedar sapiens*; a *Cedar sapiens* plays soccer; a pair of *Cedar sapiens* frolicking among the pumpkins; center: Trick or Treat?

Sanctuary Folk Art;
Mardi Gras on Every Wall

Artist Reb Roberts has a right to trim his startling artworks with Mardi Gras beads if he wants; he was born in New Orleans, home of the big festival and a hotbed of outsider art, in 1954. He left his southern roots for Michigan to work for friends who owned a pre-school in 1972, but brought along his beads and paintbrushes. He began exhibiting his art in 1994, and in 1999 opened the Sanctuary Folk Art Gallery as a showplace for many of the city's outrageous and often untutored artists.

The gallery at 140 S. Division Avenue is a riotous maelstrom of color, glitter, and transformed objects. To Reb, it's the very antithesis of the straight-laced, restrictive Catholic school he attended in Louisiana or the engineering career he was expected to pursue as a youthful math and science whiz. Although he displays artful conglomerations and enigmatic canvases by other like-minded spirits, his own slogan-sloshed paintings dominate the gallery. Ranging from the elegant simplicity of "War Sucks" to the admonitory "Don't be no big chicken," his crudely lettered words swim around the black outlines of giant animal heads, trotting long-horned steers, and blonde ladies.

He admits he discovered his huge attraction for bright paint and glitter during those years teaching preschool, and he still works with youngsters at the Grand Rapids Children's Museum and area schools.

Reb Roberts

Just Hanging Out

Many people consider Sigmund Freud a brilliant psychoanalyst. But, in Grand Rapids in December 2007, the departed doctor gave local folks the scare of their lives nearly 70 years after his passing.

When people saw a man dangling from a pole above the building housing the Open Concept Gallery, they naturally thought he needed help. Numerous people called 911 to report the man hanging on by his fingertips, about to fall to his death. Turns out the man needed no one's help—he can hang on forever. The man in peril was a sculpture by Czech artist David Cerny.

The life-size sculpture, called "Man Hanging Out," depicts Sigmund Freud who—perhaps due to a Freudian slip—hangs by one hand from a pole. Cerny's sculpture, which adorns the Louis Avenue building as part of an international tour, was set to remain on display until Spring 2008. The art gallery's owner said she had permission from the city to display the sculpture. Authorities say nobody informed them of the alarming artwork, and passersby certainly had no clue.

At night, without lighting to clarify the situation, passersby mistook the sculpture for a real man. In response to the 911 calls, fire crews rushed onto the roof. There, they found a statue suspended from a beam bolted to the roof.

 ## Haunts of Holmdene

One of the most beautiful old buildings on the Aquinas College campus—and the oldest —Holmdene Hall once was home to a very wealthy Grand Rapids clan, the Lowes. It is now used for administrative purposes, but even the college's official Web site notes that it is haunted by more than one spirit. A young boy said to have drowned on what was once a private country estate is just one of the ghosts that have been seen flitting about the building. Manifestations include water faucets turning on and off for no known reason, and lights that refuse to stay off for the night. Students like to drink a spooky alcoholic concoction known as "Holmdene's Ghost."

Holy Cross Cemetery

Holy Cross Cemetery at 2000 Walker Avenue, NW, commands a sweeping view between old and new areas, but the view is said to turn bizarre on nights when the full moon shines. Then, it is rumored, a long-deceased nun walks the grounds of the cemetery and can be seen glowing with a soft light near one of the tombstones.

Strange Michigan showed up one evening with a couple of local friends when the moon was full, but the nun didn't show. But then, we never did find out exactly which tombstone is the ghost nun magnet, and this place has a lot of tombstones.

Gun Lake
Kent County
Goofus Art

Mike Molenar's Web page, www.goofuscreations.com, while under construction read, "Please excuse the rust." His studio near Gun Lake where he assembles whimsical creatures from old metal potato planters, forks, shovels, spark plugs, and other farm tools could easily bear the same warning.

"It all started as a joke in my sister's flower garden," Molenar told *Strange Michigan.* "I had made her a birdlike critter out of farm tools and left it there, but she loved it and kept it and said I could sell them." Although Molenar did not have any previous artistic leanings, he took his sis at her word and began combing auctions and junkyards for more raw material.

She was right. He found as he began taking his rusty assemblages to art and craft fairs, people did buy them. He believes their appeal lies in the fact that people get a kick out of identifying the old tools and implement parts that make up each bird, bug, dragon, or comical human. "They see it and laugh," said Molenar.

Fans of tractor-part pterodactyls and the like can go to Molenar's Web site for a schedule of shows where his work may be viewed in person, or to contact him.

Gwinn
Marquette County
Even a Bigfoot Gets Thirsty

At 8:30 p.m. on June 28, 2006, David was out canoeing on the southern tip of a private lake near Gwinn when he sniffed an odd skunky odor. Then something on the shoreline caught his attention. To his amazement, a dark, hairy creature hunched at the water's edge some 30 yards away, drinking water from the lake with a concave piece of wood. At first, David took the creature for a bear—until the beast stood up straight, revealing its entire 7- to 8-foot height. It was a Bigfoot, David realized.

Seconds after David spotted it, the Bigfoot spotted him as well. The two eyed each other for about 20 seconds, then the creature turned and limped off into the woods. David lost sight of the beast as it retreated into the wilderness, though he could hear its feet crunching leaves and sticks for several more seconds. David immediately paddled to shore to look for footprints. While he found no tracks, he did discover possible knee imprints and snapped saplings. The creature's limp made David wonder if it had been injured. He reported his sighting to Backyard Phenomena Investigations, a Jacobsville-based paranormal research group.

In the same area, in 1959, David's great uncle saw what he described as a "gorilla." David's family has owned property on the private lake for several generations. David, a 34-year-old printer and musician from downstate, minored in biology in college. His studies, he says, gave him a good background for ruling out known animals.

What did David see that summer evening? Was it a Bigfoot? Only the creature knows for sure.

Helps
Menominee County
The Green Glow

As God as my witness, this is a true story. Back in 1985, I was deer hunting in northern Menominee County in the UP (near the Escanaba River State Forest). Around 9:00 a.m. I had a small yearling out in front of me, much too small to shoot. All of a sudden, the swamp appeared to take on this weird greenish hue. I mean…the trees, the ground, the sky all appeared this greenish color. Even the air. I don't know how to explain it.

At the same time, I had this weird feeling, one of sadness, remorse, shame, sorrow. It was so weird. I wanted to stick my head out of my blind and look up into the sky but I just couldn't do it. The little deer in front of me was shivering and eventually laid down with its head on the ground, like a dog taking a nap. I've always thought this deer must have had the same feeling as me.

This whole experience lasted maybe three minutes, but it seemed longer, like 15 minutes. Eventually the green hue began rolling and disappearing through the swamp. Sometimes you can see the rain coming down the road, then BOOM it hits ya. Well, it was the same concept.

As the greenish hue went over the top of my blind, the sorrow/sadness feeling was, like, sucked out of me. But then I had this feeling that I wanted to call out, "Hey! Wait! Don't go! Come back!" I was instantly very happy. Strange!

And then the greenish hue went past the small deer. Once it did, the deer sprang up and BAM! darted off towards a creek to the north of me. It was gone, heading the same way as the greenish hue.

I don't know, I can't explain the feeling I had and how weird things looked. I was on the verge of crying, but not crying…no tears. I felt so bad and then really happy.

I told my dad and brother this story. My brother insists that I was simply in the middle of a low-pressure system. Well, I'll tell you what, it was no low-pressure system. It was way more than that. It was something else. This is the weirdest thing that ever happened to me.

—Glenn Arntzen

Photo illustration

Hickory Corners
Barry County
Creepy Crawly Dogman

Most people in the southern part of Michigan believe themselves safe from the depredations of the Michigan Dogman. But on June 30, 2006, a man from Hickory Corners—only a few miles north of the Indiana/Michigan border—had a frightening encounter with the beast.

The man, who requested anonymity, was driving home at 2:50 a.m. at about 55 to 60 MPH when he spotted what he at first took for a deer near the road in an open field. But as he drove closer, he realized with a shock that it was not a deer but some type of manlike animal, 6 to 7 feet tall, covered in fur but standing on two feet. It turned to look at him as he passed, with round, "distinct" eyes. The creature was too slender to be a man, he said, and as he came closer, it dropped to all fours and then flattened out and began crawling, army commando-style, into the cornfield. The corn was only a foot-and-a-half high, and the man could see its "long, lanky arms" pulling the creature's body through the short stalks. He turned his car around as soon as he could slow down enough and came back but the creature was nowhere to be seen.

The man was particularly frightened because his mother and two brothers had claimed to have seen the exact same creature in that area six months earlier. "It seems too unreal," he wrote *Strange Michigan*, "but I am sure of what I saw. This was no animal/creature I had ever heard of."

Illustration by Nate Godfrey

Hillsdale
Hillsdale County
Cat-Scratch Fever

Lightning is known for the many weird effects it can have on victims…shoes blasted off, memory loss…but one of the strangest lightning injuries ever was suffered in 1887 by a farmer who lived near Hillsdale in Fayette Township. A bolt of lightning, reported an article in the *Chicago Tribune*, hit Amos J. Biggs and left a perfect silhouette of a cat etched onto Biggs's bald head!

According to the *Tribune*, Biggs had hurried outside on a stormy day to chase away a group of cats that were fighting wildly on his woodpile. Just as he reached the woodpile, it was hit by a great crash of lightning that instantly killed the cats. The farmer said he felt his muscles contract in a "prickly sensation," as the lightning also passed over him. It exploded his watch, tore the left leg off his pants, and ripped the sole off his left boot, but he was able to walk back to his house.

When his wife saw him, she fainted dead away, said the article. When she came to, she pointed to her husband's head and exclaimed that the devil had set his mark on him. There on the farmer's forehead was the five-inch-high, perfectly proportioned reproduction of a black cat, right down to the whiskers. The pair rubbed the mark with a variety of household cleaners, and it disappeared within 24 hours.

The supposed ability of lightning to etch pictures onto nearby surfaces…such as bald, shiny heads…is known as keraunography, and was a favorite topic of newspapers in the 1880s.

Tim Péwé

Horton
Jackson County
Getting A Head of Himself?
The Art of Tim Péwé

Tim Péwé holds degrees in business and sociology, but spends his days in his Horton garage-turned-studio creating the giant concrete heads that dot his lawn like misplaced Easter Island relics. "I'm just inspired by classic, old Greek heads of the Collossi (giants) and primitive Easter Island statues," he told *Strange Michigan*. He also creates lively wooden, marionette-style art dolls of famous figures like Abraham Lincoln or Paul McCartney, as well as other sculptures of granite, wood, and inlaid marble.

Péwé started out with an office job after college, he said, but discovered he didn't enjoy sitting in an enclosed space all day. He switched from white to blue collar employment after getting a job with a window manufacturer, then bounced around for a few years with other contractors to learn how to work with ceramics, marble, and granite. "I learned how to handle construction materials," he said, "but I wanted to do my own thing rather than what was specified."

He began putting a significant chunk of time into his own art around 1998. "I tried doing some art fairs," he said, "but I found the 500-pound concrete heads were too heavy to move around." Péwé switched to displaying his art on his yard, working on commission, and developing an Internet site, www.timpewe.com. "People pull in here and wonder what's going on," he chuckled. "And some are frightened and wonder what I'm up to."

The stone heads, in particular, do resemble ancient gods abandoned by some forgotten civilization, and they appear none too happy about it. Péwé's sketchbook pages posted on his Web site reveal his raw and original visions that inspire the sculptures.

The 44-year-old artist also harbors a secret dream project; he wants to build a giant sculpture that also serves as a livable home. That is, he says, if he can ever convince his wife and two sons that living inside a giant work of art could be comfortable and fun. Péwé envisions a massive abstract construction made from granite, wood, cement and all the materials he works with. It would, after all, make the perfect backdrop for his yard full of inscrutable stone heads.

Houghton
Houghton County
A Blizzard of Beasts

The UP probably has more snow than anyplace else in Michigan. What to do with all that white stuff? Yoopers, practical breed that they are, would scarcely waste anything—not even snow. The solution? Sculpt it!

For more than three-quarters of a century, students at Michigan Technological University have found chilling ways to express themselves. Back in 1922, the students put on an Ice Carnival for one night only. Today, the Winter Carnival lasts several days, and making the snow statues can take weeks.

The carnival took a four-year hiatus after the 1929 stock market crash, and during World War II took a two-year break. The year 1936 saw the introduction of snow sculptures, which replaced ice as the medium of choice for the enormous, highly detailed statues. Each year, student organizations, fraternities, and sororities compete for the title of best snow sculptor in the Keweenaw. While most ice sculpting competitions invite professional sculptors to participate, the Winter Carnival exists for the students, which makes their accomplishments that much more impressive.

The students pack their snow around a designated theme each year. The 2008 theme was "Frightful Creatures with Chilling Features," and the results proved frigid and fantastic. A monster the height of a two-story building gaped at passersby: Watch out for that tongue! King Kong beat his chest, roaring at the dinosaur he had just felled. The *Ghostbusters* battled a gigantic marshmallow man while wide-eyed spooks peeked out from clear ice windows. The sign for the *Ghostbusters* sculpture declared "Ice Ain't Afraid of Snow Ghost!" Each statue included a title crafted from frozen Jell-O and mounted on a snow podium.

Winter Carnival happens every February, even during a thaw. If there is snow, it's a go!

The Haunting of Douglass House

In Houghton County, you will find many ghosts of the past—ruins of the copper mining era, mining pits cut by ancient peoples, abandoned buildings. But in downtown Houghton, you'll find a real ghost...or so say visitors who have stayed at the Douglass House Hotel.

The city of Houghton was named after Douglass Houghton, the first state geologist of Michigan. The Douglass House Hotel also took its name from the geologist. The copper boom of the mid-19th Century caused Houghton's population to skyrocket, bringing with it the need for respectable lodging. The Douglass House Hotel opened in 1860 to fill that need, and by 1899 had expanded to accommodate its growing clientele. In 1901 a fire gutted the hotel, leaving only the addition intact. Two years later, the hotel was rebuilt to its former glory.

Legend has it that during the 1940s someone died in a third-floor room of the hotel. Subsequently, guests began to report strange goings-on in the room. Doors in the room slammed in the middle of the night. The closet doors refused to stay shut. Ghostly feet paced the floor, and curtains billowed sans breeze. Guests who stayed in the haunted room got no sleep—even those who knew nothing of the supposed haunting reported the same events.

In 1983, the Douglass House underwent renovations, becoming an apartment complex for senior citizens. The front part, which housed its saloon, continues in that tradition today in the guise of the Douglass House Saloon, Houghton's oldest bar. The stoplight on Shelden Avenue, in front of the Douglass House building, reportedly marks the third-floor room where spooks resided. Perhaps they still do live there...stopping by for the occasional whiskey.

Howell

Livingston County

Close Encounter with Glowing Cigar

One winter night in 1958, Nelson and his friend encountered something unexplainable on Kellogg Road, east of Howell. The two teenagers had gone into town, but by 1:30 a.m. decided to make their way home on foot. The snow had packed down hard on the ground. The moon lit their way as they headed down Kellogg Road, past a summer camp operated by the city of Detroit. A fence encompassed the camp and a small lake. The time was now 2:00 a.m.

Nelson heard a sound, which he dismissed as a jet. When the sound ended, he thought nothing of it. Then, to his right, a glowing object appeared above the treetops. The object glided toward him from the northeast, spinning, lowering as it approached as if coming in for a landing. The craft made no sound. The object was massive, the size of a small house, with no wings. It seemed cigar shaped, and had three "creases" in its tail end. The craft appeared to glow from within with a pale yellow light, as if its shell consisted of only a thin sheet draped over its glowing interior, like a lamp shade. The glow was constant, not glittering or blinking. Intermittent bursts of flame shot out from the creases in the tail end of the object.

Nelson and his friend froze, their gazes fixed on the object—which now hung directly above their heads. Nelson says, "It was so close I could almost touch it."

As the craft moved past them overhead, it turned west, heading over a small lake and orchard. The craft remained at treetop height, about 50 feet in the air. Despite the flame bursts, the object gave off no heat. The craft descended beyond the lake. Nelson felt sure it must have landed.

The two boys ran home. Nelson considered going back to look for the craft, but fear dampened his curiosity and he stayed at home. In his adult life Nelson has worked as a design engineer on projects from submarines and aircraft to oilfield equipment. He knows what modern technology can do. Yet he still has no explanation for what he saw that night in 1958.

Indian River

Cheboygan County

The World's Second Largest Crucifix, Cross in the Woods

It's not *quite* the biggest; the 55-foot crucifix at the Cross in the Woods Shrine on M-68 near Indian River comes in second to a 60-foot crucifix in Bardstown, Kentucky. But the seven-ton statue continues to inspire legions of people of all faiths who flock to worship and experience the peaceful forest setting. It dates from back in the 1950s, when the Catholic Church purchased land in the Indian River region. Church officials decided they would like to put up the largest crucifix in the world so that people driving by on the highway would stop and worship.

They erected the redwood cross in 1954, and the church commissioned sculptor Marshall Fredericks to create the Christ figure. It took Fredericks four years to complete his task. He had the statue cast in Oslo, Norway, making it one of the "largest castings ever to cross the Atlantic," according to the shrine's guidebook. Twenty-eight steps lead to the cross, because that's the number tradition claims Jesus had to climb to reach the throne of Pontius Pilate. Holy relics (usually body parts of saints or other items closely associated with them) were originally placed in each stair step, but have since been removed. Many pilgrims climb the stairs on their knees.

Other statues on the grounds include the Stations of the Cross, the statue of the resurrected Jesus, and the Shrine of Our Lady of the Highway, patroness of travelers and pilgrims. There is also a bronze statue of Kateri Tekawitha, a Native American born in 1656 who converted to Christianity and was known as the "Lily of the Mohawks." Her penchant for placing crosses in wooded areas as devotional reminders was the original inspiration for the Cross in the Woods.

Second to Nun: the Nun Doll Museum

What's black and white and read all over? A nun doll museum full of signs and labels. In the basement of the large gift shop on the Cross in the Woods Shrine grounds, visitors can learn everything they ever wanted to know about the habits of nuns. Habits in the sense of robes and wimples, that is. The collection of over 500 authentically dressed dolls is augmented by almost two dozen life-size mannequins. In all, they represent diocesan clergy and more than 217 religious orders of priests, sisters, and brothers. The collection, donated in 1964 by Saginaw couple Sally and Wally Rogalski, was started by Sally in 1945; and has led to a citation from Pope John Paul II for the couple's lifelong work and contribution.

This giant assemblage is the place to observe the difference in dress between a postulant, a novice, and a professed sister, or to examine the various aspects of a priest's ceremonial garments without feeling like you are staring impolitely during mass. Many of the dolls are shown in miniature diorama settings, such as the teaching nun in her classroom or the all-nun orchestra. Admission is free, and no nun-sense is tolerated.

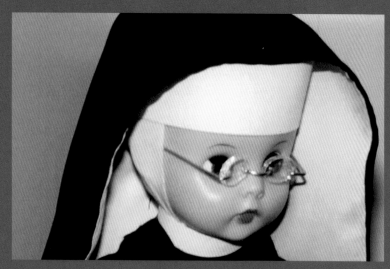

The diminutive religious at the Cross of the Woods Shrine

Inkster
Wayne County
Boomerang UFO

This incident occurred sometime in February 1978 at seven o'clock in the morning in Inkster. I had been at my new job as a driver for a workshop for developmentally disabled adults for about a month. I had to take a bus to the job every day that let us off on Michigan Avenue next to a row of one-story buildings that ran along the road. The van I drove was parked near the Inkster ice arena and you had to go through a large parking lot to get to it.

As I walked by the buildings to the van, I looked to the west above the Inkster police station. Above the station was the full moon. Above the full moon was what appeared to be a boomerang-shaped cloud. The sun had risen and the sky was clear except for the moon and this object. It was a bit larger than the moon. It was stationary and solid white and pointing up. There was no noise throughout the sighting. I stood outside the van for a few minutes watching this thing hang in the sky not really doing anything. It was very cold outside so I decided to go inside the van and warm it up. After about ten minutes I went outside the van to see it again. Much to my disappointment, the full moon was still there but the object was gone. Though there were several sightings reported in the western Wayne county area around this time, I never reported mine.

—George

Ionia
Ionia County
The Ghost of Minnie-Minnehaha

A cemetery on a deeply wooded hill, the filmy figure of a long-dead woman floating past the grave stones, dark and empty eyes turning to stare at a graveyard trespasser…these are among the mournful images visitors to Highland Park Cemetery have claimed to see. *Strange Michigan* learned that this historic cemetery holding the remains of over 3,000 people is supposed to be the eternal home of a deceased witch with an unlikely name: Minnie-Minnehaha.

One person told us that this site, now near the junction of East Main and Prairie Creek roads, was a Native American battleground, and that the strong energy from those conflicts still causes spirits to appear. Whatever the source of the legend, those seeking spirit thrills may find that Minnie-Minnehaha received her name for a reason… she always has the last laugh.

Welcome
Highland Park Cemetery

CEMETERY RULES

1. SEXTON RESERVES ALL RIGHTS TO TRIM, CUT OR REMOVE ALL SHRUBS, TREES & FLOWERS.
2. ALL TREES & SHRUBS MUST BE APPROVED BY SEXTON BEFORE PLANTING.
3. ALL TREES, SHRUBS & FLOWERS MUST BE PLANTED IN LINE WITH HEADSTONES.
4. NO OFF ROAD VEHICLES ALLOWED IN CEMETERY AT ANY TIME. NO DRIVING OFF MAIN ROADS.
5. NO TRESPASSING AFTER GATES ARE CLOSED. VIOLATORS WILL BE PROSECUTED.

GATES CLOSED
• MONDAY- THURS. 8 PM
FRIDAY-SUNDAY 5 PM

MAUSOLEUM OPEN MAY 15 - JUNE 1
REGULAR HOURS
Thereafter by Appointment Only

Iron Mountain
Dickinson County
World's Tallest Miner, Big John

Big John's painted smile may look innocent enough, but beware… he carries one mean pick-ax. And local legend has it that he possesses his own spirit, one capable of literally frowning on disaster.

Towering 40 feet high over US Highway 2 east of Iron Mountain, the tree-level wooden cutout figure was created to draw attention to the Iron Mountain Iron Mine. The old site is a popular attraction in the area, offering tours of its defunct mine shafts and the underground electric railway that rain-coat clad visitors may ride through the 2,600 feet of tunnels below.

Dennis Carollo, son of Albert Carollo who was one of the original owners of the mine tour, told *Strange Michigan* the statue was inspired by the giant Paul Bunyan in Bemidji, Minnesota. The year was 1958, when the song "Big Bad John" was popular, and the owners decided a statue of "John" would attract attention. For a model, the group chose Carollo's uncle, Gene, also an owner. Gene dressed up like a miner and posed with a pick-ax for sign artist Ted Palow of Crystal Falls. The original Big John's face bore a suitably crusty scowl, and the frowning figure did pull crowds off the highway.

In 1975, things changed. The owners decided to give Big John a friendlier look, and had a new, smiling face glued over the older, surly one. Very soon after that, according to Carollo, a bolt of lightning hit the gift shop and mine entrance, burning the building to the ground. Big John was not charred, but strangely, the intense heat caused the new face to fall off. "We noticed the smiley face was gone and the old Big John was frowning at the burnt-down building," said Carollo.

About ten years ago, the sign needed repainting once more, and again an odd incident occurred. The attraction usually closes for the winter in October, and plans were to have the sign taken down in January so that it could be put up refurbished in the spring. But in December, the mine owners were listening to a local radio station reading letters to Santa sent in by area children when one handwritten plea caught their attention. It was from a little boy whose grandmother lived near the mine, said Carollo. The little boy's only request was a new set of clothes for Big John. The owners were so touched that they gave the little boy a lifetime pass.

Although the statue's original scowl may have been more representative of the back-breaking labor the real "Big Johns" endured, the smile may also be appropriate. Big John, after all, commemorates a whopping human achievement. Over 22 million tons of ore were produced at Iron Mountain from 1870 to 1945, providing material instrumental in building our nation.

The mine tour graphically depicts both the vast enterprise and the intense labor involved. After the tour, visitors may browse a large and well-stocked gift shop while listening to "Big Bad John" and other selections from the miner's hit parade played over the loudspeaker. Also of interest and free for the viewing in the parking lot is the bright red "ax tree," a telephone pole with a huge variety of axes and shovels stuck into it at regular intervals.

Alas, unlike the Bemidji Paul Bunyan that spawned him, Big John has no blue ox. But drive a little farther into Iron River to see a statue of a pointy-headed cow and calf standing in front of the local Beefaroo. If some tender-hearted urchin ever asks Santa for a buddy for Big John, perhaps this could be a match made in roadside oddity heaven.

The Chippewa Club

Flipping lights on and off must be the Haunting 101 assignment of freshman ghosts, as it seems to be standard in hauntings of restaurants, theaters, and other public buildings. Whoever inhabits the gracious old Chippewa Club in Iron Mountain has the task mastered, however, and would probably merit an "A" on his spook report card. But the ghost known as Willie has gone on to earn an advanced degree in haunting ability, according to Dixie Franklin in her book, *Haunts of the Upper Great Lakes*, by demonstrating the amazing ability to cause a piano to play by itself. He also has been blamed for the audible cries of a nonexistent baby, and for exuding the scent of bayberry candles when none were present. He even seems to have the ability to plunge the temperature of the ladies' room down into refrigerator range. The room was previously a bar area, which also would grow inexplicably cold, once becoming so frosty that (according to local legend) a man was found dead on his barstool after shivering so hard that he'd wrapped himself in the club's American flag.

In his earthly life, Willie was only six years old when he disappeared one day near the village of Commonwealth where his father, Capt. William Edmond Dickinson, was supervisor of an iron mine. He was never found, although his parents searched for many years.

One of his sisters, Charlotte, later married another mine superintendent, O.C. Dickinson, and they eventually moved to Iron Mountain and lived in the company's superintendent's home. Charlotte and O.C. bought the property a few years later, and in 1945 developers bought and remodeled it for use as the Chippewa Club. Franklin theorizes that poor little Willie came to the house to live with his sister and never left. *Strange Michigan*, impressed as we were on our own visit to the handsome building and peaceful grounds, doesn't blame the lad for staying.

The Literate Ghost; Haunted Book World

Although a ghost named Charlie is believed to inhabit the Book World store on S. Stephenson Highway in Iron Mountain, it may be the building itself rather than the books that attract the spook, according to an employee who spoke with *Strange Michigan*. "This used to be a Payless Shoe Store," she said, "and the workers would come in and find pairs of shoes placed nicely on the floor. Now Charlie leaves books on the floor."

Sometimes workers will find other items lying around when they open the building in the morning, things that they knew were placed securely on racks at closing. And a maintenance worker at the time the building housed the shoe store claimed he would hear phantom footsteps and doors opening and closing after hours when he was the only (live) person in the store.

Iron River
Iron County
Hairy Thing in the Woods

Picture this: You're hunting in the woods, huddled in a blind waiting for a buck. Below you, something treads closer and closer to your blind. You raise your rifle, close on eye, and sight through the scope. A hairy, black shape moves into view. Your heart thuds. Too dark for a deer. What then? A bear, you presume, and go back to listening.

The dark shape moves off into the woods.

Then it hits you. The figure you just saw had walked upright on two legs. What do you do?

An event like this happened to Jay in November 1990. When he realized the animal he'd seen through the rifle scope had been upright and two-legged, Jay left his blind to find the spot where the creature had stood when he first spotted it. He found no footprints. But the branches through which the creature had walked hung several inches above Jay's head, making the creature taller than Jay's 6'2".

While Jay doesn't know if he saw a Bigfoot, he feels certain that the tall, hairy figure was not a bear.

Lode Creek Bigfoot

Michael was driving home from work on July 7, 2004, at about 7:00 p.m. He has lived in the UP all his life, hunting and fishing in the woods near Iron River. But what he saw that night looked like no animal he had ever seen before.

As he looked toward the woods alongside the road north of Iron River, near Lode Creek, he spotted a "large, upright figure" moving off into the trees. He feels certain what he saw was no bear.

Other Bigfoot sightings have occurred in the area, especially around the Paint River.

Ironwood
Gogebic County
The Blonde Bear-Man

In what might be one of the earliest documented cases of either the Michigan Dogman or Bigfoot, a 1917 article in the *Eagle River (WI) Telegram* reported that a "blonde bear-man" had been seen in the Ironwood area since that October. In the most recent event, two men had watched from a distance in unbelief as what looked like a "giant man" covered in light-colored fur snatched a deer one of them had just shot. Unlike a bear or wolf or other wild animal, this creature ran away on two legs while carrying the deer carcass in its arms. While this would be a feat few humans could duplicate, officials warned that if they found that some fur-clad person had committed the brazen crime, he would be charged with larceny for taking the dead deer. Unfortunately, not enough detail was included to be able to declare the creature canine or primate, but the witnesses swore it was not a bear or anything else they could identify.

Pressie:
The Lake Superior Monster

The waterfalls and whirlpools are awe-inspiring as I cross a primitive log bridge over the Presque Isle River. On Saturday morning, Memorial Day Weekend 1977, I am bearing east on an established hiking trail meandering through a section of the Porcupine Mountains Wilderness State Park north of Ironwood, Michigan. Mosquitoes are saturating the air and I find it hard to breathe without sucking them in. I decide to leave the trail and traverse toward Lake Superior, hike its beach, and let the bugs fend for themselves.

Exiting the trail, I pass onto a plateau of wet, spongy ground covered by ferns. Spikes of sunlight shining down through the ancient forest's canopy accompany me and a short time later, I reach the edge of the plateau. The beach is 100 feet below me down a steep, moss-covered slope. Short, scrubby, dead trees protrude from the moss. Snubbing up my backpack, I step down onto the slope and my feet slip out from under me. The moss has beguiled me by concealing a granitelike rock called scarp. As the moss peels away it's difficult to control the rapid descent. Dead, rootless trees break away from my grip during the effort to steer the slide, ending feet first in soft beach sand.

Lake Superior's ice melt has strewn the beach thick with debris. From the looks of it, there's going to be no easy way to trek this isolated place. Certainly I will not turn around and go back from where I came. Pools of lake water along with an assortment of junk, piles of sticks, and logs have flooded segments of the beach. Maybe I should

turn around, but instead I decide to ad lib the voyage. Negotiating this kind of terrain will be hazardous, but I'm not an inexperienced backpacker and am up for the challenge, having a lot of practice working for the Forest Service in the rugged terrain of Idaho and Montana.

After wading, twisting, and climbing through a few of the debris-filled pools, I remove the backpack and sit on a small boulder to eat a snack. The lake surface is glassy smooth, mirroring the daytime sky. The warm sun is above, the bugs are few, and I begin taking in the tranquility. Distant land is cresting the northeastern horizon and two ducks can be seen out in open water diving for their lunch. One duck goes down and up, then the other. Reaching into the backpack I retrieve a spotting scope to monitor the ducks' activities, and witness an astounding transformation. The two objects I assumed to be ducks now are joined by a third (a tail?) object. The three objects veer to the right and swim nearly to the shore. The undulating bumps are linked and swim several hundred feet in seconds. I can see the thing is BIG, and now is swimming parallel to the shore toward me, around and between boulders, like a huge snake. If it continues on its present course, I'll very quickly be face to face with it.

Climbing the scarp to escape will be impossible and reentering the debris pool is unthinkable. The approaching nemesis appears to be cruising the shoreline like a crocodile hunting for prey. I grab my backpack, snatch my camera, and crouch behind the boulder. If I am caught I feel I will surely be just another missing person who failed to show up at camp before dark. Hopefully, the creature will just pass by. Silently, the snakelike monster comes to a stop directly in front of me, possibly seeing movement as I adjust the camera settings. The head of the creature is shiny, dark gray, almost black in color. The head is the size of a horse and the port-side eye of the monster is large and dark, gazing straight at me.

On the nose of the creature is a whisker close to a foot and one-half in length. This appendage is wiggling intermittently...pulsating as though electrified. A distance behind the head is another black-colored part of the animal. The creature's head dips under the surface. In unison the rear part raises an even greater distance above the surface of the water and is several feet in girth! The monster continues a teeter-tottering action. A fleeting question enters my thoughts, "What kind of reaction will there be if I stand up and wave my arms or throw a stick?" The mind's overseer says, "I am in a perilous situation and given the appearance, size, and speed of the monster, I must decide to remain hidden."

Waiting for the chance, when both the head and back portion are above the water, I take a picture. The air is uncannily still while the camera shutter reports a resounding snap! Fear paralyzes me. Seconds later, the denizen resumes its course in a low-profile undulation, quarters out to open water, submerges under a thin layer of fog, and vanishes from sight.

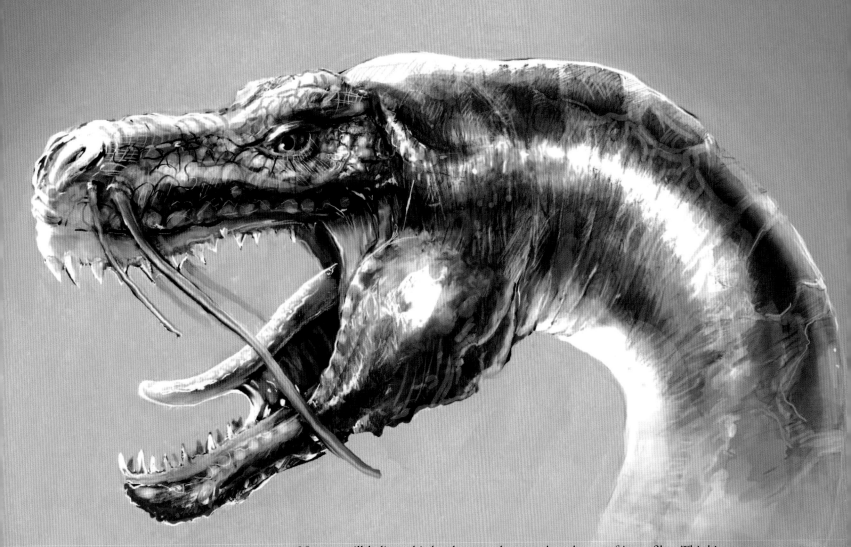

No one will believe this has happened to me, but the proof is on film. Thinking my encounter over, I survey up and down the beach and scan the water. With caution, I slowly raise from the boulder's cover. Cold sweat, nausea, and a racing heartbeat subside. Nothing in all the time I have spent working in the outdoors, hunting, and fishing has ever given me such a jolt. I must endeavor to resolve this bizarre event. Scouting the beach, I find a stick that is close to 6 feet long. I measure the number of sticks from where the camera was positioned at the time the picture was taken to the water's edge, carefully interpolating from the shore's edge to where the monster stopped in the water. I was 20 yards from the monster. Entering the water to find the exact depth of the water will be foolish. The bottom is visible and my best guess is that it is from 8 to10 feet. The weather turns chilly and windier as I hike back to camp. Mark, my camping partner, fell quiet after hearing what happened. A park ranger speculated it had been a sturgeon. He added that people do disappear near the Presque Isle River.

It has been 30 years since the sighting. One prominent professor and cryptozoologist examining the photo, measured the cryptid's head at 2 feet from snout to base of skull—the entire length at thirty feet or more! To this day I occasionally dream of being consumed by the Lake Superior Monster.

— *Randy L. Braun, contributor*

Unearthly Sparkler in the Sky

At about ten o'clock on the night of February 19, 2005, Suzanne stood in her kitchen. When her dogs started barking, she hurried to the sliding glass doors in the living room, expecting to see a rabbit or other small animal outside. What she saw instead left her awed and puzzled.

An amber light hovered above the treetops, south-southeast of the house she shared with her husband Carl. When she saw the object, Suzanne shouted to Carl, who was upstairs. He rushed down to her and sighted the same object in the sky. Suzanne and Carl went outside to get a better look. They estimated the light's size as bigger than the car headlights on the road a quarter mile away seem when viewed from their house.

Once outside, the couple noticed a car down in the road. People in the car talked loudly, using expressions of excitement such as "wow," leading Suzanne and Carl to suspect the car's occupants saw the amber light too. Carl, noting the fiery nature of the light, at first took it for a plane on fire—until he recognized the object traveled faster than an airplane. What he first took for flames seemed more reminiscent of a child's sparkler. The "big fiery glob" moved north-northwest across the sky.

Distracted by the vocal motorists, Carl looked away for a moment, though Suzanne continued to watch. The object swooped down, then up again. As Carl returned his attention to the object, it spewed white sparks. The motorists in the road shouted, "Woo-hoo!" The silent object went behind the trees, out of sight.

Ishpeming
Marquette County
A Roof Made for Jumping

Ishpeming claims the only roof in the UP that seems tailor-made for jumping—the roof of the U.S. National Ski Museum. The wild double slope of the roof looks something like structures in which skateboarders love to rock 'n' roll. But the roof is meant to evoke a soaring jump ramp. Visitors should resist the urge to climb up there and try their ski-jumping skills.

Da Yoopers Tourist Trap

"I'm Married to Da Couch Dat Burps and Looks at Da TV," "Rusty Chevrolet," "Da Second Week of Deer Camp"…dese are just a few hits from dose rustic Michigan musicians known as Da Yoopers. To our disappointment, *Strange Michigan* had a hard time finding anyone in da UP who really talks like dat, but no one has a better time making fun of demselves than da real UP-ers, as demonstrated in da outlandish displays outside Da Yooper Tourist Trap store in da quintessential Yooper town of Ishpeming (actually just west on US Highway 41). Da Tourist Trap bills itself as one of da Seven Wonders of Yooperland, partially because it offers two bathrooms with flushing toilets. But dat's not all.

In Da Yooper Innovation Museum, mounted deer in overalls and other human togs inhabit two-story outhouses and shuffle poker hands in Camp Go-for-Beer, and frightening human mannequins are posed in equally frightening vehicles of every description. Dere's even a Man Camp (as opposed to deer camp) where da deer hunt da men.

As a bonus, visitors can catch a photo op with Big Gus, World's Biggest Working Chainsaw (as attested in the *Guinness Book of World Records*) and Big Ernie, da World's Biggest Working Shotgun. (It isn't loaded, thankfully.)

Cameras aren't allowed inside the store but dat's OK. Da good stuff is all outside. Still, youse might be interested in some Yooper Technology, such as a Yooper Washer and Drier (clothespin) or a Yooper Bathroom Deodorizer (a stick holding three matches). Or youse could buy a CD produced by You Guys Records to play on da

way home from Yooperland.

Our personal favorite souvenir was Da Yooper Quarter Pounder, which featured a real quarter set into a hole with a peg to pound it deeper. Nothing tickle your fancy dere? Den try "Da Fart Section." Youse can get corks to stop diarrhea, remote controlled whoopee cushions, and for da Yooper dat has everything, a gaseous, noise-emitting tightie-whitey key chain. Dere's also da Rock Shop, owned by Jim DeCaire who is da main man in Da Yoopers musical comedy group. He and another of da singing Yoopers started da whole place in 1990.

Dere's really nothing more to say, except..."It's da second week of deer camp, and all da guys are here. We shoot da breeze and shoot da bull but never shoot da deer..."

Lisa Shiel views the Yooper Tree

Jacobsville
Houghton County
Da Yooper Tree on
Bare-Naked Beach

In Michigan's Upper Peninsula, the people have a unique sense of humor. They call themselves Yoopers, a takeoff on the abbreviation UP. They create stores like Da Yooper Tourist Trap. They hold outhouse races. But some of the best Yooper artwork remains hidden in places no one will tell you about, even when the creations sit on state land. Take the Yooper Tree on Bare-Naked Beach near Jacobsville, for example.

The remains of Jacobsville lie on the Keweenaw Peninsula, the UP's little finger. The northern Keweenaw actually exists as an island, cut off from the southern portion by the canal that connects Portage Lake to western Lake Superior. Near the Portage River, directly across the water from Chassell, sits the vanished town of Jacobsville. All that remains are the town's Lutheran chapel and the old schoolhouse, now a community heritage center. Just north of the former town, on a seasonal road dubbed Sunrise Lane, you will find a rocky beach known to locals as the Bare-Naked Beach.

Warning: Seatbelts are mandatory on Sunrise Lane! As the road winds through the Copper Country State Forest, potholes, ruts, and rocks will jar the fillings from riders' teeth. At the road's dead end, a small hill leads down to the beach. The forest extends to the cusp of the beach, where it terminates at a three-foot cliff. The surf has worn away the sandstone bedrock, forming miniature peninsulas that stick out from the forest. Forlorn trees cling to the tips of the mini peninsulas.

Local lore says Bare-Naked Beach got its name from a period in the 1970s when folks liked to sunbathe there *au naturel*. You'd expect that a beach nicknamed Bare-Naked would offer nice, sandy stretches. You'd be wrong.

Bare-Naked Beach is a slippery jumble of stone platforms and hollowed-out spots. Occasionally a big storm will sweep sand back up over the rock; later, another storm will strip it away. But the slabs of slimy sandstone that make swimming a challenge also make this beach one of the most beautiful in the Keweenaw.

At first you will see no sign of the Yooper Tree. But if you venture south down the beach, around several mini peninsulas, an odd shape will come into view. A tangle of roots stick out from the bottom of the overturned tree trunk like a forestry version of Medusa's hair. Walk around the trunk and you will see what Yoopers do for fun.

They balance rocks on this tree stump.

Nobody knows exactly when the stump washed ashore. Today it serves as a curious "I was here" proclamation. People take flat slabs of rock from piles at the base of the cliff and balance them on the roots of the stump. Someone has also applied a complementary strip of duct tape to the stump. Leave it to the Yooper spirit to find a way to dress up Bare-Naked Beach.

The Mystery Fog

Dense fog often settles in woodland clearings near Lake Superior's shore. But the fog one Jacobsville resident saw may have a less-earthly origin.

The morning was calm and sunny. At about 8:00 a.m., a woman stood at her livingroom window watching her husband head out to the garden to tend the remaining crops. He stopped about 50 feet away from the window, within the garden fence. As the woman watched, she noticed a strange cloud between her husband and the woods, about a hundred feet from the window where she stood. The cloud was white, wispy like a cloud in the sky, but solid enough to block her view of the trees behind it. The cloud hung suspended about 20 feet off the ground, well below the 80-foot treetops.

The witness estimated the cloud was 10 feet in diameter, almost circular but slightly ragged. As she observed it, however, the cloud grew until it reached 20 feet wide by 20 feet tall. She rushed outside, shouting at her husband to look at the strange cloud. He glanced at the cloud without comment. The witness estimated the cloud hung there for five minutes. She looked in all directions for fog banks or other clouds. She saw none.

The mysterious fog seemed to have stuck around only long enough to watch her husband saw some wood. Was it a ghost? A UFO in hiding? Or some other kind of entity? The witness knows only one thing for certain; she has never seen anything like it before. She reported her sighting to Backyard Phenomena Investigations, a Jacobsville-based paranormal research group.

Kalamazoo
Kalamazoo County
The Kalamazoo Dogman

Multitudes of witnesses have seen a human-sized, fur-covered, wolflike creature walking on two legs around Michigan, mostly in the northern half of the state. But the southern counties such as Kalamazoo are not exempt from the Dogman's prowls. A man named Rob called *Strange Michigan* to tell us that in 1995, he and a friend were driving around some alleged haunting spots on the edge of Kalamazoo at about 2:30 a.m., hoping to see ghosts, when they noticed what looked like a large dog standing by the side of the road on all fours. It was eating what appeared to be roadkill. "I said, 'didn't that look like a strange dog?' Rob told us. "So we turned around and came back."

As the two men in their car approached the creature, it turned its head toward them, said Rob. "We could see blood dripping off its mouth. We watched it for maybe 20 seconds and it went from being on all fours to getting up on its hind legs and taking off. No one really believes in werewolves but that's what it looked like." The creature ran on its hind legs for about 20 yards before disappearing into a cornfield, Rob said. He described the creature as dark brown or black with pointed ears on top of its head and a muzzle more pointed than that of a husky.

Rob added that an acquaintance also saw the same creature within five miles of his sighting not long after the incident.

 ## Elvis in the Building?

Of all the places Elvis might have picked to spend the rest of his life—if the tabloids are right and he IS still secretly alive—Kalamazoo seems an unlikely choice: None of his favorite southern foods, more snow in one winter than Memphis would see in decades, and few places where a white, spangled cape would look appropriate. And yet, according to a 2006 *Kalamazoo Gazette* article, a resident of nearby Vicksburg was sure that she saw Presley many times, dining at a Burger King in Kalamazoo or picking up some necessities at Felpausch's store in Vicksburg.

Louise Welling went straight to the *Weekly World News* with her story, adding that she had seen Priscilla and Lisa Marie at a mall, as well, and that the family tooled around K-Zoo in a red Ferrari. Rumors flew that the King was going by the name of John Burrows. Welling's stunning revelation was repeated in both the *Gazette* and the *New York Times*. As far as *Strange Michigan* knows, Welling never did get a picture to prove her claim.

Kaleva
Manistee County
Carver of the Dogman

Artist Big Joe McCuaig says he was once kicked out of art class. And his self-description on the Web site Flickr.com reads, "I'm fairly tall but uglier than sin...I'm so ugly people scream and run away with their eyes and mind scarred forever."

Strange Michigan has met the self-deprecating wood carver in person, however, and we hasten to note that McCuaig is a master of the art of exaggeration. Most folk artists are, however; it's how they get their point across.

We drove down narrow lanes of pine forests to reach his rural Kaleva home, finally bumping along a two-rut path to reach his woodsy paradise. McCuaig is a country man and proud of it. But his property doesn't look particularly artsy at first glance. "I don't put a lot in the yard because people think I'm weird anyway," he told us.

He did show us a few pieces that sat on his covered backyard deck...a seven-foot-long fish sculpture with each fish devouring another, a large head of Frank Zappa (Dylan, Springsteen, and Elvis are already sold), some bare-breasted mermaids, and one of his favorite stocks in trade, the Michigan Dogman.

McCuaig, who worked for the phone company and various farmers before he became a full-time artist, says he got into his craft by accident. "A friend of mine was carving and at first I didn't have the patience; he had me doing a stupid boot. I started with knives but my hands were getting bad with arthritis, so now I use power tools and a chisel."

Although McCuaig may live far from any of the usual urban art markets, he has been able to sell his art worldwide thanks to eBay. He recently finished a carving of Noah holding a white dove for a collector in Massachusetts. His works start at around $100 for the smallest pieces.

"I kind of try to take things to the edge," he said, "and I do a lot of nudes. I put breasts on women but I don't put too much detail on the male figures. I don't know about inspiration, just all of a sudden I get this weird thing in my head and just get going on it." He did have a bad case of carver's block at one time, though, he admitted. "I carved so many crows, so many owls, so many fish, I needed something new."

What he came up with was a combination of animals and humans...snake woman, crocodile girl, and bear woman, to name a few popular examples. The snake woman is just a fantasy idea, he said. "I couldn't put a woman on a pig or an uglier animal. A guy would have to go on a pig."

Now in his mid-50s, the only thing that irks McCuaig about his profession is that others sometimes steal his ideas and images. He had done a carving of heaven and hell with devils and angels, he said, and a female artist called him to discuss it. When he later visited her Web site, he discovered she had since made something very similar.

The jovial McCuaig, who has also started creating humorous, "naïve" paintings, says he has no greater aspiration than to make a living for himself and his family with his art. But he is always on the lookout for helpful publicity. "There's a psychiatrist I've sold pieces to," he told *Strange Michigan*, "and I've been waiting for him to say I'm crazy. That would be a plus." See more of McCuaig at www.joemccuaig.com.

Big Joe McCuaig

Kalkaska
Kalkaska County
Giant Trout, Wolverine, and Robin

The oversized fish, mammal, and bird gracing downtown Kalkaska make a perfect giant statue trifecta. The wolverine, of course, is Michigan's state animal, the robin the state bird, and trout the state fish. Kalkaska, however, has hosted a trout festival since the early 1930s when a couple of fishermen persuaded the town to close all businesses every May 1, the start of trout season. The leaping trout weighs 600 pounds and stands 11 feet, ready to pose with would-be fishermen for the quintessential "one that got away" photo. All three were created by Larry Robinson of Robinson Scenic Gardens and Statuary.

 ## Before Electrolysis:
Grace Gilbert, Bearded Lady

Kalkaska had probably not seen many babies like little Grace Gilbert. The child born in 1880 was covered with lovely red hair, including a luxuriant beard that would eventually measure 18 inches. Since this was the era of sideshow exhibits and P.T. Barnum, Grace went to work as a "bearded lady" while yet a teenager and traveled from town to town with Barnum & Bailey and other outfits for 14 years.

At the age of 30, she attracted a suitor, farmer Giles E. Calvin from her hometown of Kalkaska. According to a story in the *New York Times*, Calvin sent her love notes and "sweet nothings" for months, then resorted to following her from town to town until she consented to be his wife. They were married in October 1910 in South Bend, Indiana, and the *Times* claimed the judge mistook Grace for the groom. The *Times* also claimed Calvin was 19 years Grace's junior, which hardly seems accurate since he would have been only 11 years old if that were true.

The Calvins enjoyed 15 years of wedded bliss before Grace died in 1925 at the age of 45. She and Giles are buried in Leetsville/Maple Grove Cemetery four miles north of Kalkaska.

![chicken logo] **Woodsy Wonderland; Robinson Scenic Gardens**

The stretch of US Highway 131 between Kalkaska and Mancelona is a heavily forested drive typical of rural Michigan. It's a startling sight, then, to come upon a break in the treeline about six miles north of Kalkaska crowded with giant animals not normally spied in the Wolverine State. There's a polar bear, a pink elephant, a sky blue horse, and a giraffe, and that's just the roadside lineup. Behind them stand a jumble of oversized fiberglass statues that practically beg travelers to stop and gawk: a bizarre conglomeration of giant chickens, fairy-tale figures, even a royal blue gorilla.

Owner Larry Robinson told *Strange Michigan* his father built the Scenic Garden 40 years ago as a religious attraction featuring sculptured scenes from the Bible. Larry bought the place about 30 years ago, but eventually the religious figures began to crumble and he took them down. In the meantime, Larry had started his own business creating fiberglass and concrete statues. He used to sell the life-sized jungle animals in 20-critter sets to miniature golf courses. The famous trout, robin, and wolverine in downtown Kalkaska are also his creations. He began to accumulate an inventory of oversized extras and overruns, so it only made sense to erect them on the Scenic Garden grounds. They have stood in place to beckon passersby ever since.

Robinson said he got out of the fiberglass business, except for special commissions, years ago because it was a smelly, dirty job crawling around inside those big sculptures. "I itched for 20 years," he said. But he still makes concrete molds and statues—3,000 different ones by his latest count—and his best sellers, true to his father's original plan, are those with religious themes. Pink elephants and giant rabbits may bring the customers into Robinson Scenic Gardens, but concrete Madonnas are what go home with them.

The Scenic Gardens are open only on Wednesday, Thursday, and Friday during the winter, and while the address is officially Mancelona, Robinson prefers to say it's in better-known Kalkaska.

Kentwood

Kent County

Who Put the Boo in Books?
Haunted Barnes & Noble

Large chain bookstores are noted for their huge selection of books, their handy cafés and for providing comfy places to riffle through the merchandise. But one Barnes & Noble in Kentwood has also gained a rep as a place where not all the customers are entirely visible. An employee told *Strange Michigan* that a ghostly woman who resembles a deceased store manager has been seen more than once, her hair wound up in curlers. In real life, the employee said, the woman used to come in early and make coffee while her hair was still in curlers. Several times cups of coffee mysteriously turned up in odd places, far away from the café, when no customers or other employees were present.

In an even more startling incident, an employee was standing in the country music section of the store when a sign rose out of its pivot stand and flew past her head. A manager witnessed the eerie happening, and reportedly laughed at the sight.

The music department is also home to a phantom black Scottie dog that scoots around under the CD stands. "Customers are always coming and asking why we let dogs in here," said the employee.

Those who attach superstition to numbers may come up with one possible explanation for all the ghostly activity; the store's corporate number is…2666!

Laingsburg
Clinton County
Blood Cemetery

A tiny old cemetery in Section 13 of Victor Township, just west of Laingsburg, bears the ominous name of a longtime local family: Blood. A map from 1875 shows that large plats of land north and south of Prospect Street were owned by the Blood family. A small lake to the west of town was named after them, and so was the cemetery which contains nine members of the Blood clan. One, Daniel Blood, was a minister. Perhaps its name has inspired many of the local legends about this cemetery; one warns that spirits of the cemetery will kill anyone who goes there on Halloween night. Some have also reported seeing the torso of a woman in a blood-red gown floating among the graves.

Lake Linden
Houghton County
The Lost Lady

Many tourists drive through downtown Lake Linden without noticing the eerie memorial that sits in front of city hall—an airplane propeller mounted on a brick monument. Beneath the propeller, centered in the brick structure, a glass-enclosed plaque names soldiers in Lake Linden's "World War II Honor Roll." The propeller itself tells a different story, a tale of lives lost in vain and of enduring mysteries.

After defeating German forces at El Alamein in North Africa, the Allies set their sights on Italy. On April 4, 1943, a fleet of American B-24D Liberator bombers from the 376th Bomb Group based at the airfield in Soluch, Libya, attempted a high-altitude raid on the harbor at Naples, Italy. Twenty-five Liberators took off that day; 24 would return. The fate of the 25th, the *Lady Be Good*, remains shrouded in mysteries.

Newly arrived from America, *Lady* was assigned a crew of rookies with no combat experience: 1st Lt. William J. Hatton, pilot; 2nd Lt. Robert F. Toner, copilot; 2nd Lt. Dp Hays, navigator; 2nd Lt. John S. Woravka, bombardier; Technical Sgt. Harold S. Ripslinger, flight engineer and gunner; Technical Sgt. Robert E. LaMotte, radio operator and gunner; Staff Sgt. Samuel E. Adams, tail gunner; Staff Sgt. Guy E. Shelley, Jr., waist gunner and assistant engineer; and Staff Sgt. Vernon L. Moore, waist

Lady's crew, from left: 1Lt. William J. Hatton (pilot), 2Lt. Robert F. Toner (copilot), 2Lt. Dp Hays (navigator), 2Lt. John S. Woravka (bombardier), TSgt. Harold S. Ripslinger (flight engineer/gunner), TSgt. Robert E. LaMotte (radio operator/gunner), SSgt. Guy E. Shelley Jr. (waist gunner/assistant engineer), SSgt. Samuel E. Adams (tail gunner)

PLAQUE BELOW DISPLAYED WITH PROPELLER AT WHEELUS AIR BASE IN LIBYA, NORTH AFRICA. USAF MUSEUM ACQUIRED PROPELLER AND PLACED ON LOAN TO LAKE LINDEN ON 23 MAY 1970.

THIS PROPELLER IS FROM THE FOUR-ENGINE B-24 LIBERATOR BOMBER, SERIAL NUMBER 41-24301, **LADY BE GOOD** WHICH CRASHED IN THE LIBYAN DESERT 880 MILES SOUTHEAST OF WHEELUS AIR BASE ON 5 APRIL 1943, AFTER A BOMBING RAID ON NAPLES, ITALY. THE AIRCRAFT OPERATING FROM AN AIRFIELD NEAR BENGHAZI WITH THE 514th BOMB SQUADRON, WAS REPORTED MISSING IN ACTION AND ITS FATE WAS NOT KNOWN UNTIL DISCOVERY OF THE WRECKAGE IN MAY 1959. SUBSEQUENT SEARCHES IN THE LIBYAN DESERT RECOVERED REMAINS OF EIGHT OF HER NINE CREW MEMBERS. Placed 19 January 1961

The *Lady Be Good* memorial in Lake Linden

gunner and assistant radio operator. Two crewmen hailed from Michigan, Ripslinger from Saginaw and LaMotte from Lake Linden. For *Lady's* new crew, who had themselves just arrived from America in March, the Naples raid would be their first mission...and their last.

On April 4, a sandstorm besieged the airfield at Soluch as the Liberators took off in small groups, usually three at a time. Just after 3 p.m., Lt. Hatton and his crew lifted off in *Lady Be Good*, the 21st Liberator to depart Soluch. Soon Hatton and crew slipped in behind two other Liberators, shadowing them across the sea. But a little over an hour later engine trouble brought on by the sandstorm forced the two lead bombers to turn back toward Soluch, leaving *Lady Be Good* alone.

With wind nudging all the planes east, *Lady* likely ended up nowhere near Naples, dangerously close to Greece and the Axis aircraft based there. Crew logs tell of several course corrections made in a vain attempt to get back on track for Naples, and of the crew's anxieties about enemy attack. By 9 p.m., Hatton gave up, finally turning the Liberator around to head home to Soluch. Bombardier Woravka dumped *Lady's* bombs over the Mediterranean. On their first and ultimately only mission, Hatton's crew failed to reach their target.

By 11:15 p.m., 21 of the 25 Liberators had landed at Soluch. Three more had ended up on safe ground at Malta, unable to make it all the way home. The pilot of a Liberator that landed at Soluch at 11:10 p.m. reported hearing LaMotte's voice over the radio, requesting a heading for his apparently lost crew. By 11:15 p.m. one Liberator, the *Lady Be Good*, remained absent. Around midnight, a bomber was heard in the skies over Benghazi, near Soluch, but the aircraft passed overhead without attempting to land.

Around 2:00 a.m., Hatton made a final radio call requesting help. *Lady* flew ever southward, hundreds of miles from Soluch, into the Calanscio Sand Sea. Not long after Hatton's final call for help, hopelessly lost and running out of fuel, the crew bailed out over the desert. The Liberator dropped from the sky, skidding to a stop 16 miles from the spot where Hatton and his crew landed.

The propeller monument

One man was missing—Woravka, the bombardier. The men spread out to search for him, without success. The crew presumed him dead and set out to find their way home, or at least to safety. When the men found tire tracks in the sand they opted to follow them, thinking the marks might lead to somewhere. The next day, they abandoned the tire tracks. What little water they had was depleting fast. Hunger, thirst, and exposure to the harsh desert conditions tormented the men. On the fourth day, a sandstorm descended on them. By day five, five of the crew had gone blind.

On April 10, the crew's sixth day in the desert, only three of the men could still walk. Ripslinger, Shelley, and Moore realized they must leave the rest of the crew behind if they had any hope of finding help. Despite their suffering, the men kept writing in their diaries. Those left behind believed that Ripslinger, Shelley, and Moore would reach safety, because they had no doubt Soluch lay just over the next dune.

The three men who pushed onward had left the remaining water with the five who stayed behind. Without water or food, exhausted from days of trudging through the desert, the three men struggled to keep moving. Twenty miles later, one of them died. A little farther on, a second died. By April 13, the last living member of the crew perished in the sand. The first five men had walked 78 miles. The last to die—Shelley—had walked 115 miles.

The day that *Lady Be Good* vanished, a search was instigated. The search lasted about a week, and found no trace of the Liberator. The crew was officially designated missing in action, presumed dead. For 15 years, the lost *Lady* would slumber in the desert.

By 1958, with the war long past, oil companies vied for concessions in oil-rich North Africa. British Petroleum (BP) had acquired a large concession that included the Calanscio Sand Sea. While conducting an aerial survey of the concession, BP employees spotted a crashed airplane near the boundaries of the Calanscio Sand Sea, remains which they immediately recognized as a B-24D Liberator with American markings. The plane was broken into several pieces. Over the next two years, the BP men and others embarked on missions to explore the wreckage and locate the bodies of the crew.

At first the searchers found no signs of the crew. *Lady* was empty, save for the relics the men had left behind when they bailed out—personal items, log books, and equipment lay as they had for 17 years. Dead birds, mummified by the desert, littered the interior. The once powerful Liberator had become a ghost.

Eventually, the searchers found the bodies of the five men from whom Ripslinger, Shelley, and Moore had parted on the sixth day of their ordeal. Woravka, the man missing after the bail out, would be found still wearing his parachute, which had failed to deploy. He died on impact. Later the searchers would find Ripslinger and Shelley. They never found Moore.

On his Web site, Lady-BeGood.com, author Mario Martinez recounts a story told by a British ex-military man who had seen skeletal remains in the region where Ripslinger and Shelley had been found. During his military service, ten years after *Lady* and her crew had met their tragic end, the soldier had seen a skeleton in the desert. The military's Arab guides had buried the body in the sand after 20 minutes. With nothing to go on but a photo of the remains, Martinez could never determine the skeleton's identity with any certainty, though the remains had reportedly been discovered not far from where Shelley's had turned up several years later.

For Robert LaMotte, the radio operator from Lake Linden, the tragedy of *Lady Be Good* finds a solemn end in his hometown. A propeller from *Lady Be Good* sits outside Lake Linden City Hall, accompanied by a plaque explaining its significance. Previously displayed at Wheelus Air Base in Libya, the propeller made its way to Lake Linden thanks to local resident Octave Du Temple, who saw the propeller at Wheelus. Du Temple helped bring the artifact to Lake Linden, where it arrived in 1970, on loan from the air force.

When LaMotte's body came home, the local squadron of the Arnold Air Society, based at Michigan Technological University in nearby Houghton, participated in the memorial service for his burial. In 1961, the squadron honored LaMotte by taking his name, becoming the Robert E. LaMotte Squadron.

Even after more than 60 years, mysteries still surround the *Lady Be Good.* How did a 20mm projectile wind up lodged in her port inner engine, without the crew realizing it and without harming the Liberator? Who named the Liberator *Lady Be Good* shortly after her arrival in Libya? How did a letter addressed to Sergeant Shea end up in the *Lady Be Good,* when no one by that name had any association with the 376th Bomb Group? How did the Liberator manage to fly level and fairly straight for an additional 16 miles after the crew abandoned her? How did she execute a perfect belly landing on her own? Why was Dp Hays's navigation equipment found boxed up neatly, as if he had never used it?

According to a fact sheet about *Lady Be Good* posted on the Air Force Museum Web site, parts from the bomber, recovered from her wreckage, were recycled into other aircraft. A C-54 that received autosyn transmitters from *Lady* experienced propeller trouble and only survived by ditching its cargo. A C-47 with *Lady's* radio receiver crashed in the Mediterranean, while an army plane that received an armrest from *Lady* went down in the Gulf of Sidra, killing 10 men. Scant few remnants of the army plane washed ashore—including the armrest from the *Lady Be Good.* Did *Lady's* remains become cursed?

The memorial in Lake Linden honors a crew who seemed doomed from the moment their bomber took off from Soluch. They struggled to survive the desert, lasting five times longer than anyone believed possible. But, ultimately, the desert proved too powerful for even the valiant men of the *Lady Be Good.*

Lady Be Good in her final resting place in the Calanscio Sand Sea

Lapeer

Lapeer County

Clanging Caskets

There is a cemetery just west of downtown Lapeer, Michigan. As a child I remember my family telling stories of times long ago, when the first graves were dug in the cemetery. There was an underground spring just underground in that very spot. My family would tell of tales about sounds coming from the cemetery at night. Sounds of the caskets clanging together! It managed to scare me!

—*Kelly Bretzloff*

Laurium

Houghton County

Digging Up the Gipper

The dead are supposed to rest in peace. Once in awhile, though, the living won't let them. Take the recent interruption of football legend George Gipp's rest after a deceased girlfriend's child claimed to be Gipp's daughter.

The story starts and ends in Houghton County, the runner-up for the farthest northern county in Michigan (behind Keweenaw County). The village of Laurium lies adjacent to Calumet—a small town now, but during the copper boom the largest city in Michigan. In that boomtown era, George Gipp was born in Laurium on February 18, 1895.

With the decline of copper mining, Calumet became a small town with few claims to fame save for Gipp, a sports legend whose purported request that his team "win one for the Gipper" was made famous when Ronald Reagan portrayed Gipp in a movie. In 2007, Laurium found itself back in the spotlight thanks to the Gipper—and his alleged love child, Bette Bright Weeks.

Gipp attended Calumet High School where he played baseball. While attending the University of Notre Dame, Gipp became a star football player—during his four-year career, Gipp thwarted every pass attempted by opposing teams. His achievements on the field earned Gipp a place in the National Football Hall of Fame.

Gipp died of pneumonia on December 14, 1920, at age 25. As with most legendary figures, Gipp's life and death have themselves spurred legends. Did Gipp contract pneumonia after getting locked out of his dormitory, or did an untreated strep infection lead to a more serious illness? Whatever the cause, pneumonia defeated the unbeatable Gipp, and he was buried in Lakeview Cemetery near his hometown. A memorial on the corner of Lake Linden Avenue and Tamarack Street in Laurium celebrates the life and career of the Gipper along with annual recipients of the George Gipp Award,

handed out by Calumet High School.

Gipp rested in peace for 87 years, until his great-nephew requested a DNA test to determine the validity of a claim made by Bette Bright Weeks, the daughter of Gipp's old girlfriend, who said she was Gipp's love child. According to some stories, Gipp preferred life on the other side of the tracks, frequenting dance halls and perhaps getting expelled from Notre Dame briefly due to his unsavory proclivities. Bette died in January 2007 but in October 2007, authorities exhumed Gipp's body, despite protests from family members. Tests compared DNA from Gipp's right femur with that from Weeks's skin.

Despite the rumors, DNA tests disproved the love-child claim. You might say modern medical science did "win one for the Gipper."

Lennon

Genesee/Shiawasee Counties

Krupps: Lawn Ornament Heaven

It may look like a convention of garden gnomes, but the small town of Lennon bills itself as the Lawn Ornament Capital of the World. Actually, a business called Krupp's is the reason for the title. The lawn ornament extravaganza was started in the early '50s by Jean Krupp, who staved off poverty by building and selling bird- and doghouses she cobbled from wood scraps. Her front lawn business eventually expanded into the gigantic ornament industry she still commands at the age of 83, with thousands of statues covering the massive sales area inside and outdoors. Krupp also still paints many of the statues herself, and *Strange Michigan* found her in spattered trousers, paintbrush in hand, an hour after closing one night. We talked and snapped a few photos as she rested a while near the devotional statue display, and later we discovered an odd effect on one shot of the Virgin Mary statues. In the photo, colored lights emanated from the palms of the largest statue and arced to the crown of another, smaller Mary!

This shot was taken inside the building with a digital Minolta camera and is not altered in any way. None of the other dozens of photos we took indoors or out, including one with Jean, showed any kind of mist, let alone colored swirling lights. Two of the building's fluorescent fixtures are shown clearly at right and they do not appear to be affecting the light swirl or causing reflections. But what this light display means, we will leave to our gentle, weird readers to figure out.

There are many other bits of statuary to ponder. Gargoyles, bunnies, cartoon figurines, fountains, bird baths, even the ubiquitous

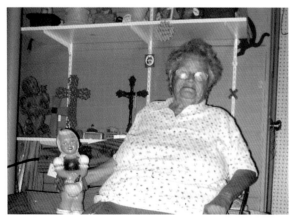

Jean Krupp

concrete deer can all be found at Krupp's. Jesus statues stand armless in a row, sold with hands to be attached separately. King Neptune, David, and St. Francis hobnob in a corner. There is a horse section, cat section, dog section, and angel section. If they don't have it, says their Web site, they will get it for you.

As for Jean, she told *Strange Michigan* she's just waiting to pass the concrete kingdom on to an interested grandchild. And it's certain, thanks to the countless lawns she's helped to adorn, that Jean Krupp's contribution to Michigan yard art will never be taken for granite.

Lewiston
Montmorency County
Something in the Air

On May 2, 2007, something appeared in the skies over Lewiston. So say Jeff Nickert and his mother Denise, both of whom witnessed the fantastic display that carried on until early the next morning. Jeff Nickert contacted the *Gaylord Herald-Times* at 5:30 a.m. to report the incident.

When Nickert arrived home Wednesday night at 10:30 p.m., he spotted the unusual activity in the sky. He described four to five UFOs, shaped like diamonds, that resembled "electricity floating through the air." The activity lasted through the night, finally abating around 7:30 a.m. Thursday. Denise Nickert saw the objects too, which she described as fast-moving, color-changing lights with "electricity floating through them."

Maj. Andrew Roberts of the Grayling Aerial Gunnery Range dismissed the lights as those of seven fighter jets dispatched throughout the area on Wednesday night. The jets flew between 8:40 p.m. and 11:00 p.m., dropping flares for training purposes. The folks from the Grayling Aerial Gunnery Range say their planes fought no UFOs that night—the Nickerts saw flares.

Yet the Nickerts insist the activity over their home lasted until morning, while the jets supposedly left the area by 11 p.m. The lights weren't flares, Denise Nickert said, because the objects could repeatedly rend themselves in two without dispersing.

Lost Nation
State Game Area

Hillsdale County
Lost Bigfoot in Lost Nation?

If there's one thing Michigan has a lot of, it's snow…the perfect tracking material for Bigfoot prints. They've been found all over the state, but one of the best-documented cases happened February 6, 1989, not in the northern hinterlands but near the southern border. The case was reported in the *Detroit News*.

An anonymous outdoorsman discovered the prints in the Lost Nation State Game Area in eastern Hillsdale County and phoned the local sheriff, who hotfooted it to the Bigfoot tracks. The sheriff had the presence of mind to photograph the gargantuan, 22-by-10-inch prints and also make plaster casts. He told reporters he took the action so people wouldn't panic thinking that the authorities were ignoring reports. Bigfoot prints are almost completely flat, with toes that run straight across, and are the most oft-cited evidence that the creature really exists. Unfortunately, they are also probably the most easily faked evidence, ensuring the controversy will never end.

Luna Pier
Monroe County
Camp Lady of the Lake

The screams of orphans who died hideous deaths in a giant fire are supposed to haunt the site of this former church camp in the southeastern corner of Michigan. The legend claims that a woman who ran the camp had gone for a walk, and returned to find the place ablaze. She died trying to save the children, and can still be seen floating over Lake Erie after midnight. Some have also reported the presence of a shadowy black spook figure. *Strange Michigan* found no historical basis for the legend of the burned orphans, but campers in the area off Erie Road still claim there are strange goings-on and that the lady has never left.

Luther
Lake County
Head of the Dogman

Luther, a small town on State Road and Old M-63 in Lake County, was memorialized in Traverse City DJ Steve Cook's song about the Michigan Dogman, "The Legend." The story goes that a cabin in Luther was attacked by some type of animal that left large canine prints but also left scratches seven feet off the ground! Although some parts of "The Legend," such as the idea that the Dogman reappears in the seventh year of every decade, were made up by Cook for dramatic effect, this particular section of the song happens to be true. Strange Michigan traveled to Luther and talked to a relative of the owner of the "cabin," which turned out to be a nice, two-story house located outside of town. They had been away on vacation when the unidentified animal evidently tried to get in, and the prints were not those of a bear.

The North Bar in downtown Luther became an unofficial headquarters for the Dogman, and for many years decorated its walls with Dogman signs and cartoons. We were most impressed, however, with the taxidermy masterpiece, "Head of the Dogman," that sits atop a game machine in the bar. Complete with glass eyes, it certainly looks canine; however, the wife of the head's owner confided to us that it had been cleverly manufactured from the rear end of a black deer. We will not go into the details.

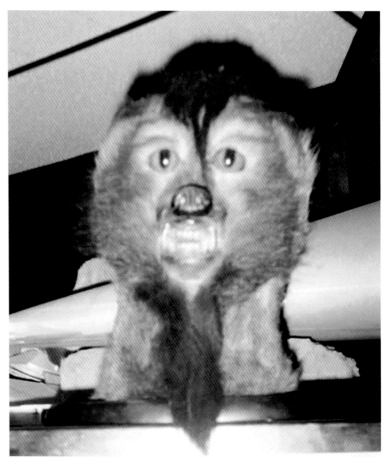

Mackinac Island
Mackinac County
The World's Longest Porch

Mackinac Island offers beautiful vistas, enough fudge to make you sick, and solitude, thanks to the lack of motorized vehicles. Yet visitors flock to one attraction: the Grand Hotel. Since its opening on July 10, 1887, the hotel has become an icon, even appearing in the movie *Somewhere in Time*, which starred Jane Seymour and Christopher Reeve. What makes the Grand Hotel so grand?

Maybe it's the front porch. The hotel boasts the longest front porch in the world, at 660 feet. You could fit a lot of rocking chairs on that porch. *Strange Michigan* may not know exactly how many rocking chairs would fit on it, but we do know how many geraniums would. The hotel's porch boasts 260 planting boxes that hold a total of 2,500 geraniums. In fact, to decorate the porch and surrounding gardens, staff plant one ton of bulbs each year.

In the 1890s, courting couples gave the porch the nickname "Flirtation Walk," and the porch became the central meeting place on the island. In 2001, to celebrate the hotel's 114th anniversary, staff planned a unique and fitting tribute. They pieced together one of the world's longest cakes on the world's longest porch. The cake measured 114 feet, one foot for each year of the hotel's operation.

The Ghosts of Mackinac Island

Reminiscent of the era when transportation was limited to bicycles, foot, or horse and carriage, Michigan's most beautiful—and most haunted—spot sits off the north shore of the mainland peninsula. Surrounded by Lake Huron, it is Mackinac Island.

The Victorian era has been preserved on this picturesque island. Vacationers invade the island in search of a simple and slow-paced life, away from the normal hustle and bustle of the real world. Loving couples walk hand in hand, and families spend their afternoons shopping in the quaint shops, swimming off the docks, and sampling fudge and taffy. In the winter, however, the streets are empty, leaving an eerie, cold feeling that doesn't have much to do with the temperature. But whatever the weather, spirits haunt every part of Mackinac Island, whether you believe in them or not.

The Mackinac Bridge, the longest suspension bridge over fresh water, holds its own haunting secrets. Five men lost their lives building the "Mighty Mac" and several others have committed suicide plunging into the straits.

As the Grand Hotel was being built, several skeletons were unearthed. Some were moved to a nearby cemetery, while others remained in place, continuing their rest below the foundation of the building. Or are they? The Grand Hotel has had several claims of unexplained orbs and other energy fields showing up on camera film. And just down the road at another resort, Mission Pointe, an Indian burial ground was discovered as the foundation was being set, stirring up even more ghosts. With so many graves disturbed it is no wonder that so many visitors have had paranormal encounters.

The Straits of Mackinac was a battleground between the French, American, and British forces as they fought for control of the upper Great Lakes. Two forts were built at Mackinac in the 17th century, and since the early 19th century many accidents have occurred as vessels tried to squeeze through the treacherous shallows and reefs.

The Straits of Mackinac, also known as the Great Lakes Triangle, have claimed several ships and planes and 7,900 lives, much like the famous Bermuda Triangle. On foggy nights, the phantom of the *W.H. Gilcher*, a coal steamer that sank in 1892, is said to be seen in the Straits of Mackinac. An older vessel thought to be the boat of an explorer, *Sebastian*, returns every seven years, trying to find his way home to his fiancée in France. Since 1913, close to 400 men have died on the waters near Mackinac Island in just the month of November; however, the mysterious and ghostly waters of the Straits continue to draw in visitors.

Several other cottages, hotels, and B & Bs on the island are also said to be haunted. The *tap, tap, tap* of a mischievous child ghost's footsteps running down the hall of one elegant and historic inn keep guests awake at night, as does the telephone ringing in the dead of night, with nobody on the other end.

However, the people who head the tourism community of Mackinac Island don't quite like the claims of the hauntings; staunch skeptics possibly fear injury to the island's elegant and historic reputation. But catch an employee in the hallway of one of Mackinac Island's old and charming historic hotels and they will whisper many tales of hauntings and offer paranormal excursions that will surely make the hair on the back of your neck stand up.

In the heart of the historic town, in the middle of Main Street, sits one such haunted Victorian inn where several spirits of children are said to play with the telephones, set off the alarm clocks, and even move towels away as the lodgers shower. Guests leave small gifts for the ghosts—jacks, a ball, or marbles—as a small means of paying their respect to little ones lost, who have not yet crossed over.

One popular and haunted tourist attraction continues to be Fort Mackinac, constructed by the British. You will find military music, cannon salutes over the harbor, and interpreters sharing the story of the Revolutionary War. You may also find an air of sickness and fear in the energy around the Fort. Still standing is the oldest hospital in Michigan, which is also said to be one of the most haunted locations. There have been sightings of spirits in the Officers' Hill quarters and the soldiers' barracks. More skeletons were found during renovations to the Fort; one in particular was found in the guardhouse, in the "Black Hole" where unfortunate prisoners were kept. Visitors claim an eerie feeling as they gape down into the abyss. On a misty morning, take a walk and see if you too can hear the music played by the phantom piper said to haunt the land near the Fort.

If you are seeking a rustic adventure, take a hike through the woods, but keep close to your partner. As you admire Michigan's fragrant lilac trees and tall pines, you may just find yourself standing toe to toe with one of the many spirits of Indians said to inhabit the surrounding forest. The island had been a tribal gathering place where Gitchie Manitou, the Great Spirit, was worshiped, until the Chief sold it to the British. During the War of 1812, the British slaughtered more than 70 Indians.

The island is also littered with caverns and caves to explore and spelunk. But to ghost enthusiasts, names such as Skull Cave, Fairy Kitchen, and Devil's Kitchen denote these places as extremely haunted, since they were used as burial sites.

— *Kristy Robinett, contributor*

The Haunted Theatre

From the moment you walk up the front steps and find yourself greeted by the Man Thing, you will realize you've crossed the threshold into another realm where legend becomes flesh. Take heart, though, for you have not entered the underworld. You've simply reached the front door of Mackinac Island's own museum of the strange, the Haunted Theatre.

The Man Thing, which looks like the love child of Bigfoot and the Creature from the Black Lagoon, stands watch at the doorway. A sign above the ticket booth reads "The Orpheum," reminding visitors that at one time the building served as a movie theater. In 1974, the Orpheum became the Haunted Theatre, a kind of museum showcasing re-creations of famous monsters and villains. Erik, the Phantom of the Opera, forever pounds away at his organ. The *Manitou* of native legends flits about in search of souls.

If that's not spooky enough for you, the building sits on an old Indian burial ground.

The Highway with Manure Instead of Cars

Mackinac Island preserves a bit of the past on every inch of its land, from the Grand Hotel to colonial-era Fort Mackinac. The state highway that circumnavigates the island sticks to the bygone-era theme. M-185 is the only truly eco-friendly highway in the nation—and the sole state highway to ban motorized vehicles.

That's right. Not a single motor home, car, or even ATV touches the pavement. No smog, no backfiring cars, no honking horns, no screeching tires. What will you find on M-185?

Pedestrians. Bicyclists. Horses pulling carriages. And the occasional pile of manure.

One type of motorized vehicle may touch down on the island—airplanes, which remain sequestered at the island's airport. High-speed ferries drop off tourists at the docks, but never set rudders on land. If you want to travel M-185, bring your walking shoes...or your riding crop.

Mandan
Keweenaw County
Mournful Mandan

The UP's Keweenaw peninsula might have been left to jut into Lake Superior and mind its own business had it not been for the rich lodes of pure, native copper found there. Copper mines brought miners, who imported their families, who required stores, schools, and all the enterprises that go into the making of a town. Such a place was Mandan, four miles north of Delaware off US Highway 41. (Delaware, 12 miles south of Copper Harbor, is often designated a ghost town, too.)

Mandan is not hard to find. A small, rustic sign marks the dirt road leading into the woods now grown up around the formerly booming community. Mandan even merited its own stop on the Keweenaw Central, the railroad that moved copper and people to and from the once-isolated area. The Mandan Mining Company was headquartered here in 1863. Most people feel it was probably named after the Mandans, Native Americans noted for their use of red dye.

Strange Michigan missed the sign the first time, but we swung around and managed to follow the little road, still named Main Street, past the mournful little assemblage of houses that were once the heart of Mandan. One place was marked as someone's summer home by a pair of slouched lawn chairs and a barbecue grill, but the others sat desolate. We passed the likely foundations of the old general store.

Remnants of other stone footings could be glimpsed in some of the undergrowth along the street. The homes once stood two rows thick on either side of this street. It was hard to believe that Mandan once occupied over 500 acres, serving both the Resolute and Medora mines.

In 1907, the town boasted around 300 residents. A school stood on the small hill facing the woods, while a steam-heated rooming house (a real attraction in chilly northern winters), and over two dozen other homes and buildings filled out the village boundaries. Church services were held in parishioners' houses. The mines played out by 1909, however, and the populace began trickling away. The Mandan Post Office managed to hang on until 1938, but its closing was the community's final death knell.

It's hard to say what ghosts remain. The only legend *Strange Michigan* uncovered here was an online claim that someone's "Great Aunt Jenny" who lived there in mining days still peers out the upper-story window of her house. And yet, the old street is very eerie. Perhaps it's the dense forest that gives the little place its air of foreboding, but we did not feel inclined to linger. Some say that a curse followed those who removed Michigan's native copper nuggets from their hidey-holes in the earth; perhaps a bit of that ill wind still blows through the trees of Mandan.

Manistee
Cow Jumping Over the Moon or UFO?

It happened this past summer (2006) toward the ending of July, in Manistee, Michigan, on Kosiosko Street. I was with my aunt and uncle and we were about to go in the house because we had just roasted marshmallows on the grill. The time was about 11:30 p.m. – 12 a.m., and my uncle looks up at the stars and asks me what that was. I looked up; it was very odd. It looked like a cow! It wasn't a bird or airplane or bat because it was too slow, and it wasn't a satellite. It looked like a cow because it had a similar outline and the spots of a cow. Who knows, maybe it was the cow that jumped over the moon!

—Ashley

Manistique
Schoolcraft County
The Magic Spring

The name *Kitch-iti-kipi* means "big cold water." The legend behind the spring's namesake tells of a young chieftain called Kitch-iti-kipi who, in an attempt to prove his love to a vain girl, drowned in the pool of the spring. The bubbling natural feature saddled with the ancient chief's tongue-tying name is, in fact, a big source of cold water and the biggest spring in Michigan.

Over 16,000 gallons per minute erupt from underwater fissures, creating the impression that the spring magically arises from the depths. The water remains 45 degrees year-round, which means that the spring never freezes no matter how blistering cold the winter. The churning waters stir up sand in phantasmal displays. Ancient trees and big fish seem to materialize beneath the waters, only to vanish again. These wonders and more await you in Palms Book State Park, on the northwest corner of Indian Lake.

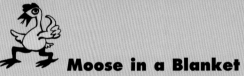

Moose in a Blanket

We all know about pigs in blankets, those bite-size sausages wrapped in breading. But have you heard about the moose in a blanket? No, it's not an appetizer....

Along US Highway 2 in Manistique stands a life-size moose statue. Unlike other moose, however, this one dons the regalia of royalty—a purple blanket adorned with gold trim and buttons. While antlers substitute for a crown, the attire leaves no doubt that this king of the north woods demands respect.

 ## Driving Underwater...Without a Tunnel

The Siphon Bridge: A span that narrows to squeeze traffic over it? Or a bridge with lots of holes in it or a canopy over the top? We feel confident you'll never guess how this old bridge in Manistique got its name.

Erected in 1919, the bridge stands 300 feet long by 66 feet wide. Designers built the bridge to siphon water under itself via a feed flume measuring 3,000 feet long, 66 feet wide, and 20 feet deep. Hence, the road surface hung suspended four feet below the actual water level, supported by the current. The bridge proved so strange it was featured in *Ripley's Believe It or Not!* and became a unique attraction in the UP.

The flume once gushed 650,000 gallons per hour but now has reduced to a trickle in comparison. The bridge itself no longer rides underwater. You can still see the bridge and its flume, plus two smaller bridges nearby, on Deer Street. If you can't find it, stop by the Chamber of Commerce (behind Paul Bunyan) on US 2 for directions. While the bridge may no longer siphon many tourists, it lives on as more than a drop in the bucket of strange history.

The OTHER Home of Paul Bunyan

Every town in the Midwest wants to claim Paul Bunyan as its native son. Oscoda, a town on the shores of Lake Huron in Iosco County, took that desire to supreme heights by having itself declared the official birthplace of Bunyan—by the state legislature! Yet some towns refuse to relinquish their claims, even in the face of legislative disapproval. So when you drive into Manistique, you will still see a Paul Bunyan statue accompanied by a log sign that declares the town the "Home of Paul Bunyan."

The proud declaration sits above a plaque listing, in much smaller letters, the "Friends of Paul Bunyan." The list includes names of businesses and individuals who presumably support the upkeep of the statue, as well as the town's proclamation that Bunyan was born here in the UP, not down there in the mitten.

Manton

Wexford County

The Sweet Singer of Michigan; World's Worst Poet

> *Have you heard of the dreadful fate*
> *Of Mr. P.P. Bliss and wife?*
> *Of their death I will relate,*
> *And also others lost their life.*
> —*Ashtabula Disaster,*
> Julia A. Moore

> *And now kind friends, what I have wrote;*
> *I hope you will pass o'er,*
> *And not criticize, as some have done,*
> *Hithertoherebefore.*
> —*The Author's Early Life,* Julia A. Moore

In the 19th century, there was no *American Idol,* so instead of bad amateur vocalists, people made laughingstocks of horrible poets. Michigan's Julia A. Moore was the William Hung (famed *American Idol* wannabe) of poetry from about 1876 to 1915. In fact, the *Literary Encyclopedia* goes so far as to call her "the most famous bad poet in the history of American literature."

Born in Plainfield in 1847, she and her farmer husband had ten children on their homestead near Manton, four of whom died in childhood. This may have influenced her tendency to write about tragic death, earning her the label, "mortuary poet."

> *She knows not that it was her son,*
> *His coffin could not be opened—*
> *it might be some one in his place,*
> *For she could not see his noble face.*
> —*William Upson,* Julia A. Moore

Her first book, *The Sweet Singer of Michigan,* was an immediate hit upon its release in 1876, as people amused themselves with Moore's maudlin, sentimental themes, mismatched rhymes, and nonexistent or offbeat rhythms. Her dearth of writing ability was understandable, however. Moore had little education and admitted she was almost completely ignorant of any of the great poets. And it took her quite a while to catch on to the fact that the crowds who flocked to her readings were laughing at her expense. When the audience would be unable to restrain themselves from boos and catcalls, Moore figured they were complaining about the musicians who accompanied her presentations.

It wasn't until the publication of her second book in 1878 that it dawned on Moore that people were disdainful of her work. Her husband was so embarrassed that he almost ended her career, although she eventually managed to squeeze out a few more awful verses for publication, along with a short story and a novel about a poor farmer whose wife rescues the farm with her writing.

Ironically, one of Moore's best-known bits of twisted doggerel is also a plea to judge her work gently.

Moore died in 1920, but not before influencing two true literary greats. Mark Twain, aka Samuel Clemens, was said to have loved her poetry because it always made him laugh, and he based his *Huckleberry Finn* character Evangeline Grangerford on Moore. American humorist Ogden Nash often wryly insisted that Moore's wretched verse was his major influence, although, of course, Nash's poetry was intentionally funny. And Moore has not been completely forgotten by her public. Every year, the Flint Public Library holds a Julia A. Moore Poetry Festival, complete with a bad poetry contest, "proferring style so awful, your ears you will close."

Marquette

Marquette County

Walking the Haunted Streets

In early November, the Landmark Inn in Marquette becomes the setting for an unusual event—Crossings, hosted by the UP Paranormal Society. While Crossings features a multitude of uncanny events, the one we enjoyed most was the ghost tour. *Strange Michigan* attended the final tour of the night, along with about a dozen other folks. Our guide, Bobby Glenn Brown, gathered us on the steps outside the Landmark Inn, from whence we embarked on our walking tour of downtown Marquette, pausing at various locations to hear the history and ghostly encounters associated with each.

Early in the tour Bobby stopped us in front of an old building which now houses Elizabeth's Chophouse but that had, in a previous incarnation, housed a funeral parlor. As he spoke the words "funeral parlor," the streetlight beside him blinked out. To the light, Bobby exclaimed, "Thank you!"

As Bobby resumed his discussion of the building's history, the streetlight blinked on again. Throughout his speech, the light dimmed off and on, occasionally winking out altogether.

Haunted Downtown

Intrigued by the ghost tour idea, but too impatient to wait for Crossings in November? Follow this roadmap to haunted downtown Marquette.

The **Landmark Inn** on Front Street apparently hosts guests both living and dead. A specter known as the red-haired "woman in white" makes occasional appearances clad in a flowing white dress with a bustle. The woman shows herself on the sixth floor, especially in the Lilac Room—a lilac scent is often associated with her—while in the Sky Room, ghost hunters believe they captured the woman's voice on tape declaring "my name is..." either Mary Ellen or Eleanor.

Just down the street from the Landmark, the **First Presbyterian Church** has its own otherworldly occurrences. A janitor seems unwilling to leave the 150-year-old building, even after his death, having been spotted hunched over holding a mop or broom.

The **harbor area behind downtown** offers mysteries of its own. In a single storm that occurred more than 85 years ago, 17 ships sank, with one never recovered. Today, in the area from downtown north to the red lighthouse, people report apparitions crawling out of the water onto the beach, perhaps the remnants of souls lost in shipwrecks.

The building at **113 Front Street**, which now houses Elizabeth's Chophouse, during Marquette's frontier days held a funeral parlor. Back then no one had a foolproof way of determining whether the "deceased" had actually expired or simply fallen into a coma. The story goes that a woman presumed dead was taken to the funeral parlor and sealed in a coffin. When the morticians returned in the morning, they discovered the woman had not

The old railroad depot

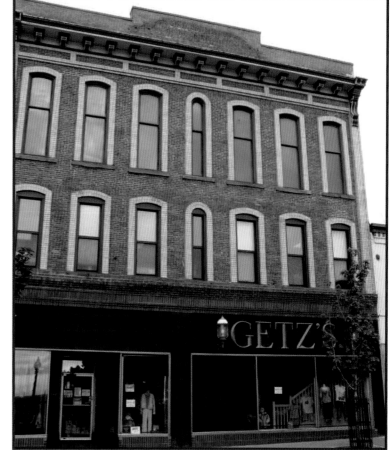

First Presbyterian Church

died—until she suffocated in the coffin. Perhaps the story accounts for the weird goings-on at the building today. Doors slam, lights flicker, glass breaks. People have heard a woman's voice begging "Can you get me out? I want out, let me out."

The **Rosewood Building** has seen similar activity from a man's ghost. Windows crack for no reason. During construction, while workers were on break, tools would fall off tables and an electric chainsaw started up on its own.

Across the street at **Getz's Department Store**, a former employee apparently lingers even though he retired in the most permanent way. The man, who worked in the men's department, was found dead of a heart attack, slumped over the slacks rack. Employees have seen, via security cameras, a man in the men's department, sometimes folding slacks. Even death can't get you a sick day!

Elsewhere downtown, the **Back Room** bar may serve the ghosts of gangsters who once owned the place. Bone fragments found in the lake behind the building could be the remains of those who crossed the gangsters. **St. Peter's Cathedral**, home to the tomb of the "Showshoe Priest" Bishop Baraga, often affects visitors with a sensa-

The dock where the railroad ended

The Delft Theater

tion of something unseen. Nuns and priests walking down the passageway to the rectory sometimes feel cold while the lights flicker.

A railroad used to run through downtown Marquette, ending at the old ore dock that still stands on the shores of Lake Superior, beyond the **Rosewood Walkway**. Many years ago, two trains collided between the old depot (now a doctor's office) and the ore dock. The wreck proved one of the worst ever, killing 39 passengers and the conductors. One conductor who tried in vain to warn the oncoming train by waving his lantern, lost his head, literally. A search of the wreckage found no sign of the man's head. In recent years, people have spied glowing orbs under the ore dock and along the path of the old railroad, leading to stories that the orb represents the conductor's lantern.

Many other locations claim spirits too, from the **Delft Theater** to the **Masonic Center** to an **abandoned orphanage**. So next time you drive through Marquette, stop in and say hello—to the ghosts!

 **Granny Doors**

On our way through Marquette, *Strange Michigan* spotted a train of folk art pieces—doors with images painted on them—displayed along the road. A walking path that doubles as a snowmobile trail in winter skirts the lakeshore on the northeastern side of Marquette. Here, propped up on either side of the trail, stood scads of "Granny Doors," part of a community art project coordinated by Mary Wright, the 1999 recipient of the Michigan governor's Civic Leader

Award. Each door was created by a different artist.

Each door honored the artist's grandmother. Some featured collaged photos; others showcased paintings of the grannies. One granny sat demurely on a couch or chair, hands clasped on her lap. Another had her photographic head pasted onto a painted body clad in a short and rather un-demure dress. More Granny Doors were displayed in Hancock, about 100 miles north of Marquette.

The Yooper Dome; Biggest Wooden Dome in the World

Why build a normal sports stadium when you can have the biggest wooden dome in the world?

At Northern Michigan University, the Superior Dome, built in 1991, rises 14 stories into the UP sky and stretches 536 feet across, covering more than five acres of land. Naturally, the dome's builders constructed it to withstand Yooper winters—60 pounds per square foot of snow and winds up to 80 miles per hour. The geodesic dome, which consists of Douglas fir beams and decking, seats a maximum capacity of 16,000. The dome also features the largest retractable turf carpet in the world.

To make the dome more weatherproof, workers installed rubberized sheets that they unfurled starting from the top of the dome. Yoopers have a devilish sense of humor, so locals decided the unusual sheath worn by the dome demanded a new nickname for the structure—the Con-dome. (In reality, the dome looks more like a giant igloo.) Most of the time, however, it goes by the less risque nickname of da Yooper Dome.

Morbid Mary & Her Band of Seven Ghost Hunters

Michiganders love their hunting—kids take off from school for the opening day of deer season, restaurants hang "Welcome, hunters!" signs. But one type of hunting has yet to gain a foothold in most Michiganders' hearts.

Ghost hunting.

Several groups throughout the state engage in this paranormal pastime. Marquette boasts one such group, the Upper Peninsula Paranormal Society (UPPS), which has investigated numerous haunted habitats and possessed places. Maryanne, the group's founder and director, has always harbored an interest in things that go bump in the night—or in the daytime, or any old time.

"My friends started calling me Morbid Mary," she says, "but every time they would hear a weird sound in their house, they would call me."

In 2004, Maryanne founded a ghost-hunting group at the local university. In 2006, she left that group to start a brand-new endeavor into the eerie—UPPS. When Maryanne and her seven cohorts enter a haunted building, they come prepared with digital and 35mm cameras, thermal temperature sensors, electromagnetic sensors, video cameras, night vision, and digital recorders.

Maryanne has had quite a few ghostly encounters on her own. While visiting a friend's house, she glimpsed a ghost girl in the kitchen. Sicilian relatives who have passed over occasionally visit her as well. Since founding UPPS, Maryanne has ghost-hunted throughout the UP, including an abandoned orphanage in Marquette well known for its unearthly activity.

The first time she visited the site, she heard children's voices outside the building. Her son, Eddie, a member of the UPPS crew, once captured a strange noise on tape while attempting to record EVPs—electronic voice phenomena—outside the building. EVPs are sounds or voices heard on recordings played back after the fact. While trying to capture EVPs, Eddie began to hear a noise through his headphones, a noise so loud it hurt his ears. He ripped off his headphones. Then the microphone started acting up, so he removed it as well. But when he played back the recording later, the noise remained audible even after he had removed the microphone.

UPPS members prefer to keep a low profile. The group has no Web site, and its members prefer not to give their last names or phone numbers. But next time you see a strange light flashing inside an abandoned house, it may be Morbid Mary and the UPPS folks hard at work trying to contact the other side.

moved west to try his luck in the iron industry. In 1875, inspiration of another sort cast its spell on Harlow.

In the woods one day Harlow came upon a tree that reminded him of a man. He had the tree cut to enhance its resemblance to the human form. But Amos hadn't finished yet. He found a knot in another tree and transplanted it onto his creation to serve as the Wooden Man's head. Fungi ears, cedar arms, hemp-rope hair, a cedar-bark sailor hat, a collar and cuffs of white birch bark, and...voila! The Wooden Man was born. To cement the Man's reputation as a true Victorian gentleman, Harlow added a cane hewn from a large branch.

By November 1875, the Wooden Man had become quite the attraction. The *Marquette Mining Journal* proclaimed that "Harlow's old man turns the heads of as many travelers on the train as an excruciatingly pinned-back dress." Perhaps those pinned-back dresses caught the Wooden Man's eye, for in 1891 wedding bells tolled for the tallest man in Marquette.

Even in Victorian times, Yoopers had a unique sense of humor. Locals held a mock wedding for the Wooden Man, with a corset saleswoman as his human bride. Of her groom, the bride reputedly said, " He was all right only he stayed out all night." At least she always knew where to find him!

To learn about the Wooden Man, and see photos of him, visit the Marquette County History Museum at 213 N. Front Street, across from the Landmark Inn.

A Real Stiff: Harlow's Wooden Man

Every town needs a hero. A solid citizen who stands above all others. Marquette boasts just such a fellow—a man so upright no one can topple him. Though he celebrated his 133rd birthday in spring 2008, this hero remains as strong as ever.

Just don't ask him to step aside so you can pass. Or smile. He's, well...a bit wooden. Harlow's Wooden Man, a statue cobbled together from bits of trees, has resided on Fourth Street in Marquette since the spring of 1875. Though now on private property, the Wooden Man remains an icon of Marquette's history and can be spied from the street, if you look hard enough. The statue stands about 14 feet tall, and is nearly six feet wide at the shoulders.

Amos Harlow, creator of the Wooden Man, is known as a founding father of Marquette. Originally from Massachusetts, Harlow

A Yooper Wonderland

Free. Fun. Original. If those words describe your perfect roadside attraction, then head on out to Lakenenland in Chocolay Township, on M-28 just east of Marquette, and discover a treasure trove of over 60 clever, often whimsical sculptures crafted from scrap metal. The sculpture park is the product of one man's imagination.

Ten years ago, construction worker Tom Lakenen gave up drinking. But he soon realized he needed a hobby to keep himself out of the bars. Ever the practical Michigander, Tom devised a unique hobby that both occupied his free time and recycled scrap metal leftover from the construction sites where he spent his days. He started making junkyard art. His first sculptures, dancing wolves, adorned his front yard in Marquette. Gradually he added more sculptures, until his yard hosted a menagerie of metal creations, and until the township ordered Tom to remove the "junk" from his yard. Forced to seek a new home for his art gallery, in 2003 Tom acquired a 37.5-acre

parcel in Chocolay Township. That fall, he carved out dirt trails on the property and transplanted his existing sculptures to their new home. Since the property lay smack-dab on a snowmobile trail, Tom decided to cater to the needs of snowmobilers by providing a warm and comfortable place for them to rest.

Since that first winter, Tom has kept a fire lit for the snowmobilers. On weekends he serves free coffee and hot chocolate. He also clears snow from the sculptures and grooms the trails. In the snow-free seasons, visitors can walk or drive down the trails to view Tom's amazing artwork.

And what wonders await the visitor. *Strange Michigan* arrived mid-morning on a late summer's day. As we pulled into the entrance, we rolled past a pond traversed by a footbridge, and an abstract sculpture placed alongside the bridge. Looking right, we spotted a giant

green dinosaur holding a fishing pole in one hand while in the other he gripped a silver fish nearly as big as the dinosaur himself.

We continued past the pond, spying outhouses on the left. As we rounded the end of the pond, straight ahead loomed two lumberjacks whose size would've made Paul Bunyan proud. The silver colossi grasped either end of an oversize saw, forever whittling away at a log bigger than our car. Signs (metal, of course!) announced that we'd stepped through the wormhole into Lakenenland, a fantastic realm where "Junkyard Art" reigns. If we had any doubts that we had stumbled into a wonderland, those uncertainties vanished as we turned right onto the first trail, passing several abstract sculptures on our way to the first denizen of Lakenenland's enchanted woods—a smiling skeleton, seated in a chair, who stretched a bony metal hand out to us. Though the skeleton seemed friendly, we declined the handshake in favor of snapping a photograph of the gentleman.

The deeper the trail wound into the woods, the more we thanked our laziness for inspiring us to drive rather than walk down the sometimes steep and often sandy path. Strange faces and funky dioramas peeked out from within the trees. A beastly biped—green and fanged—hauled a buggy. Little green coil-men poked their heads out of a flying saucer. A manlike being with big eyes glanced away from his telescope to smile at us. A silver eagle swooped down in front of a pine tree to nab a rabbit. A cougar paused in mid-stride atop a real log. After witnessing wonders too numerous to count, we emerged from the woods and passed between the sawing lumberjacks and their ax-wielding friend. Back on the highway, we drove past a final piece of Lakenenland—a sign set back in the grass alongside the road.

What's ahead for Lakenenland? The fisherman-saurus foreshadows a new attraction. In May 2007 Tom stocked the pond with 1,000 bluegill and perch, which means any day now the pond will be ready for fishing. So if you visit the UP's hidden wonderland, you can both ogle fantastic creatures and snag your lunch.

Of course, if you catch a big one, you may have to fight the dinosaur for it!

 **Jilly & Her Sisters Hang at Jilbert's**

Yoopers know the name. In stores in every corner of the UP you'll find Jilbert's milk, Jilbert's cheese, Jilbert's ice cream. But only in Marquette can you find the company's mascots, a bevy of big bovines who congregate at the Jilbert's Dairy store on Meeske Avenue. The identical triplets share a name too: Jilly.

Jilly Number One perches atop the store building, gazing out at traffic on nearby US 41. Jilly Number Two stands in a little picnic area behind the store, gawking wide-eyed at the tourists slurping down Jilbert's products. Jilly Number Three resides on a flatbed trailer. Since Jilbert's rents out the moooveable Jilly, she may not be around when you stop by the dairy. When *Strange Michigan* stopped in she was keeping an eye on her sisters from the parking lot.

Jilly and her sisters have been around awhile. Jilbert's started out in 1937 in Lake Linden, then moved up the hill to Calumet in 1955, remaining there until 1983 when the dairy moved to its current home in Marquette. Demand for Jilbert's products keeps the three Jillys busy. The dairy processes four million pounds of milk per month, which averages out to 1.3 million pounds per Jilly.

Marshall
Calhoun County
What the Sam Hill?

It's a delicate way of avoiding out-and-out cussing, and has been since the 1830s. Just say "What the Sam Hill?" and people will know what you really mean. The phrase is used nationwide, but one Michigan historian, Charles L. Tucker, claims the original Samuel Hill was born and died in Marshall, 1816-1888. Supposedly Hill could barely choke out a full sentence without the air turning blue around him, so that his very name became a synonym for swearing. Besides, Hill does sound a lot like hell, making it a perfect euphemism.

Not everyone agrees with this version of the story. Other sources argue the original "Sam Hill" was a Guilford, Connecticut, politician who represented his hometown so successfully that when he died and his son took his place in the legislature, the people cried, "Give 'em Sam Hill." And still others insist Sam Hill from Connecticut lost so many local elections the phrase, "Run like Sam Hill" was born from his humiliation.

Strange Michigan thinks Tucker's story is more plausible, and fits the time frame better. But regardless of which Sam Hill gave the world his name as a substitute for hell, Tucker has documented there once lived a Sam Hill in Marshall whose speech could make a sailor blush. Who in Sam Hill can argue with that?

The Petunia Tree

Do petunias grow on trees? Usually, no. But near the Marquette Welcome Center on US Highway 41, south of the city, the answer is yes. There stands a supertunia tree, a piece of roadside art constructed from steel and real, live supertunias (a breed of petunia). The steel trunk looks amazingly lifelike, save for the coloring, and the petunias overflowing their holders resemble the foliage of a genuine tree.

The supertunia tree owes its existence to artist and inventor Earl Senchuk of Marquette, whose other creations can be seen on his Web site www.OxyAce.com.

Metamora

Lapeer County

Ghost in Riding Boots; the Haunted White Horse Inn

Lorenzo Hoard enjoys stomping around Metamora's White Horse Inn in black riding boots. That wouldn't be too remarkable, merely a bit eccentric, if Lorenzo hadn't died 120 years ago, in 1888. According to owners and staff of the popular restaurant, the man who turned the original store and inn into a stagecoach hotel in 1850 is in it for the long haul…and shows no signs of leaving.

Owner Tim Wilkins can't say he wasn't warned when he and his wife took over in 2001. The sellers offered full ghost disclosure. But Wilkins told *Detroit News* reporter Neal Rubin that he didn't believe in spooks and was not scared. It only took a month before Lorenzo revealed himself by dimming the lights repeatedly despite the fact that no one was touching the switches. Customers and staff told Wilkins how plates would fly off counters, phantom footsteps would pound the upstairs floorboards, and that servers would hear a disembodied voice whispering their names. Once, Wilkins observed a human torso floating in the reflection of an upstairs hall mirror.

Lorenzo soon developed a particular affection for a pair of old riding boots the Wilkinses kept in the upstairs apartment. Every day, the Wilkinses would find the boots either facing a different direction or set someplace else in the building. Wilkins told the *News* that he figured Lorenzo was wearing the boots. Perhaps Lorenzo once owned a very similar pair, back in the day. The Wilkinses and their staff and clientele respect the revenant's original right of ownership of the whole place; so to Lorenzo the boots probably just seem like gravy. And gravy, in a restaurant, is always good.

Mio

Oscoda County

Elephant in the Pink

It doesn't necessarily mean you've had a few too many cocktails if you spy a pink elephant while driving through Mio (pronounced *My-oh*) on Highway 33 east of Grayling in northern Michigan. The giant, bubble-gum colored fiberglass creature really is there, trunk raised to bring people into a pizzeria. What do pink elephants and pizzerias have in common? Well, they both start with "p." But *Strange Michigan* is never one to dis any weird roadside attraction, and somehow we find the unrelatedness of the elephant to any surrounding business rather endearing. The only problem is that, at press time, the pizzeria had burned down. Luckily, the elephant escaped unscathed. And according to a Mio native we talked to, Pinkie did once nicely illustrate the name of the Pink Elephant Bar, former occupant of the pizzeria building. But nowadays, the Mio pink elephant just "is." And that's all anyone can ask of a roadside oddity.

Monroe
Monroe County
The Monroe Monster

It was the Depression era, the mid-1930s, when a farmer near Monroe became aware that some hulking and hairy "person" was lurking around the riverbanks on his property. But this was no out-of-work transient trying to live off the land between freight train rides. It was a creature completely covered in hair, manlike but not a man. Bigfoot? Interestingly, the hairy, humanoid primate so familiar to monster fans today was not widely known in the '30s. But in 1978, a Monroe librarian wrote a letter to the woman whose in-laws had owned that farm, recalling the stories her own father had told her about the creature and asking if she had any more information. *Strange Michigan* doesn't know whether the woman ever answered. But it's possible the hairy farm lurker stuck around Monroe for at least 30 years.

Monster mania struck Monroe in the mid-1960s, as newspaper headlines screamed "Monster Mob Clogs Roads" and "Is Monster Loose Here?" Mrs. Hubert Owens and her seventeen-year-old daughter, Christine Van Acker, were the main focus of the clamor. The women claimed they were attacked in their car near Mentel Road around midnight on Friday, August 13, 1965, by a hairy seven-foot-tall monster as they drove home from visiting Mrs. Owens's parents.

Christine was at the wheel, driving slowly due to bald tires on the family vehicle. She slowed down even more when she saw some kind of a figure in the headlights. Then, to her horror, the "figure" reached in through the driver's-side window and grabbed Christine by the hair as if to drag her

out of the car. It banged her head against the doorpost until she fainted and her head fell against the horn. That brought area residents running to the women's aid, and the creature retreated.

As many as 15 area residents claimed to see the monster over the next week or so, although one "sighting" turned out to be nothing more than a horse. Some said the creature "grunted and groaned like a mad dog." But both Mrs. Owens and Christine flunked polygraph tests questioning them about the incident, and local authorities began investigating rumors that the monster was actually a local young man in a gorilla suit. At least one witness said it appeared there were men's pants visible under the beast's torso. By January 1970, the local newspaper was looking back on the Monroe Monster as the "Hoax of the Decade." It noted Monroe had enjoyed worldwide notoriety for 10 days, until police decided the whole thing was a joke.

Witnesses, however, continued to stick to their stories. Mrs. Owens, after failing her polygraph, insisted the test had been "rigged." "How can I make people believe?" she asked. Two hairs purported to be from the animal were sent to a state police laboratory in Lansing, but newspapers did not report the outcome. And then there is the fact that a similar creature had been reported without fanfare in the same area 30 years earlier. Was the Monroe Monster a case of hysteria or a cover-up of something that police preferred to keep quiet? The episode is still controversial, and *Strange Michigan* can only hope that the creature will show up once again (behaving more politely this time) to settle the matter.

 **Painting the Horse (Partly) Orange**

In most people's minds, George Armstrong Custer is inextricably linked with that famous last stand in Montana. But he spent many of his formative years in southeast Michigan, living with his half-sister and other family members in Monroe, and several buildings remain as historic reminders of his presence. Most notably, a larger-than-life statue on Elm and Monroe streets portrays the cavalryman at his Gettysburg victory with the Michigan Brigade. Custer sits mounted upon a magnificent bronze stallion…a bit too magnificent, perhaps. The highly regarded artist, Edward Potter, was careful to sculpt the horse with great anatomical correctness, a fact that has fascinated the town's youth since the statue's unveiling in 1910.

It has become a tradition in the town, *Strange Michigan* was told, for teenagers to paint the horse's underside parts a bright orange. Our informant confessed that she had at one time herself engaged in the time-honored vandalism. Since we are never in favor of defacement of public monuments, *Strange Michigan* hopes visitors to the statue will spare the horse further humiliation and focus on other aspects of the great work. After all, Custer's last stand was embarrassing enough for one general's lifetime.

Incidentally, despite the occasional prank, this bronze horse might be thought luckier than most of Custer's live mounts, since no fewer than 11 steeds were shot out from under him during his years of military service.

The ABC Ghost Towns

Shards of pottery, brown glass apothecary bottles, crumbled brick…the remains of discarded civilizations lie under Michigan woods and fields as stubborn reminders that people like us once farmed, ate, shopped, bore children, and worshipped on these desolate sites. We call the places "ghost towns," after the only beings who still may live there.

In the mid-1950s, three forgotten ghost towns came to light in the county of Monroe. All 100 years old or more, their names were Athlone, Briar Hill, and Clark City. A, B, C. And they may have remained buried and unremembered if a Harvard professor named Reginald Isaacs hadn't chanced to get his hair cut in the village of Carleton while on a quest to discover the whereabouts of Clark City. The barber asked Isaacs if he had been to a cemetery on a nearby farmer's property which contained graves of Civil War soldiers.

Isaacs headed for the Kamin farm about three miles north of Carleton, just south of the Wayne-Monroe County line, and discovered headstones with many of the names of people he already knew lived in Clark City. The farm fields were full of old bricks and other debris…this was the site of the former community of 2,300 inhabitants! The town's upwards of 700 houses, Isaacs learned from old-timers, had been physically removed in winter in the late 1880s, dragged over ice slicks by teams of oxen to a better locale. Even the schoolhouse was ferried across the frozen tundra to Waltz.

As he poked about in the open field, it must have been hard for Isaacs to visualize that in the early 1800s, the spot on which he stood boasted a bustling Main Street with stores, a hotel, a dentist, a gunsmith, and other buildings, and was described as an "up and coming

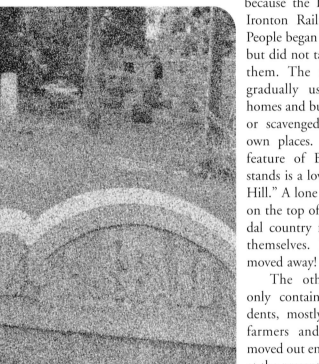

village" in county historical records. All it up and became, finally, was a cow pasture.

Several weeks later, inspired by the discovery, other local historians got busy and dug up two more buried ghost towns within four miles of Clark City.

One, Briar Hill, population 300, was founded by a charcoal factory magnate in 1800 and lasted until the factories closed down. It sprang up on Briar Road, about three miles south of Flat Rock, because the Detroit, Toledo, and Ironton Railroads crossed there. People began leaving around 1890 but did not take their houses with them. The few who remained gradually used the abandoned homes and buildings for firewood, or scavenged materials for their own places. The one remaining feature of Briar Hill that still stands is a low rise called "Suicide Hill." A lone apple tree once grew on the top of the knoll, and suicidal country folk used it to hang themselves. No wonder people moved away!

The other town, Athlone, only contained about 100 residents, mostly German and Irish farmers and lumberjacks, who moved out en masse in 1890. It sat at the present intersection of Lobo and Exeter Roads. Its Catholic church still exists at the site. One descendent of the settlers told a *Detroit News* reporter that Athlone seemed doomed after the post office closed in 1895.

It almost seems fitting that the only visible reminders of the ABC towns should be a handful of rounded old headstones and a hill known for suicides. Just like the people who once inhabited them, these villages died in their own ways. *Strange Michigan* hopes the villages and villagers all now rest in peace.

Local Catholic authorities, acknowledging the settlers' hardships, specifically allowed the "rats" to be eaten for Lent since they swam like fish. The practice later received church approval as a time-honored custom. That is the legend, at least.

Monroe gradually became famous for its muskrat cuisine; an 1891 newspaper article noted an enterprising townsman was selling muskrats, or "marsh beef," from a wheelbarrow he dragged around town. Annual muskrat dinner fests are still held to this day. One of the most popular recipes is the muskrat cigarette—the flesh of Francoise's brethren rolled up into a thin tortillalike crust.

Marsh Beef in a Sportcoat

Visitors to the Dorsch Memorial Library in Monroe must make their way past an oversized, gentlemanly looking muskrat statue dressed in a motley patchwork jacket and visored hat, placed in a spot of honor in the lobby. Similar statues guard the Holiday Inn Express Hotel and Suites on Dixie Parkway and the *Monroe Evening News* at 20 W. First Street. The expression on the statues, all from a model originally named "Francoise," is strangely content considering what the artworks actually memorialize is a long-standing fondness for roast muskrat in Monroe.

Ghost of the Irish Gothic

The Boyd House, the only standing example of Irish Gothic architecture in North America according to a Monroe brochure on historic buildings, looks eerie enough with its tall, pointed arch windows. But clinching its aura of mystery are whispers that the 1848 building is haunted. The spirit is said to be that of a three-year-old girl, a daughter of William Boyd whose brother founded Boyd School for Girls in Monroe. The little girl died of scarlet fever in 1860. In addition, the house was reputed to be a stop on the Underground Railway for slaves on their way to freedom in the North.

Mr. Elastic

During our formative years, we each struggle to become individuals and find our own unique place in the world. Some discover athletic talent, others musical gifts. In 1975, 14-year-old Moses "Moe" Lanham discovered he had a truly unique talent—he could twist his feet around backwards and walk that way. He may be the only person to walk backwards into the history books!

One day in 1975, Moe took a tumble in gym class, accidentally twisting one foot around backwards. The seeming injury caused Moe no pain and he later experimented with his newfound gift, learning he could turn both feet around and walk in that alignment. Medical tests proved Moe had no deformity or injury, but that extra ligaments and cartilage in his ankles, knees, and hips gave him the ability to swivel his joints.

After a few appearances on TV shows, in 1975, Moe gave up the spotlight at his father's behest to concentrate on school. In college he used his unusual ability to surprise classmates by occasionally donning a suit backwards, flipping his feet around, and strolling the campus.

Through the years Moe used his gift to wow friends and family, but gave little thought to pursuing fame. Then, in 1995, Moe and his wife, Felicia, visited a *Ripley's Believe It or Not!* Museum at Niagara Falls, Canada. Inspired, Felicia encouraged Moe to submit photos to *Ripley's*, and to send videos of himself to the TV programs *America's Funniest Home Videos* and *The World's Funniest*. The following spring, both programs aired Moe's videos. *Ripley's* featured Moe in their internationally syndicated comic strip. Moe found himself in the spotlight once again, thanks to the strange gift nature had bestowed on him. As international offers for media appearances poured in, Moe took full advantage of his celebrity this time around and accepted every offer he received.

The story doesn't end there, however. Moe's son Trey has inherited his father's gift, giving Moe the chance to teach his son the art of walking backwards. We hope Mr. Elastic, as his business card names him, continues stretching his horizons!

"Moe" Lanham; inset: "Moe" and his son Trey

Norway
Dickinson County
The Hairy Hitchhiker

Alone in his car, in a parking lot off US Highway 41 near the Michigan-Wisconsin border, Kevin sat thinking. As weariness descended over him, he decided to take a nap. The time was 2:15 a.m. The date was August 25, 2006.

Before dozing off, however, Kevin set the alarm on his cell phone to wake himself half an hour later. When the alarm roused him, for a reason he can't explain Kevin glanced in the rearview mirror of his car in time to see a large creature mosey past his car. Although Kevin could make out no more than a silhouette, he noted that the figure walked upright on two legs, stood perhaps seven feet tall, and looked apelike in some respects. The figure walked with its palms down, moving in "awkward strides."

Kevin compares this movement with the motion of the creature in the famous 1967 Patterson-Gimlin film. The creature behind Kevin's car resembled a muscular, bipedal gorilla. Kevin's sighting lasted between five and ten seconds, at which point he skedaddled—or, as he put it, "I freaked out." The sighting occurred not far from where several witnesses heard a strange scream in December 2006.

Miner's Castle, Pictured Rocks National Lakeshore

Munising
Alger County
Snake in the Lake

Pictured Rocks National Lakeshore, on the banks of Lake Superior, attracts scores of tourists each year. The tourists come to see the fantastic, colorful shapes into which nature has carved the 200-foot rocky cliffs, outcrops with names like Miner's Castle and Chapel Rock. Yet if you visit the lakeshore, you might also spy something stranger just offshore.

In the 1930s, two fisherman caught more than a few fish—they also caught a glimpse of a serpentine creature swimming in the waters off Pictured Rocks. The beast resembled a snake and traveled an estimated nine miles an hour, leaving behind a powerful wake. The men didn't venture closer for a better view of the creature, and who can blame them?

Why would a giant serpent haunt Lake Superior? For the view, naturally! Pictured Rocks boasts some of the most spectacular vistas in the state, rock formations so stunning even a relative of Nessie can't resist pulling over for a look.

Valhalla in Michigan

The names of some towns tell you all about their heritage. Norway, situated on the Michigan-Wisconsin border in the UP, bears a name that calls to mind the Scandinavian settlers who came to toil in the area's iron mines. Everywhere in Norway are reminders of the Viking past. Yet perhaps the town has invoked the Viking spirit a little too much, becoming a nomad itself like the Norse warriors of old. Norway, you see, has moved twice!

Visitors approaching the town on US 2, from either side of Norway, first notice the massive Viking ships. The ship on the eastern approach sails in the highway's median, while the western ship seems to have grounded on a hillside. The town sports numerous Viking references, from the Viking Motel to the odd little theater on a side street—a band shell decorated with a mural depicting the Norse warrior's heaven known as Valhalla.

The town's secret, however, proves less visible. Norway's mining operations forced the town to relocate twice by the year 1900 due to cave-ins. The old Aragon Mine caved in first, and now spends its afterlife as Strawberry Lake, a recreational park. The old downtown, abandoned after the cave-in, has reverted to fields. In 1900, the town moved for the second time, though in this incarnation the town's leaders saw fit to plan ahead, rebuilding important structures and including all the creature comforts a small town deserved. In 1903, an exploratory shaft drilled by a mining company produced Norway's most widely known resource—Norway Spring, an artesian well from which Norway Spring bottled water originates.

Norway's existence reminds us of the resourcefulness and resilience of Michigan folk. Rather than forfeit their town to a literal underworld, the Michigan Norwegians have successfully kept their town alive and kicking.

A Scream in the Night

Have you ever heard a strange sound in the darkness, one you couldn't identify? Most of us would say yes, at some point we've experienced that moment when an unknown sound vibrates our eardrums and seizes our hearts. Yet most of us find a mundane explanation lies behind the sound. A wolf howled. A cat screeched. A hunter fired his rifle. Once in awhile, though, a sound defies explanation.

On December 19, 2006, one young man and his friends encountered such a sound.

Night falls early in the UP in December. By 6:30 p.m., darkness had enveloped the woods near Norway in the southwestern UP, just over the Michigan-Wisconsin border. Dan and his friends were at Dan's family home when they heard a strange cry outside. The cry started out resembling a dog's bark, then segued into a high-pitched scream. The young men rushed outside so they could hear the sound better. Just then they heard something scramble up the steep hillside, faster than a person could have scaled the slope.

Dan's description of the scream sounds reminiscent of recordings purported to capture the screams of Bigfoot. When Dan called Backyard Phenomena Investigations, just a few minutes after the incident, his first words were "What does Bigfoot sound like?"

The truth is...no one really knows.

Novi
Oakland County
The Haunted Tunnels of Northville Asylum

It was a gargantuan monster of an institution. With a hivelike complex of sturdy, pleasant buildings and a 22-mile maze of steam tunnels sprawled over 1,040 acres, the Wayne County Training Center suffered a schizoid name split for most of its life. Situated almost on the township line, people called it either the Novi Asylum or the Northville Asylum but it didn't really matter. Everyone knew the place. "People always said they could hear ghosts there," a woman at the local library told *Strange Michigan*. "There used to be a cemetery, and you could hear crying babies in it. A former resident wrote in a book that there was abuse of children."

The legends make it sound like a place where few people would wish to grow up. But hundreds of children did spend their tender years on the labyrinthine property between Five Mile and Six Mile roads. Originally named "The Wayne County Training School for

Feebleminded Children," it opened in 1926 with the admirable intention of providing vocational training to the developmentally disabled. The place had taken three years to build with only hand tools and horse carts, but it was almost a complete village. The 400 students lived in "family" cottages, enjoyed their own theater, a black-and-white tiled swimming pool, and even a bowling alley. The complex drew power from its own plant and employed its own fire department. It even had a hospital, dentist's office, and dairy cows for fresh milk.

The children's cottages were decorated with fleur-de-lis insets, and the administration buildings had brick and masonry walls and marble thresholds. The grounds were a marvel of landscaping, designed to make students feel they were living in a flower-filled park. The children, aged six to 18, were trained as cooks, laundresses, or semi-skilled industrial laborers.

The school soon began to veer from its original purpose, however. In the 1930s, nationwide economic hardship increased both the number of orphans and abandoned children. Around Detroit, these young unfortunates were funneled into the Training School so that they could learn a trade. The school operated for nearly fifty years, the population climbing as high as 1,000. But by the 1950s, the disabled were moved to other institutions or into group homes, and there were fewer orphans and street children to house. As the inhabitants dwindled, the Training School ground to a slow halt, finally disgorging its remaining residents and turning belly up in 1974. One day, everyone simply left without even boarding the windows.

Northville Police Lieutenant John Sherman later told a local reporter, "It was a classic *Twilight Zone* scene. Like everyone was beamed out." Dental tools and Novocaine were left lying on a tray in the school dentist's office, school supplies lay dropped on teachers' desks, even a cup still half-filled with coffee was noted by someone who walked the grounds soon after its desertion. Furtive looters spirited away any valuable artifacts, from books to architectural remnants.

Entropy and decay set in as vandals and nature worked hand in hand to erode the formerly bustling grounds. By 1992, a *Detroit Free Press* article reported "all 36 of the school's buildings (there were at one time as many as 60 structures) have been smashed, burned, defaced, and strewn with rubble. Some have been burned to the ground….Big holes have been smashed in the walls of the theater." Local teens called the place "the Northville Tunnels" (translate as "party place"), and neighbors began deriding the ruined city as a nuisance and hazard. The chief of police even admitted in the newspaper that they had found "animal remains they believe were used in Satanic rituals."

In 1997, a reporter for *The Community Crier* dared to explore the overgrown paths and multi-story brick shells of the buildings still standing. Bryon Martin recorded the detritus left to rot: rusting desk frames, discarded shoes, ubiquitous broken bottles. Martin seemed unnerved by the experience. "And although the place is totally abandoned," he wrote, "there is a presence inhabited and startled, as if someone was here just moments before the tour arrived. Creepy."

He and his companions also noticed that even though there were abundant trees joined by almost impenetrable thickets, no birds sang in the old compound. At its inception, the school's planners had seen to it that at least one of every tree native to Michigan was planted here, including one dropped into the ground at the center's opening by silent screen star Lillian Gish. Now the arbor served as a rustling green shroud, tangling its branches to conceal the institutional skeleton.

Today, there is nothing left to see at the site of the old Northville/Novi Asylum, as people still call it. That's what *Strange Michigan* was told by the Northville Historical Society, which takes a keen interest in the lore that has grown up around the memories of the place. The tunnels have been filled in or sealed, and the rubbish finally carted away. A few people, like the librarian we met, still talk of hearing the voices of all those disabled and abandoned youth who lived there over the years…whispering, crying, even laughing. Maybe that's why the birds don't sing in those woods; the spirits of the long-gone children make all the music the land can bear.

Northville Asylum's Satanic Teen Murders and the Moaning Nude Woman

The Novi Asylum was something; lots of heavy metal graffiti, some bats, and a really scary red room that no one would go into. The most overheated rumor about the Novi Asylum pertained to underground tunnels, which definitely existed (as I once had displeasure of touring them) but which may or may not have led to some kind of chamber, where hooded Satanists were supposed to have held—like, I don't know...whatever hooded Satanists hold—down in hidden chambers.

If I'm not mistaken, though, Northville/Novi may have been host to some Satanic teen murders during the '80s, the kind that were usually blamed on Ozzy Osbourne. I seem to remember this being talked about on the news, and it was part of the lore that these murders took place at the Novi Asylum or the abandoned butcher house nearby.

One other tidbit; an art student I knew back in the early '90s had a picture on her fridge of a nude girl lying on the floor of the Novi Asylum. The story behind the photo was pretty funny. Turns out an intrepid photo student and this equally intrepid model were at the asylum taking nude pictures when they heard the approach of some thrill-seeking high school students. Light bulbs went off over their heads.

The photographer quickly hid, and when the teens made it up to the room they found a thin, naked woman crawling towards them across the hardwood floor. She was moaning, "Help me, come closer, help me...."

The teenagers turned and ran screaming from the building. As you would, I guess. Or at any rate, as I would!

—(name withheld on request)

Exploring the Northville Tunnels

On the northwest corner of Five Mile and Sheldon roads there used to be a large complex of buildings that were once ran by the State of Michigan. I believe this complex had originally opened in the 1940s. Before it closed in the early 1970s it had been a mental health facility. The complex was huge, fenced, and spread out amongst several dozen acres. It had its own athletic/recreation fields that were on the west side of Sheldon. A tunnel underneath that road connected the two pieces of property.

One night, right before Halloween, a large group of us went exploring on the property after hearing about it from some other classmates who had been there the weekend before. It was like an abandoned city. It had been very self-sufficient, with its own medical clinic, dental clinic, bowling alley and underground swimming pool. Everything was just as it had

been when the facility was closed. It was like the state had just locked the doors and abandoned it. The health clinics were still stocked with supplies, the bowling alley still had balls and shoes on racks—very bizarre!

As we explored, we discovered that most of the buildings were connected via underground tunnels, no doubt as a shield against the brutal Michigan winters. The tunnels were accessed via the basements of each building. In one building, there was what appeared to be a crude, home-made altar of some sort. Symbols usually associated with Satanism had been spray painted on the walls. These were obviously recent, very recent, and so we decided to call it a night and leave.

The following Monday in school, a classmate whose uncle worked on maintenance with another state facility just down the road from the "tunnels" complex, told us that the state workers there had reported seeing people in black robes moving around the complex at night. Apparently, the Michigan State Police/Northville Township Police had tried several times to catch this group to no avail. We never went back after that, figuring people who were into that might be capable of anything. About ten years ago some developers bought that property from the state and demolished all of the buildings. Today, there are luxury homes on that site.

—J and S

Omer
Arenac County
Michigan's Smallest City

Some titles inspire debate. The right to call itself the birthplace of Paul Bunyan has led to many an argument between Michigan towns. But although not every town can claim the world's largest lumberjack as its hometown boy, there are other titles—such as smallest city in Michigan—to go for.

In the 1990 and 2000 censuses conducted by the U.S. Census Bureau, Lake Angelus won the smallest-city contest. The city, with 11 fewer residents than Arenac County's Omer, brought the title home to Oakland County. The story did not end there, however, because by January 2006 Omer had lost enough residents to edge out Lake Angelus, with 313 bodies compared to Lake Angelus's 314. Official census data shows a number of cities with even smaller populations, though, so Omer may have to duke it out with those mini-metropolises. In spite of the controversy, the city of Omer now calls itself the smallest city in Michigan, with a road sign to announce the accomplishment. While most cities want to gain residents, Omer proudly proclaims its losses.

The city of Omer—a nice place to visit, just don't move there. You wouldn't want to cause them to lose their title!

 ## The Water Bill That Started a Civil War

Some towns have a tradition of strangeness. Omer—self-proclaimed smallest city in Michigan and next-door neighbor to the Cussing Canoeist—could qualify as such a town. In 1897, a tornado plucked up a house from Omer and absconded with it. No one saw the house again. Then there's the annual sucker run, when fisherman converge on the Rifle River to camp out in hopes of catching the ugliest fish around. The town's very origins seem a bit offbeat. The first postmaster, George Carscallen, wanted to call the town Homer; alas, another town had beaten them to that name. The solution was to drop the "H" and call it Omer.

Then, in 2002, the strangeness reemerged. The Perry family had just built a house on the outskirts of town. Although the water lines didn't extend to the Perry property, the city told the family they could receive city water. After the Perrys built their house, the city reneged, saying the Perrys would have to pay to extend the water lines. The estimate for the project started at $1,000. Later, the estimate went up to $3,000. Meanwhile the Perrys continued to receive bills for water taxes, adding up to about $40 per year, perhaps for the water that fell from the clouds now and then. Angered by taxation without irrigation, the Perrys acquired the necessary signatures (four) to petition a special election.

They wanted to secede from Omer.

On December 17, 2002, both Omer and Arenac Township opened their polls from 7:00 a.m. to 8:00 p.m. for the election. Winning would change the Perrys' official address from Omer to Arenac Township, without physically moving an inch. The story drew national media attention, with ABC News, the *Detroit Free Press*, and the *Chicago Tribune* covering the special election.

The election drew 140 voters and, although the Perrys lost in Omer, they won enough votes in Arenac Township to win the battle. The civil war ended without a shot fired—except, perhaps, by the mystery man who shoots off his cannon during the sucker run.

Ontonagon

 Ontonagon County

Ontonagon's Haunted Poor Farm and the Vibrating Potter's Field

Michigan death notice, August 19, 1893: "Joseph B. Drake, an inmate of the Ontonagon county poor house, locked himself up in the poor farm barn and set fire to it for the purpose of destroying himself. This he did afectually (sic), as his charged remains were discovered after the fire."

Drake was evidently one of those unfortunate enough to have lost his property, health, and/or mind, and in those times, that often meant consignment to the local "poor house" or "poor farm." Ontonagon's was a lovely brick building just a few miles out of town on what is now M-38, and it still stands today, although empty and a shelter only to homeless mice and other small wildlife. Just down the road lies its "potter's field," a weedy cemetery of mostly unmarked graves where Drake's "charged remains" were likely interred after the disaster.

Poorhouses or poor farms were a sad but necessary fact of life in those days. A nationally known, maudlin but very popular 1870s poem by Michigan native Will Carleton titled, "Over the Hill to the Poor House" described the agony of an elderly woman wending her way to the county home to live out the rest of her days.

O'er the hill to the poor-house - I can't quite make it clear!
Over the hill to the poor-house - it seems so horrid queer!
Many a step I've taken a-toilin' to and fro,
But this is a sort of journey I never thought to go.

The poem was actually written about a southeastern Michigan poor house, a cobblestone building still just outside Hillsdale where Carleton went to college. Carleton's verse was published in *Harper's Weekly* and a silent movie was made based upon it. Some have even claimed that it helped goad the nation into providing the Social Security program we have today.

But the poet's poor old lady might not have felt so distressed if she had found herself in Ontonagon's spacious institution. With its slate roof and top-grade Georgia pine interior, it was designed for beauty as well as for practicality, with separate sides for women and men. The high-ceilinged interior had 19 rooms plus attic and basement, and featured two beautifully crafted wooden staircases. The place is remembered by area neighbors as well-tended. Conditions were probably as good as things got at a county "home" in those days. Nonetheless, as everywhere, Ontonagans would make their children behave by threatening to send them to the poor farm, and hard-working citizens did their best to avoid ending up there.

The cornerstone of the brick building reveals that it was built in 1900 (Joseph Drake evidently lived in an earlier structure), and it operated into the 30s. In 1940 Sylvia and Sulo Laitala purchased the farm and continued the dairy operation. The couple lived in the grand building with their six daughters, and after the dairy closed out in the late 1960s, Sylvia opened Syl's Café in Ontonagon. Syl's flourishes to this day and is run by Sylvia's granddaughter, Kathy Wardynski, who also now owns the Poor House.

Wardynski took a few moments out of a busy café morning to talk to *Strange Michigan*. Unfortunately, she said, the Poor House is just a shadow of its former dignified self. The windows have been broken by vandals, some of its doors were given to the Ontonagon Historical Society to use in its lighthouse museum and the staircases

were taken to be used in a new home built by family members. "Unless I win the lottery, nothing in the way of restoration will be able to happen," said Wardynski.

A tuberculosis sanitorium also once stood on the grounds, she said, and she remembers playing around its old foundation as a child. She and her husband use the Poor House building mostly as storage for straw bales, although some decorative elements like the two-toned stenciling remain. "There was one room that was kind of spooky; they always said that was the 'dead room,'" Wardynski told us. "It was where the patients would go to die, like a hospice."

The poor farm is rumored to be haunted by the spirits of the desolate souls like Joseph Drake who lived and died there. Although Wardynski said her family never experienced anything ghostly, a local historian took *Strange Michigan* to the site and told us that because of the Upper Peninsula's frigid winters, the undertaker could only come out once a week to pick up bodies. Anyone who died in between "pickup days," then, was stacked in the "cold hall" to lie blue and frozen. It must have been a grisly site for the other residents.

"You see blue lights in the windows at night," he told us. "There was a room upstairs in the vaulted attic where moaning patients were put so others couldn't hear them. People who worked there at night would hear strange sounds and voices coming out of the walls."

He also took us to the burial plots adjacent to Evergreen Cemetery on M-38 southeast of Ontonagon, and pointed out some of the unmarked graves, identifiable by the shallow, rectangular depressions they made in the soil. "You can almost feel the stirring of lost souls," he said, and lay facedown on one of the graves. We did likewise, and must say we felt a strange vibration to the earth.

"It's just a force you feel emanating from the ground here," he told us. He estimated the "potter's field" is eternal home to about thirty bodies.

No one knows how many spirits still live in the red brick Poor House. Although the property owners bar trespassers, Wardynski sometimes gives tours either through the Ontonagon Historical Society or Syl's Café at 713 River Street.

 The Ontonagon Boulder; Copper Nugget "Ore" Manitou?

The Native Americans of northern Michigan, long before white traders and settlers came, believed a massive boulder that had lain in the west branch of the Ontonagon River since the last glacier possessed miraculous and magical powers of healing. They revered the stone and claimed that it had its own spirit.

Prehistoric Michigan was chock-full of large, glacially deposited chunks of copper, all of which were considered sacred by the indigenous people. A copper boulder entrenched in a river, which the indigenous people often believed was a doorway to the spirit world, would have been doubly honored. Even small pieces of copper were thought to carry spiritual power. The Ojibwe often kept copper "pebbles" in their medicine bags and handed them down as family heirlooms.

The big stone's resting place in what is now Lake Victoria, near the Lake Victoria dam, served as a Native American shrine and place of worship. In fact, according to Ontonagon historian Bruce Johanson, one Jesuit missionary wrote that the rock was used as a surface for human sacrifice and that it "was to the Ojibwe a *Manitou*, a go-between to the Great Spirit." But the white prospectors who eventually moved into the area did not entertain the same notions.

The hunk of nearly pure copper was estimated to weigh a whopping five tons by English trader Alexander Henry in 1760. The stone was also documented by Henry Schoolcraft in 1819 during an expedition led by Governor Lewis Cass. The group was taken to the boulder by an Ojibwe named *Wabishkipenace*, or "White Bird," who ran into big trouble with his tribesmen for taking the whites to visit their sacred rock. Schoolcraft wrote that seven years after the incident, when he again ran into *Wabishkipenace* at Sault Ste. Marie, the man was still suffering greatly from feelings of guilt and from tribal disap-

proval of his actions.

White Bird wasn't the only one to pay a penalty for revealing sacred copper to the white invaders. In *Kitchigami, Life Among the Lake Superior Ojibwe* by Johann Georg Kohl, the story is told of another man, *Keatanang*, who showed a fur-trader the site of a 50-pound chunk of copper that lay buried in the forest near what is now the city of Ontonagon. Secretly, by cover of night and for the trade of some cloth, ribbons, jewelry, blankets, and tobacco, *Keatanang* allowed the trader to remove his revered rock. Kohl wrote that the trader said, "Old *Keatanang* bitterly repented afterwards the deal he had with me, and ascribed many pieces of misfortune that fell on him to it." And that was a minor piece of copper, compared to the Ontonagon boulder.

Between the expeditions of Henry and Schoolcraft, enough visitors came and took samples to reduce the boulder to about one and a half tons. But Detroit businessman Julius Eldred saw money-making potential in the boulder as a natural wonder. He was said to have paid a local chief $150 for it, although it is hard to imagine why the chief would have sold the sacred boulder. Perhaps he rationalized that the white men were going to take it anyway. Or he may have figured that anyone who violated such a sacred object would receive divine retribution beyond the punishment a mere human could inflict.

But before Eldred managed to get the copper chunk back to Detroit, a Wisconsin lead miner named James Paull staked a claim on it and Eldred had to pay $1,800, according to *Prehistoric Mining in the Lake Superior Region*, to reclaim it himself. Local legend has it that Eldred finally moved the boulder to Lake Superior by the backbreaking, painstaking process of shoving it onto a small railroad car and then laying tracks in front of the car, pushing the car to the end of the tracks, then picking up the tracks and laying them down again. But *Prehistoric Mining* reveals that it was actually Paull who moved the boulder out of the Ontonagon River. Paull used a cart and windlass to drag it below the rapids, and then he was able to load it onto a flatboat. Once in Ontonagon it was weighed in at 3,708 pounds, with hundreds of chisel marks testifying as to how much had been chipped away from it over the years.

At this point, history gets a little fuzzy. *Prehistoric Mining* says that Eldred arrived in Ontonagon with a federal official, Major Cunningham, to seize the boulder from Paull. Other versions say that Eldred had it moved to Detroit and the government in turn seized it from him. At any rate, from Ontonagon it was loaded onto a schooner and after a succession of boat transfers, finally arrived in Detroit in the fall of 1843. Detroit held a parade!

The boulder was loaded onto a brightly festooned wagon and dragged up and down Main Street behind a decorated team of horses. The excited people of Detroit all crowded in with chisels and hammers trying to cut their own souvenirs from the boulder, and had to be held back along the entire parade route. The boulder's celebrity status helped assure Eldred's main claim to fame; his tombstone in Detroit's Elmwood Cemetery reads, "owner of richest copper mines in Upper Peninsula 1841."

The giant spirit stone was just beginning its journey, however. The boulder was shipped to Washington, where it lay ignominiously in a War Department yard until 1855. Then someone from the U.S. patent office took a shine to it and displayed the mammoth chunk for decades until yet another bureaucrat relegated it to a dusty basement. The Smithsonian Institute finally rescued the boulder and made it a permanent exhibit.

But Ontonagon wanted it back. State Representative Dominic Jacobetti waged a futile, one-man fight for years to have the boulder returned to its native soil.

The Smithsonian wasn't interested in returning the copper treasure, however. They did allow it to be exhibited once more in Michigan, but the massive stone has stayed in Washington, D.C., since then. Not to be thwarted, the state had a replica made which is now on display in the Ontonagon Historical Museum. And it remains to be seen whether the Smithsonian will endure any cosmic punishment from the curse of *Wabishkipenace* for taking the sacred Ontonagon *Manitou* boulder so far from its riverbed home.

Oscoda
Iosco County
The Old Woman House of Oscoda

I was born in Tawas City and lived in Oscoda until my family moved from there in 1989. The house we lived in was built in 1848. Our house was one of the only buildings to survive the 1911 fire that destroyed the town. I lived there with my parents and older brother and had many strange things happen.

My mother had someone push her while she was coming down the stairs, and was once awakened in the night by a little girl. She told me the little girl touched her with an ice-cold hand, then disappeared. She got out of bed thinking it had been me, and when she checked on me I was sound asleep.

Both my mother and dad told about seeing an old woman at the foot of their bed at night. On one occasion my dad felt our cat jump up onto the bed and lie down. He could feel the cat purring next to him, but when he went to pet it nothing was there.

My brother used to talk about some things he had seen but now won't discuss it. I vaguely remember an old woman in my room, too. My parents sold the house to a man who worked on the air force base there, but the base closed in 1993 and the house has sat empty and boarded up since then.

—Julie Allen

Mystery bacteria chomps toxic waste

Discover Magazine calls them "bizarre creatures from the deep," naming them #28 in their list of the top 100 scientific discoveries of 2003. The people of Oscoda call them tiny heroes. But the person who found the miniscule critters, environmental engineer Frank Löffler, named them BAV1. That's the scientific term, at least, for this newly discovered species of bacteria that love to chomp vinyl chloride.

Oscoda first discovered its special status as a monster-bug breeder in 1996 after groundwater specialists found that pollution from an abandoned dry cleaner store on Bachman Road had crept into the local water table and subsequently made it into Lake Huron. Löffler found the bacteria lurking in a "toxic plume" twenty feet underground, said an article in the *Oscoda Press*. The plume, or underground water stream, was discovered running smack be-tween the Bavarian Bakery and the local bowling alley.

Löffler performed further experiments, dumping a load of hungry BAV1 into a test pit at the contamination's ground zero point. He reported that the voracious critters had devoured all the vinyl chloride, a carcinogen produced by old dry cleaning solvents, in just six weeks. Since vinyl chloride is one of the industrial world's most common pollutants, scientists have big hopes for the bacteria, which is a strain of *Dehalococcoides*. The microbe even looks weird, said Löffler in an online article for *Chemical and Engineering News.* Shaped like a Frisbee, the bug is rimmed with "peculiar filamentous appendages." Nobody knows what the filmy tentacles are for, but as long as the town's aquifers get decontaminated, no one in Oscoda cares.

Word isn't out yet whether the community plans to celebrate their newfound mascot with an annual festival called *Dehalococcoides* Days.

Ossineke
Alpena County
Monsieur Le Bunyan & the Cursed Gun

On the corner of US Highway 23 and Nicholson Hill Road in Ossineke stands a unique statue of Paul Bunyan, the legendary lumberman so popular with roadside statuary artists. In this incarnation, Paul has become Monsieur Le Bunyan, the French-fried lumberjack. The gentleman dons a beret and keeps a neatly folded handkerchief in his back pocket, should he need to lay it down to help a lady cross a mud puddle. Yes, this Paul has the air of an aristocrat.

Then there's Babe. The poor old blue ox has lost his, er, manhood. The statues used to stand on Lookout Hill, across the street from a bar. Apparently, back in the 1950s a drunk who disliked the way Babe looked at him blasted Babe's private parts to smithereens with a gun. The same gun showed up a week later as the weapon in a murder. Whether the same drunk perpetrated both acts remains a mystery.

Though Babe appears fit, he has never fully recovered...certain parts of his anatomy remain absent. Now we know the real reason Babe is blue. *Mon Dieu!*

Owosso
Shiawassee County
Big Bear Statue

Perhaps counting on passersby to make a hairy connection between bearskin rugs and rooms swathed in plush carpeting, Owosso Carpet Center at 2090 West M-21 hails motorists with a giant statue of a dark brown bruin. The statue is never bear-naked, though. On the day *Strange Michigan* cruised by, he wore a black fireman's hat and yellow slicker with the letters OTFD. A photo on the store's Web site, www.owossocarpet.com, shows the bear roaring in a white toga. *Et tu, Bruinus?*

The store's owners, Diane and Jim Krajcovic, told *Strange Michigan* that the bear came with the store when they bought it, and has been there since at least 1984. He has a name, too: "Oliver," after an Owosso native, author and woodsman James Oliver Curwood who wrote the book (later made into a movie) *The Bear*. The name was chosen from many suggested in a town contest.

Oliver's wardrobe is extensive, said Diane. The one-bear fashion parade includes leprechaun, Santa, Easter Bunny, and pilgrim costumes. He even sports a tutu for the week of local dance festivities. And it turns out Oliver was wearing his fireman's outfit—the letters stand for Owosso Township Fire Department—the day we took his picture because Diane serves on the township board and thought it would be a fun way to honor the department's service.

There is one somewhat disconcerting twist in Oliver's history, however. Diane believes that Oliver once also had a cub. Since bear cubs stay with the mother, is it possible Oliver should really be named Olivia? Perhaps, allowed Diane, but she and Jim are sticking with Oliver. Either way, Owosso Carpet's mascot is probably Michigan's best-dressed local landmark.

Paris
Mecosta County
Ghost Lights

Paris has a longtime legend. Sometime in the 1800s, an old farmer's horses got out of the corral and took off down the road on a very dark night. The old farmer grabbed his lantern and went out to look for them, for he could not afford to lose them. The road the farm was on is very hilly, and when the farmer started up one of the hills, the horses came running toward him and trampled him to death.

The legend tells that if you go out to this remote part of Michigan on a very dark night, you will see the old farmer's lantern moving erratically, looking for the horses. My roommate and I are always up for an adventure, so we decided to check it out. I am VERY skeptical of the "supernatural" and can always come up with a rational scientific explanation for anything weird.

It was a pitch-black night and the harvest moon was huge. Coming from Big Rapids, you head north on State Street, also called Northland Drive. About five miles down, after going through the small village of Paris, you make a right turn on Meceola Road. You head down that road about a half of a mile, then make a left turn on 200th Avenue. It is a bumpy little unassuming dirt road. Be careful not to mistake the "Rails to Trails" snowmobile on your left for 200th Avenue. We mistakenly went down the trail one night, only to get stuck, and the plow trucks do not go down the trails. 200th Avenue is fairly well-marked with a white street sign.

After making the left turn, you proceed down the hilly road until you come to a stop sign. Turn completely around at the stop sign and head back down 200th Avenue. Disregard the first small rise in the road, but then count the larger hills, and come to a stop at the top of the third hill. When stopped, you should see another large hill in front of you. The road is not visible from here, nor are any houses. The only thing you may see is a tiny red tower light in the distance. When stopped at this spot, stop and shut your light, radio, and car off. Legend says that you must be very quiet.

There is no noted waiting time until the lantern light is supposed to appear. We had been sitting on the hill for about five minutes until I noticed a tiny green light floating somewhere near the middle of the hill in front of us. I was certain that it was just a reflection of the red tower light, but it was flashing very randomly. Moments after I saw that tiny light, a bright light flew across the road at the bottom of the hill in front of us. My roommate and I both saw it and were very startled. Our friend in the backseat did not see it.

We kept watching, and the tiny light reappeared, closer this time. I watched it carefully, and just as it flashed closer, the bright light flew back across the road from the direction it came from. This time our friend saw it too. We all screamed at the exact same second. We explored every possibility of what it could have been, and we determined that there is just no other explanation for it other than it was the old farmer's lantern. I have to say now that I am no longer a total unbeliever. . . .
—Name withheld

Paulding
Ontonagon County
Bigfoot Trio

For a bump-in-the-road town, Paulding seems to have more than its share of mysteries. The Paulding Light frequents an old logging road, making nightly appearances. On that same road on November 11, 1988, two brothers glimpsed another kind of mystery—the hairy kind.

The youngsters spotted three "brown, hairy figures" walking upright in the dense woods along the road. The lead creature stood about six feet tall, while the two smaller creatures behind the taller one measured perhaps four or five feet tall. The three creatures traipsed out of the woods and across the road in formation, the taller one leading the smaller two. One of the brothers, Aaron, thought the taller creature must be the parent of the smaller ones. All three creatures had long arms that swung like pendulums.

Aaron and his brother did not see the Paulding Light that night. But, one must wonder, could the Bigfoot have stepped out of the mysterious light that also haunts the old road?

Bunny Man of Choat Road Woods

Paulding, a tiny community on US Highway 45 in southern Ontonagon County, has already given its name to the mysterious lights that appear some miles south of it near Watersmeet. Now it appears the woods near Paulding hold yet another secret...a pure white, man-sized bunny rabbit! A believable, middle-aged woman named Lil told *Strange Michigan* that it was in 1958 when her mother had a forest encounter that she never forgot. "She used to work in the woods near Choat Road, between Paulding and Bruce Crossing," said Lil. "And she said she saw what looked like a white rabbit, only it was five feet tall. When it saw her, it ran away...on two legs. She said, 'Lil, I just couldn't believe it.' But Mom wasn't the type to make things up. If she said it, I believe it." Choat Road runs north and south about five miles west of Highway 45.

Pellston

Emmet County

The Pellston Mothman

Our true story began at around 10:00 p.m. The area is known as the Larks Lake haunts or other references are the Stutsmanville swamps. Larks Lake is heart shaped and spring fed and is part of the haunts and the swamps. A road tours around it. The Stutsmanville name comes from a road about five miles south of Larks Lake. Many who live in the area do not wish to travel the roads of the Larks Lake haunts because of some strange sightings. The locals are known to take alternative routes to avoid driving through. Sightings of Bigfoot, flying creatures (which I have personally seen many times), flying orbs, and wolf men have been noted.

The flying mud orbs that I have seen many, many times are like a round mud ball that wooshes by your car. The orbs are gray/brown in color and about a foot long.

To go back to our story, we were going north on Canby Road on the way home from a picnic. The date was Wednesday, July 25, 2007. Suddenly, a huge creature flew from above and hit our windshield. The height of this creature was around 9 to 10 feet tall and the wing span is hard to guess. This thing looked all white in the front with a black back. It had two back feet and what appeared to be two front feet—all white.

It was so big that it covered the width of the windshield. In an instant, it disappeared as fast as it came. No sounds were heard. Even when this thing hit the car there was no sound or bang or anything. We looked high and low to see where it went. Funny thing…we did not get out of the car. My friend turned the car around to drive the other way and nothing was to be found on the road or in the sky. The plausible explanation may have been that an eagle, turkey, or hawk flew into the car. Yet, I have never seen an eagle, turkey, or hawk that was totally white in the front of its body. When we got back, my friend took a flashlight to see what was on the car. From the bike rack, he picked off what appeared to be a feather of sorts. Many have said that our sighting may have been of a Mothman.

—*Jennifer Cupples, contributor*

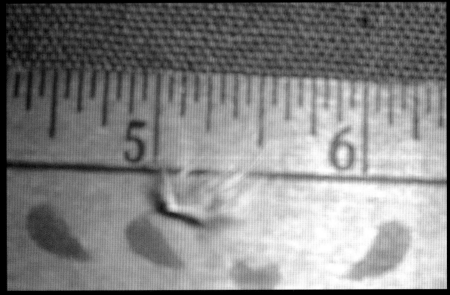

Pellston Mothman feather

Pequaming
Baraga County
The Haunted Bungalow

When Henry Ford abandoned his sawmill on the Abbaye Peninsula, did he leave behind more than an empty bungalow? Guests who have stayed at the Henry Ford Bungalow in recent years say something otherworldly inhabits the building. The uninvited guest just might be Ford himself.

Pequaming, a resort town northeast of L'Anse, came into being in 1878 when Charles Hebard and his business partners founded a sawmill at the location. The town's architecture reflected Hebard's English heritage. In 1914 Hebard's son, Daniel, built the bungalow and, in 1923, Henry Ford purchased both the mill and the bungalow. Ford needed wood for his cars, and a bungalow presumably to sleep in whilst tending to his business in the UP.

The bungalow saw many notables, including Thomas Edison and Harvey Firestone, during its heyday as Ford's summer retreat. In the '40s, however, Ford shut down the mill and Pequaming became a ghost town—literally. Today the bungalow lives on as a venue for weddings and reunions, providing overnight accommodation to as many as 20 guests, though the site remains closed to the public.

Guests who have slept in the bungalow have reported many strange occurrences. Footsteps clap on the stairs in the dead of night. Doors slam for no reason. Lights switch on and off as if some invisible hand operates them. Pillow cases vanish. Guests have shared their tales in the bungalow's guest book, a trove of creepy chronicles such as the tale of the six-year-old who felt "skin" snuggling up to him in bed one night. If you stay in the bungalow, when you hear footsteps on the stairs best not call for your mummy. You might find your call answered by another kind of "mummy" altogether!

Other guests report feeling uneasy in the bungalow. One person told of sneaking a Ouija board into a wedding at the bungalow, in order to hide in the bathroom while attempting to channel Thomas Edison and Henry Ford. Unfortunately, the bride kept banging on the door, interrupting the séance. If you want to hold your own illicit séance in the bathroom, make sure you put a "Do not disturb" sign on the door! The identity of the ghost (or ghosts) at the Henry Ford Bungalow eludes us still. But it's fun to imagine old Henry himself haunting the halls, unwilling to relinquish his former retreat.

Petoskey
Emmet County
The Petoskey Sea Panther

Native American elders are notoriously closemouthed about revealing sacred tribal legends to outsiders. But in 1981, the *Petoskey News Review* published an interview with Petoskey resident Simon Otto, who claimed he had just such a conversation regarding something local elders observed in Lake Michigan off the Petoskey shore around 1900.

They reported seeing the mythic "underwater sea panther," or *Mishipichoux* (spellings vary), from a variety of points that also included Cross Village, Harbor Springs, Northport, and Torch Lake. Although the creature's body was lizardlike and spiked, its head resembled that of a big cat. It was usually depicted with a long tail.

Otto added that his grandfather had seen it too while working in the woods near Manistee. The lumberman's term was "big snake that lived in the woods."

Pierson

Monroe County

The Pierson Beavers: the Only Animals Ever Threatened with Fines by the State of Michigan

Humans generally think they have it all over the rest of the animal kingdom, but creatures not classified as *Homo sapiens* sometimes do get a break: Animals don't have to pay taxes or follow governmental building regulations.

Some beavers in the Pierson area found themselves the exceptions to those rules when area resident Ryan DeVries received a letter from the State of Michigan in December 1997. The *Detroit News* and *Wall Street Journal* both reported that Michigan's Department of Environmental Quality sent DeVries a notice that the "contractor who did the unauthorized activity" of constructing "two wood debris dams on the outlet stream of Spring Pond" faced charges of $10,000 a day if said unauthorized activities weren't stopped.

DeVries passed the letter on to his landlord, Stephen Tvedten, who fired back a letter still on file with Montcalm County. It stated a couple of beavers were the contractors engaged in the unauthorized activity, and that Tvedten did not authorize or pay for the illegal dams. Tvedten further suggested that all beavers in Michigan should be required to fill out permits to build dams if the Spring Pond beavers were so required, and suggested the wardens instead go after some bears in the habit of despoiling the adjacent woods with defecation.

Eventually, the department figured out the whole episode was triggered by a neighbor who complained fearing flooding on his property. The responding agent simply wrote the cease-and-desist letter to the "dam builders" without inspecting the property. When Spring Pond was finally inspected by a DEQ employee, the agency dropped its investigation and the beavers were finally left to their own dam devices.

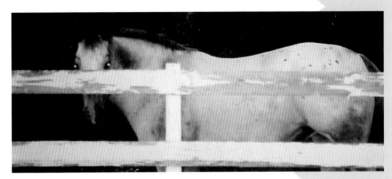

Pipestone

Berrien County

The Horse Mutilator

Horse tongue is generally not prized as a delicacy in the American kitchen. So when horses in Sodus and Pipestone townships started turning up with their tongues cut out in November of 1905, area residents were upset and mystified. Was the culprit someone with an unusual appetite, a malicious prankster with some unknown grudge, or the devil himself?

The first two horses to suffer tongue-ectomies belonged to farmer Bert Talbot. He complained to the county sheriff but the vandal had left no clues. And the mutilator did not strike again until the next November, in 1906. He took three bloody prizes away with him this time. Two mutilations followed in May 1907, in Pipestone.

The baffling case finally broke the following September when farmer Dennis Murphy's champion stallion was attacked. Various elements of the crime had started to add up for the sheriff, who began to suspect a farm worker named Max Minney. Minney fled when approached for questioning but later surrendered and was charged with multiple horse mutilations. Weirdly, the lawyer who represented him was named "Gore."

Minney was convicted partly on the testimony of a witness who claimed Minney had suggested they cut the tongue from someone's horse to enact revenge for a third party. But Minney's conviction was later overturned by the state's supreme court. While it was never proved conclusively that Minney was the mutilator, it's true that after his arrest the horses of Berrien County had no problem holding their tongues.

Plymouth
Wayne County
The Theme Park of Graveyards; United Memorial Gardens

If it's true that we are judged by the company we keep, even in the afterlife, perhaps United Memorial Gardens Cemetery is onto something. At 4800 Curtis Road outside of Plymouth, lies a vast acreage of cemetery space divided into separately themed "garden" or burial areas so that its occupants can be buried near others with the same sphere of interests. Like chat rooms of the dead.

There is a tombstone tour of Michigan section, for instance, so people can choose what they like best about their state, and then be planted next to a pillar engraved with an illustration of their favorite Michigan factoid. The altar-shaped pillars are arranged in a loop so that visitors can walk the long circle and make their abeyances to the eternal goodness of the Wolverine State. It's a very long, shadeless jaunt on a hot summer day, *Strange Michigan* found out, but worth the effort. It seems the list of Michigan greatness really is endless. And just in case anyone misses the point, it's called the "Garden of Praise." Only Michi-philes allowed.

The messages are pithy rather than poetic. Double entendres are fair game. The area designated for worn out duffers declares, for instance, "There are more golf courses in Michigan than any other state. This proves that Michiganders are swingers." For those with a fatal case

BIRDHOUSE MAUSOLEUM

of "shopaholism", a pillar engraved with a big empty shopping bag and a stack of greenbacks is dedicated to "Michigan's Great Malls." And those who can't bear the thought of heaven without Rice Krispies can snap up a plot next to the pillar adorned with three graduated sizes of cereal boxes and the epitaph "Mmm Good." (Except it's oddly spelled "MUM Good." And isn't that the jingle for Campbell's soups?) There are additional pillars for everyone from the sportsman (promising a deer for every hunter) to those who wish to be forever associated with the salt mines that lie deep beneath Detroit…diagram provided for the geographically ignorant.

The Garden of Praise is only one of the cemetery's many distinctive groupings, however. Another titled "Facts of Life" is already filled with headstones, but they are for people who never actually lived. Still, those who like moralistic humor couched in rhythmless verse might want to be stuck somewhere in their vicinity. A small grove of trees shelters a grid of flat stones with names such as "Flip Chip," whose faux epitaph reads, "I had a chip upon my shoulder I didn't plan to have a boulder." Or "Tricky Dick, watchin' and stealin' to get ahead, now I'm dead." Our favorite was the ominous, "If you think the 'o' cults are wild, you are thinking as a child. Satan has a long-term plan, intent on capturing girl and man."

More obtuse is the gravestone of "Katie Did," which reads, "I was used and abused, now I'm resting, my bod's in sod." Our award for the most tasteless goes to "Bubbles, Heavy sex can cause you trouble, could make you look just like a bubble." The section, also known as "Humor in Stone," is attributed to Ed Wensley.

Evidently seeking universal appeal, the cemetery also caters to every religion. There's an Islamic Garden with a giant Koran, a Jewish Garden with a replica of the Old Testament Tabernacle, a Masonic Garden, a Turkish Garden and more.

Corpses of other species will probably want to be placed near the Animal Gateway to Heaven. The pet area is complete with a lofty "Birdhouse Mausoleum" and statues of various canine breeds near the granite doghouses. A memorial fire hydrant adds realism to the pup scene. Cats, of course, have their own area where ghostly little claws may scratch.

And in the "things you never really wanted to know but now you do" category, perhaps the smallest and most unusual area of the cemetery is the "University of Michigan Cremation Garden." This special corner is distinguished by a huge metal placard bearing the names of all those who donated their bodies to the university's science department, and whose remains were subsequently reduced to ashes and interred here.

The beauty of the place is that just in case the designers did accidentally leave some small facet of Michigan life unrepresented, there is still plenty of room to add whatever additional garden may come to mind. (We'd suggest the Garden of Strangeness, of course, but that may be redundant.)

Potterville

Eaton County

Gizzard City: A Chicken Gizzard in Every Pot

Chicken gizzards, like rutabaga and haggis, are an acquired taste. Gizzards, for those not up on their bird anatomy, are muscular food-grinding organs found in the chicken's digestive tract. Not exactly the other white meat. But one Michigan town has turned the tough little morsels into their claim to fame. Potterville, just southwest of Lansing in, appropriately, Eaton County, claims to be the chicken gizzard capital of the world: Gizzard City. Every year in June around 15,000 visitors throng to Joe's Potterville Inn, which holds a contest to see who can eat two pounds of deep-fried gizzards the fastest. At the 2004 fest, over 1,400 pounds of gizzards were gobbled by hungry attendees.

The festival is presided over by a giant chicken brought into town just for the event. One year its head was stolen but festival sponsors saw to it that their mascot was recapitated in time for the

next gizzard-off. Diners hungry for bird stomach parts can order gizzards from Joe's any time of the year, however. The gizzards are served with cocktail sauce and fries.

Ramsay
Mailbox Mania

Winters are long in the UP. What else is there to do but construct elaborate, miniature, total replicas of your entire house and farm and then mount them as mailboxes? And who other than big-hearted Yoopers would spend so much time and energy just to bring some daily joy to the heart of their rural mail carrier? *Strange Michigan* spotted this beauty of a mailbox assemblage in Ramsay, off US Highway 2 between Wakefield and Bessemer on Sanders Road. Another yard a few houses down sports a colossal barber pole in the backyard, so perhaps the urge to be original is contagious. And we can only hope that perhaps next the unknown artist will create a scale model of downtown Bessemer.

Rapid River
Delta County
Taking the Crap Out of Scrap

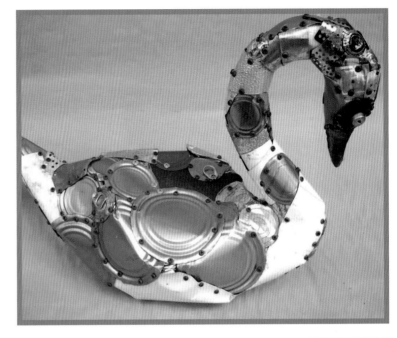

Beer and fish—the two seem made for each other. After all, many fishermen like to drink beer while they await the big one. But Ritch Branstrom prefers to avoid the waiting. He simply makes his fish out of the beer cans.

In his Ad Hoc Workshop, Ritch crafts some of the most inventive artwork you'll ever see from found objects, scrap metal, and anything else the average person might toss in the trash. Ritch gathers scraps from the beach, roadsides, and from friends and fans who drop off unwanted odds and ends at his workshop in Rapid River. The workshop has also become an unofficial community center where Ritch and friends gather to create art, eat good food, and chat about world events.

Strange Michigan met Ritch at the Poor Artists' Sale in Calumet where people flocked to his booth, entranced by the strange metallic creatures like his beer can fish. Ritch's other works include humanoids with lopsided grins, gargantuan insects, birds as tall as semi trailers, scrap metal rock bands, and a swan pieced together from can lids. The menagerie at the *Star Wars* movie's bar couldn't begin to compete with Ritch's backyard!

One sculpture depicting ZZ Top sprang to life from a wooden thermometer that survived a house fire. The wooden phoenix rose from the ashes to become the beer can of ZZ Top's twin guitars. Another musical sculpture features a rock band whose saxophone evolved from an exhaust pipe and muffler, while the lead singer got her shapely figure from a chrome truck bumper, chimney flue, snowblower chute, and leftovers from previous sculptures. The sax player himself can trace his roots as far back as World War II— a chunk from the tip of a drop tank from a World War II aircraft helps form his legs, along with bits of a Corvette bumper.

Ritch has found a unique way to clean up the environment while doing what he truly loves. How many of us can say that? Rather than turning cans in for cash, he turns them into art. So to Ritch we say...cheers!

Ritch Branstrom

Reed City
Osceola County
Double Dogman Dare You!

Sighting June 7, 2006. Interview June 8, 2006, by phone with *Strange Michigan*. Location: near Reed City, Michigan, on an isolated gravel road near a small, old building.

I'm a college kid and I live in Big Rapids, and I heard people saying there is this (building) around Reed City where this 'thing' hangs out.

We (myself and two friends) arrived there at 2:30 in the morning and there we sat. After about half an hour something caught our eye. About 50 yards to the right of us we saw something moving. We didn't think anything of it until we heard big twigs start to snap. I got out my Maglight and shined in the area...I saw something that was not human.

There were crickets all around and all of a sudden they all stopped. I kept on seeing something move over in the woods, kind of a silhouette. I thought it was a deer until we shined the light on it. Must have been 6' 9"; It was huge...tall! It was a humanoid; I could see below the midsection, could see thighs but not feet. I'm believing it's bipedal. The hair was either dark brown or black, probably dark brown...must have covered most of the body, maybe an inch long.

It was behind a tree, in a little wooded area, and it stood half behind the tree and half exposed; didn't move at all when we had the light on it. His arm was longer than a human's. When we saw it in the light when it was standing still, it looked a little hunched.

I only got a small view of its face. I could tell that it was very hairy but the way the eyes set made me think of a human face. I could not see the ears; I remember the mouth to be narrow but I don't recall seeing a nose on the end of the "snout." All I could really tell about the eye color was yellow, and the eyes were a little slanted. It has a very big forehead.

All of a sudden my friend spotted something behind us. I pushed my clutch in and slowly rolled back to get a closer view. My friend shined the light on him and two yellow eyes stared at us. I thought it was a regular road reflector until I saw it blink. Then a feeling came over me; I felt that this thing wanted to harm us. I could tell that this thing was on two legs at the time we saw the eyes. I fired up the car and floored it; we must have of been going 40 MPH and I could see in my brake lights that something was chasing us on four legs. I don't know if this is a dogman or not but this thing is NOT human, is NOT natural, and is NOT friendly. I don't think this was paranormal; it was biological. Not ghostly. I was not aware that other things like this were going on at the time I saw this thing. The only reason I refer it to a dogman is the fact that I have heard through local legend that it was a dogman. So, I really had no idea that there were other sightings of dogmen or the body style it had.

—John

This would not be John's last encounter with the upright canine-like creature. He returned with a male friend and a female friend some weeks later, and saw a similar creature that appeared to be a different individual—it was gray and slightly larger—coming at the back of their car. Again, John floored it and quickly left the area. *Strange Michigan* conducted an onsite interview and investigation and spent a spooky night out on that road with some kind of animal that shook its coat like a canine, had yellow eyes, and stood tall enough to block out a reflective, six-foot-high road sign just outside the reach of our spotlight.

His sighting was reenacted on the History Channel show *Monsterquest*, on the episode titled "American Werewolf," after Linda Godfrey's book *Hunting the American Werewolf.* John has returned a number of times, and although he has not seen the creature again, he feels it is still lurking somewhere in the wild underbrush of rural Reed City.

Richland
Kalamazoo County
Rockin' at the Blackhawk

The Blackhawk Grill in Richland can serve you more than good food. They might also give you a glimpse into the afterlife. You just might spot a ghostly woman in the rocking chair by the fireplace, said to be her favorite spot before she passed over to the other side. Now, they say, she refuses to give up her spot by the fire. A ghost also reportedly haunts the basement. A little food, a nice fire...and some not-of-this-world conversation.

A Corny Tribute

Grand Rapids has the Gerald Ford Presidential Museum, a strange place indeed, with its fake ATM and disco dolls. But when a farmer wishes to pay homage to the late president, what can he do?

He can have Ford's likeness hacked out of his cornfield.

While corn mazes have become popular around the country, few depict presidents with the eerie accuracy of the Richland maze. Gull Meadow Farms hired the Maize, a company that constructed nearly 200 mazes around the world in 2007.

The Ford maze will probably be gone with the cornflakes by the time you read this. So take a moment to ponder the picture, and marvel at the weird ways the people of Michigan find to honor their heroes.

Rochester
Oakland County
Curse of the Bear Walk

The repatriation of Native American skeletal remains from museums and unearthed burial grounds has been ongoing for decades. In most cases, tribes have only had to make the request and authorities have complied. But in the fall of 1977, a Detroit leader of Native American Strategic Services threatened Oakland University with an ancient curse called the "bear walk" if the institution did not hand over 20 skeletons university anthropologists had removed from an ancient site in Oakland Township.

The bones were discovered in October by children playing at a building site. The property's owner called in university anthropologists, who estimated the bones' age at between 700 and 1,000 years, vastly predating European settlement. The anthropologists had promised to turn them over to the state's Indian Affairs Commission within a few weeks, but missed their deadline and asked for more time to study the remains.

According to a United Press International story November 23, 1977, Frederick Boyd of the Detroit organization advised the university that if the skeletons were not returned, the school would be put under a curse. The story quoted Boyd as saying, "I am in touch with one of three people in the state who can do the bear walk…No one will know if the secret spell is cast…until people get very sick or start dying. I'm not superstitious, but I know the bear walk power works. Some might call it voodoo."

The bear walk, a tradition of many Algonquin-speaking tribes, is said to involve a priest or shaman taking on the form of a bear to visit intended enemies and induce sickness or death. As far as *Strange Michigan* could determine, the 20 skeletons were duly returned and no out-of-place bears were ever observed on the Oakland University campus.

Rockford
Dinerland; Eat and Time Travel at the Same Time

A visit to this little string of three vintage diners on 14 Mile Road outside of Rockford feels like a trip to the set of the TV show *Happy Days*. The artist who originally assembled the refurbished eateries had only intended to open one diner, formerly Uncle Bob's in Flint, as an art gallery for himself and his wife. But people, governed by the needs of their stomachs as people usually are, kept missing the point of the gallery and asking where the food was. So artist Jerry Berta, along with his artist wife, Madalyn Kaczmarczyk, finally gave in and bought another vintage diner from Little Ferry, New Jersey. This became Rosie's Diner, the main restaurant of the three. The third antique diner, hauled to Rockford from Fulton, New York, serves as a bar and club car.

Rosie's was once used as a location for a commercial for Bounty paper towels. The diner's TV waitress, played by Nancy Walker in those commercials, was named Rosie, so Berta decided to name the diner after her.

Strange Michigan marveled at the décor built into this deluxe model manufactured by the Paramount Dining Car Company in 1946. A blue and gray retro color scheme coupled with the stainless steel ceiling, ancient linoleum flooring, and a glass block entryway all complement the curved, red Naugahyde booths for the most authentic diner experience possible. To complete the look, waitresses wore long pink scarves and ponytails.

The diners have changed ownership a few times, but have never changed their mid-20th century looks. Last time we checked, Berta and Kaczmarczyk were still selling their clay pieces onsite. And the artwork Jerry Berta creates? Miniature diners, of course, made from clay and little neon signs.

Rogers City
Presque Isle County
Earthbound Moonscape

Heading northwest on US 23 into Rogers City, on the shores of Lake Huron, a sign pronounces the town "The Limestone City." The reason may seem less than obvious, unless you take a detour onto a side road that peels off to the north. Easily missed, the road is just southeast of town. Down the side road you'll find a viewing area, little more than a gravel turnout bounded on its far side by a chain-link fence. Beyond the fence lies an astounding sight: An enormous hole that resembles the surface of the moon.

You won't find green cheese here, though, only rocks. The hole comprises a section of Michigan Limestone's Calcite Plant, the world's largest limestone quarry. It is served by the busiest cargo port in Lower Michigan, known as the Port of Calcite. The quarry stretches several miles to the east, all the way to Lake Huron, and several more miles to either side. What at first look like pencil marks crisscrossing the quarry, drawn by the hand of Atlas himself, are in fact roads traversed by large machinery. Far in the distance, huge equipment at the port appears as tiny as toys.

There is no Hard Rock Café here, but there's enough calcium carbonate (limestone) to start an antacid factory—or build your own pyramid. Rock on!

Roscommon
Roscommon County
The Witch of Pere Cheney Cemetery

I live in Roscommon, and there is a cemetery called Pere Cheney Cemetery that is well known around here for weird happenings. I went there to just check it out and as soon as you walk through the gate, the temperature seems to drop about ten or more degrees.

It's said there is an old witch that used to practice there. There are candles and mementos left at the graves. Every day they are removed and every night they are back. As I walked through the cemetery, I felt lots of spirits moving around and lots of sadness.

There are a lot of young children buried there, and it is said the witch watches over them so they don't leave the grounds. People go there to practice their religion and people also go there to party, hoping to see the witch. It's pretty well known in Michigan, and is one of the most scary places I've been. I do believe the ghosts abound there and get upset when people leave the cemetery a mess after their parties.

—Peg

Saginaw
Saginaw County
Gooey Brown Rain

A Richland Township man needed more than an umbrella when sticky brown stuff fell from the sky in late January 2006, and covered his truck and home with a nasty-looking mess. A *Saginaw News* article by LaNia Coleman documented the reaction of the homeowner, Timothy J. Rohn, who said the brown "rain" did not look like "friendly stuff."

Local police officer Gary Wade thought the material was some kind of sky-borne manure, but neither he nor Rohn could imagine a giant flock of birds all defecating at one time. And while it's true that Rohn's house lies on the flight path of a nearby airport, modern aircraft are constructed so that the waste hatch cannot be opened while in flight.

The worst part, said Rohn, was that this was the second time it had happened. And his greatest fear was that it would occur a third time while his family was outside.

Michigan seems prone to falls of brown substances. Paw Paw was covered with brown dust that looked like some kind of plant material on February 16, 1901, well before airline traffic lanes filled the sky. And there was not even enough wind on that day to run a windmill, said the *Monthly Weather Review* published that year.

Unidentified brown stuff also fell on the Detroit suburb of Westland in November 1998. And in April 1954, blue rain that stained clothing sprinkled Detroit.

St. Ignace
Mackinac County
Bounding Buck Statue

In case anyone has the slightest doubt about what may lie inside the Deer Ranch in St. Ignace, the big, bounding buck at its entrance cinches it; there are white-tailed deer of every size, age and gender here, including a rare white deer. Visitors may gawk and stroll the shady trails at their leisure.

The Patriotic Moose

On the south side of US Highway 2 in St. Ignace, near the Mackinac Bridge, sits a Quality Inn. But this incarnation of the motel chain offers something few of the other branches do—a moose painted in patriotic colors.

The husky moose stands in front of the Quality Inn sign, appearing content, perhaps because he has enjoyed a restful night at the motel. Then again, maybe his serenity stems from the Purple Monkey Ice Cream he scarfed down earlier. A purple monkey on a sign behind the moose advertises the ice cream, just in case the red, white, and blue moose fails to satisfy your thirst for brightly painted wildlife.

 **The Red Tongue of Castle Rock**

The dictionary defines a curio as something unusual or rare, a curiosity. Castle Rock Curios in St. Ignace lives up to that definition. Aside from the knickknacks for sale inside the store, visitors can discover two unusual and strangely connected attractions—Paul Bunyan and his blue ox, and Castle Rock itself. Just what connects a rock tower and an oversize lumberjack?

Oversize footprints, of course.

As you pull into the parking lot, you can spy Paul and Babe inside their small chain-link enclosure. A second fence along the edge of the parking lot bars entry to the area. Above Paul's head towers Castle Rock, a 200-foot natural pillar of stone topped by an unnatural metal viewing deck.

Ever wanted to walk in Paul Bunyan's footsteps? At Castle Rock Curios you can—literally. Inside the store, footprints painted on the floor lead out a doorway to the Bunyan area and up a long set of steps to the top of Castle Rock. Once outside, you can approach within mere feet of Paul and Babe. Unlike most Bunyan statues, this one sits wide-eyed on a white box, as if stunned by the cars zooming by on the road in front of him. Although he may appear dazed, Paul still carries a big ax (in his right hand). Beside him, Babe the blue ox mocks the traffic by sticking out his red tongue.

 **Mystery Spot**

Is it a place that actually traps gravity and magnetic forces to create its own topsy-turvy world, or are tourists the only things really trapped in St. Ignace's Mystery Spot? Similar attractions dot the U.S. with names like The Vortex in Gold Hill, Oregon, or Wisconsin Dells' (now closed) Wonder Spot. Michigan's Mystery Spot is typical…a slant-walled cabin set into an inclined natural area, where balls seem to roll uphill and furniture can never quite align with the walls. *Strange Michigan* joined a tour and watched a procession of brave people try to stand upright on a table that appeared to be horizontal, but wasn't, quite. They were able to balance on a chair tilted backward, and perform various other feats of gravity-bending amazement that would never be possible in more ordinary environments.

Some mystery sites, like Oregon's Vortex, come with legends. There, it is said, the local Native Americans had long noted that birds refused to nest on the oddly tilted spot, and horses would whinny and shy away. The tribes pronounced the ground "forbidden" and refused to go there.

As for the Mystery Spot, three surveyors allegedly discovered the anomaly in 1953 when their magnets and equipment wouldn't work and they felt "light-headed" within a certain 300-square foot area. The attraction's brochure claims that even blind persons are affected by the physical sensations.

Some speculate that the ground underneath must contain some sort of rock strata with electromagnetic properties, others wonder if it is a window into another dimension. Part of the show is admittedly illusion, with the "cabin" walls built at wacky angles to enhance the experience. Still, the crowd seemed to find it entertaining the day we visited, and more than one person became disoriented and dizzy, whether from odd architecture or mysterious earth forces. The Mystery Spot can be found just west of St. Ignace on US Highway 2.

 **The Saint Ignace Curio Fair**

Most tourists who visit the Upper Peninsula want to see a laundry list of expected sights; lighthouses, Native American artifacts, and the vintage Victorian architecture of many old UP towns. But thanks to one man's genius, time-conscious motorists can hit all three goals in one fell swoop just outside St. Ignace on US 2. There they will find Curio Fair, a giant lighthouse, Victorian railway station, and Native American teepee all rolled into one amazing package. As if that weren't enough, Curio Fair also has a crackly Florida shell coating on the outside and a creamy souvenir filling inside.

The curious blend originated in the enterprising visions of St. Ignace native Clarence Eby. Sparked by a desire to provide UP tourists with an unobstructed view of the Mackinac Bridge after it was constructed in 1956, Eby took hammer in hand and began to build the conglomeration. It soon became the dominant landmark around St.Ignace. Eby's grandson, Chuck Tamlyn, now owns Curio Fair and is proud to talk about his grandpap's exploits.

Eby had been a longtime promoter of tourism for the St. Ignace region, and already owned a couple of other attractions, a big natural stone formation called Castle Rock, and the Indian Village handicraft store. But when the new bridge went up over the Mackinac Straits, Eby realized the area lacked one great place from which to view the scenery. Figuring if he built it, tourists would come, he constructed an eight-story faux lighthouse that looked over not just the Straits but the nearby Hiawatha Forest, as well. Eby charged ten cents a person to climb the tower and have a look at the spectacle. It's still only fifty cents today.

About that same time, the old Victorian railroad depot in downtown St. Ignace came up for sale. Not one to miss an opportunity, Eby shelled out a whole dollar for it and had it moved to the lighthouse location where the two buildings were joined. To this day, old coal dust drifts out of the cracks in the depot section when the wind blows off the lake. But Eby wasn't done. To balance the depot, he built a giant teepee of wood on the other side of the lighthouse.

The store entrance didn't seem fancy enough to Eby, however, so he hauled truckloads of conch, starfish, and abalone shells from Florida and encrusted them in stucco on the base of the lighthouse section. "To do that would be pretty expensive nowadays," said Tamlyn. "Those big shells can cost $20 apiece."

But probably the most unique feature of the whole place is the birch bark that lines walls and ceilings, harvested and attached by Native American workmen.

"Clarence was part Chippewa," Tamlyn explained. "The whole place was built by Chippewa Indians. He hired Indians to work for him 'til the day he died. The Indians knew how to take bark off trees without killing the tree. They would go out and peel bark until they had as much as they could put up in a few days, plus the green willow sticks for the edges." The result is a woodsy patchwork that makes the interior of the Curio Fair feel more like the inside of a rustic wigwam than a souvenir shop, despite the rows of snow globes and ceramic figurines for sale.

Curio Fair is weird in another, less obvious way, too. In this age of mega-stores of every kind, it's one of the few old-style souvenir stands left. "These are the last of the mom-and-pops," Tamlyn told *Strange Michigan.* "They either get handed down or torn down."

Weird Michigan Wax Museum

While you need not travel far in Michigan to find strangeness, sometimes the strangeness screams out at you from the roadside. Take, for instance, one of the state's newest strange attractions, the Weird Michigan Wax Museum.

If the name sounds familiar, then you've probably read the book from which the museum's founders took their inspiration and their name, *Weird Michigan* (authored by Linda Godfrey, co-author of this book). A few miles west of St. Ignace, overlooking US Highway 2, lurks a red metal building that seems normal enough from the outside. *Strange Michigan* pulled into the ample parking lot at 10:00 a.m. on an August morning, unsure what to expect.

White block lettering on the building informed us we had arrived at the Weird Michigan Wax Museum. A smaller sign in one of two windows announced the place's name in creepier yellow lettering, while a modest "open" sign glowed in the other window. Behind us, traffic whizzed past on the highway.

The museum lies a glowing orb's throw from the Mystery Spot, the most famous attraction in St. Ignace. With this fact in mind, we crossed the threshold into the realm of the uncanny. Immediately inside the doors we found a gift shop brimming with Weird Michigan merchandise, and a reception desk where a lone attendant sold us our tickets.

Fiends and freaks conjured from the pages of *Weird Michigan* came alive before our eyes as we tiptoed down a hall of dioramas bathed in eerie light. The Dogman peeked out at us from behind a tree, stalking a group of young men gathered around a campfire who remain unaware of the dog-faced thing wearing a plaid shirt. In another scene, a Melonhead terrifies his victims. The Calumet Theater ghost, the spooks of Soop Cemetery, and the slightly less frightening King of Beaver Island haunt the hallway as well. Plaques explain the scenes to the uninitiated.

When we got home after our visit to the museum, we discovered an eerie anomaly in our photo of the exhibit featuring the Grand Rapids Wooden Leg Murderer. Behind the killer and his victim, between them and a bed, hovers a translucent purple mist. No glass or anything else that could cause reflections separated the camera from the display. Could the brand-new museum have attracted a ghost? If anyplace would draw wayward spirits, the Weird Michigan Wax Museum seems the perfect candidate.

On your next trip through St. Ignace, watch for the plain red building that hides a plethora of mysteries within its walls. From mid May through late October you can experience the bizarre in person all-day long at the Weird Michigan Wax Museum. Perhaps by then they will have added a *Strange Michigan* wing.

The Grand Rapids Wooden Leg Murderer with a strange purple mist in the background

Saugatuck
Allegan County
Melonheads No More?

Every town has its urban legends. Saugatuck, south of Holland on Lake Michigan's eastern shore, has an unusual legend all its own—the Melonheads. These creepy beings with deformed, mangled heads supposedly originated at a mythical place called the Junction Insane Asylum, where as inmates they were tortured until their heads acquired their freaky form. But, according to one local resident, the legend has a far more mundane origin. Michael says the story sprang out of a Halloween prank perpetrated by him and his buddies.

Michael first remembers hearing about the Melonheads in the mid 1970s. From 1973 to 1977, Michael attended high school at St. Augustine Seminary, a boarding school nicknamed "St. A's." Since he and his buddies lived locally, they could leave the campus during off-school hours. Michael and his family lived about a mile from the school, and he would often hang around in the area between his home and the school.

On Halloween, probably 1974, Michael and his buddies got tired of harassment from the other local boys so they decided to go home. On the way, they ran across some pumpkins in a yard and decided to "borrow" the melons. The boys took the pumpkins back to St. A's, where they proceeded to hollow out the melons in order to put them on their heads.

Upon finishing their task, the boys took up positions alongside the road, where they donned their melon masks. When they moved their heads, the melons would jiggle. So when a car passed by them, they would yell "wobble-wobble-wobble" as they jiggled their pumpkin heads. Mysterious figures along the road, on Halloween night, shaking their melon heads at passersby...sounds like the perfect campfire story.

After the Halloween incident, Michael never gave the Melonheads a second thought—until October 2006, when an article appeared in the Holland newspaper about the Melonheads. Both he and his sister contacted the paper to report the possible origins of the legend, but they received no response.

Michael doesn't know for sure that he and his buddies started the legend. But he does wonder: Did a teenage prank give birth to an urban legend?

 ## Sault Ste. Marie
Chippewa County
Shiny-Topped UFO

On June 28, 2006, a citizen of Sault Ste. Marie looked out his window at 20 minutes to noon and saw a "metallic large object the size of a house, hovering 1,000 feet above his home." Soo Police Chief Lou Murray made that statement to *Strange Michigan* via phone call July 6. Chief Murray said the man, a local contractor, estimated the height of the object by comparing it to a TV antenna of known height. "He said the object was 'in sections,'" with a dark top that was similar in color to an astronaut's face shield, said Chief Murray. The object had a 200-foot antenna or 'tail' coming out the back.

The chief also said the man reported the craft was totally silent and stationary, only moving a few feet several times as if to reposition itself. From the time the man noticed it until it finally "went straight up and left," was close to an hour. "His mother-in-law and neighbor also saw it," said the chief. "In fact, his mother-in-law actually called us to report it after he had just called the dispatcher to ask a few questions."

The man, his mother-in-law, and neighbor are "regular, credible people," said the chief. "The investigating officer believed them."

The chief also said the man tried to shoot the UFO with his video camera but the battery was dead. The sheriff said he called the Green Bay FFA office, and they were not able to explain the sighting in terms of any known flights in the Soo area that day.

 ## Antlers Taxidermy Restaurant

Aficionados of the strange will love being met by a stuffed, two-headed calf rather than the standard one-headed hostess when they enter the Antlers Restaurant on Portage Avenue in Sault Ste. Marie. And although a live human will eventually greet and seat each diner, the restaurant's population of dead animals far outstrips the number of daily customers who come to sit among the mounted fish, fur, and feathers that fill the walls and ceilings of this popular eatery. Antlers from every hoofed ungulate that ever walked the planet, mountain lions, beaver, coyote, mink, and more complete the taxidermy zoo.

The place had a colorful start as the Bucket of Blood Saloon and Ice Cream Parlor, the ice cream part tacked on for legitimacy during Prohibition. Town legend has it that many of the animals in the Antlers were traded by hard-up trappers in exchange for booze. Tourist guides claim that a thirsty but cash-poor patron named Tiny traded the moose head, a Pontiac automobile, his gun, and even a relative to slake his thirst. A giant log was left outdoors in an unsuccessful liquor barter attempt made by another soused lumberjack. The place is so rustic that the old TV show *Gunsmoke* filmed three episodes within its colorful walls.

The restaurant is also known for boat whistles, horns, and hair-raising noises of all kinds that blare from the PA at regular intervals just in case anyone gets too complacent. Diners sensitive to unexpected screeching or those who get nervous eating with hundreds of beady little eyes trained upon them should be forewarned. Everyone else will have a blast, literally.

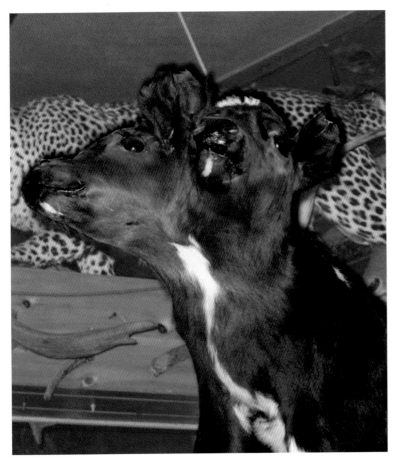

on the day of her departure. In spite of darkness and bad weather that set in that evening, those aboard a passenger ship called the *Huronic* said they spotted the *Bannockburn* on the evening of the 21st. The *Bannockburn* featured three distinctive masts, which folks on the *Huronic* recognized.

The *Bannockburn* never arrived at the Soo. While erroneous reports claimed the ship had grounded on Michipicoten Island or Caribou Island, another ship had run across wreckage near Stannard Rock. Bad weather kept the crew from searching the wreckage, and nothing turned up except a life jacket and an oar retrieved by a rescue crew on December 12.

Theories about the *Bannockburn's* fate abound, though little evidence supports any one theory. Not long after the ship's disappearance, at the end of the season, the Soo Locks were drained. A hull plate was found at the bottom of the locks. Whether it belonged to the *Bannockburn*, as many believed, remains a question without an answer.

Two-headed calf at the Antlers Restaurant

The Disappearance of the Bannockburn

Many ships have sunk in Lake Superior. Storms can turn its deep waters into a freshwater hell that tears ships asunder. Sometimes, though, the exact fate of a ship remains a mystery even after more than a century has passed. Such a ship is the *Bannockburn*.

The month of November has proved especially deadly for vessels traversing Lake Superior. The *Bannockburn* and her crew began their fateful voyage on November 21, 1902, setting out from Port Arthur in Ontario (now Thunder Bay) laden with wheat, headed for the Soo Locks. The gods seemed to frown on the ship from the start—she grounded a bit on the way out of Port Arthur, but sustained little or no damage. Once she reached open water, the Bannockburn would vanish.

Two crews on separate ships claimed to have seen the *Bannockburn* after her departure from Port Arthur. The crew of the *Algonquin* reported seeing her east of Isle Royale during the afternoon

The Kinross Incident: UFO over Superior

What happened over Lake Superior on November 23, 1953? The answer eludes investigators to this day. We know one thing for certain: The U.S. Air Force lost both an F-89C jet and its two-man crew on that evening more than 50 years ago. The circumstances surrounding the disappearance of the jet and her crew remain murky.

The events began at Kinross Air Force Base south of Sault Ste. Marie, in Michigan's UP. In October 1953, several F-89C jets from Kinross's 534th Air Defense Group had been sent to Arizona for training. To replace the absent jets, the air force temporarily reassigned to Kinross F-89s from the 433rd Fighter Interceptor Squadron based at Truax Air Force Base in Madison, Wisconsin. First Lieutenant Felix Moncla and 2nd Lieutenant Robert Wilson took their F-89 to Kinross as part of that detachment.

Born in Louisiana, Moncla had served in the army during World War II, in the Pacific Theater. After the war he attended college but, when the Korean War broke out in 1950, Moncla reenlisted—this time as a pilot in the recently formed U.S. Air Force. Moncla left behind a wife and two children, including a daughter born five months before his disappearance. He was 27 at the time of his death.

Oklahoma native Robert Wilson joined the air force less than 18 months prior to his death. His fellow pilots described him as soft-spoken and dedicated to his air force career. Wilson died at 22, unmarried. Wilson served as the radar operator in the F-89C Scorpion piloted by Moncla. On November 23, 1953, Moncla and

Wilson sat on five minute alert, meaning they must be ready to take off in five minutes or less.

Sault Ste. Marie boasts the busiest shipping locks in the world, the Soo Locks, built in 1855 as a way around rapids that made it difficult for ships to enter Lake Superior. The locks became a vital link for shipping. So at about 6 p.m. on November 23, 1953, when radar operators on the Keweenaw Peninsula spotted an unknown target heading off Lake Superior toward the locks, they realized no aircraft were supposed to be near that area. The military considered the Soo Locks a prime target for enemy attacks, as striking the locks would cripple shipping. No one could ignore the unidentified blip hurtling toward Sault Ste. Marie. At 6:17 p.m. Moncla and Wilson were scrambled to intercept the unknown. Within two minutes, the F-89 piloted by Moncla—designated Avenger Red—raced toward the unknown blip.

The F-89 had enough fuel for 1 hour and 45 minutes of flight. Almost as soon as Avenger Red took off, radio problems began. Kinross could barely hear them and, at 6:41 p.m., passed communications over to the Calumet radar station, but Calumet also could barely hear the transmissions from Avenger Red. Moncla reported he could hear Calumet fine. On the receiving end, though, problems persisted. A few minutes later, the Detroit radar station informed Moncla of possible icing dangers ahead, a message Moncla acknowledged.

Radar operators on the ground watched as Avenger Red approached the unknown target over Sault Ste. Marie. Suddenly the unknown altered course, heading back toward Lake Superior. The ground controller informed Moncla of the change in course. Avenger Red streaked after the blip at 500 miles per hour, past Whitefish Bay, northwest over the open waters of Lake Superior. Over the next nine minutes Avenger Red struggled to close the gap between the F-89 and the unknown.

Because Wilson had trouble tracking the target on the F-89's radar, the ground-based radar stations had to direct Avenger Red en route. At 6:51 p.m., radar operators told Avenger Red the unknown target now lay 10 miles away at their 11:00 position. Moncla acknowledged the report. The closer Avenger Red got to the unknown target, the worse the static in Moncla's transmissions became. The unknown moved from port to starboard, from Avenger Red's viewpoint, but transmissions informing Moncla of the change went unacknowledged. On the radar screens, the blips for Avenger Red and the unknown merged. At about the same time, Avenger Red's identifying signal, which marked them as a friendly aircraft, stopped transmitting.

Calumet attempted to contact Avenger Red, receiving no response. They assumed Moncla and Wilson were too busy navigat-ing around the target, flying above or below it, to respond. The two targets—Avenger Red and the unknown—stayed merged on the radar screens. Radar operators thought perhaps Moncla had decided to fly in formation with the object or, their worst fear, Avenger Red had collided with the object. Calumet tried repeatedly to contact Avenger Red, without success. Finally, Calumet asked Kinross to attempt contact. Kinross's attempts failed too.

The merged blip vanished from radar screens.

The Detroit radar station ordered Kinross to scramble two more F-89s to search for Avenger Red. When neither of the newly scrambled jets could establish radio contact with Moncla, Kinross called them back to base. In his deposition, recorded after the fact, the pilot of one of the F-89s stated that both he and his radar operator thought they heard Moncla's voice over the radio. The transmission lasted a few seconds.

On returning to base, one of the pilots reported some icing conditions. The minutes ticked closer and closer to the time limit on Avenger Red's fuel.

By 10:07 p.m., everyone knew Avenger Red would have depleted all its fuel. Capt. William Bridges, the Officer in Charge of the 433rd, informed the base's Commanding Officer that Avenger Red was overdue. Bridges also tried, unsuccessfully, to notify the 433rd commander at Truax of the situation. An hour and a half later, Bridges took off in his own jet in an attempt to find Avenger Red, but deteriorating weather conditions forced him to turn back. All night planes with flares searched the area, and the next day boats were dispatched to comb the lake for hundreds of miles around the presumed crash site. An intensive search and rescue mission found nothing.

Avenger Red had vanished 100 miles from Sault Ste. Marie, 70 miles off Keweenaw Point.

Eventually, the air force would deny Avenger Red had merged with anything on the radar screens, blaming radar operators for misreading their screens. The air force floated the story that the unknown blip had been a Canadian airliner. Two air force officers sent to inform Moncla's family of his death told Moncla's widow that he had crashed into the lake after flying too low while looking for the airliner. The Canadian government denied having any aircraft in the vicinity. Then a second air force duo showed at the Moncla household—this time claiming Moncla's jet exploded at high altitude.

A year later the air force gave up the airliner story, switching to a new explanation that still blamed our northern neighbors. The new story alleged that Avenger Red had crashed while intercepting a plane from the Royal Canadian Air Force. To this day no one knows the exact fate of Avenger Red, or the true identity of the

An F-89 similar to the one flown by Moncla

unknown blip.

In the summer of 2006, a company calling itself the Great Lakes Dive Company (GLDC) leaked a story in online discussion forums that they had located the wreckage of the F-89 as well as an unknown object. Both lay 200 feet apart at the bottom of Lake Superior. The GLDC website contained two small sonar images of twin objects—one of which resembled a virtually intact airplane, and the other which looked like a smooth, oblong craft. Experts disagreed on the validity of the sonar images, though most everyone agreed that in this age of digital imaging you can't trust a photo... or a sonar image.

The claim made waves, and GLDC's spokesman appeared on the national radio show Coast to Coast AM. UFO investigators failed to verify the claim, or the existence of GLDC as a legal company. By the end of the summer, GLDC yanked their website offline. Silence ensued. GLDC had claimed their employees had been harassed and threatened. Did the company vanish out of security concerns? Or did the hoax become so obvious that GLDC had to back out of the limelight? Whether or not GLDC and its claims resurface, the mystery of November 23, 1953, perseveres. What happened to Avenger Red?

The Cursed Mirror of Sault Ste. Marie

A dying patient in Sault Ste. Marie's old War Memorial Hospital uttered a curse, according to author Deidre A. Stevens, that baffled dozens of hospital employees and area residents. Stevens told the strange tale of Jeffrey Derosier's death in her book, *Thunderstruck*.

Derosier was on his deathbed when he asked a nurse to hand him a rimless piece of mirrored glass that lay on his nightstand. She complied, and after Derosier stared at his reflection for a few moments, the nurse heard him cry, "I'm dying!" He dropped the mirror back on the nightstand and the nurse heard him say in a serious monotone, "You won't be able to pick up that mirror." And then he did indeed die.

Later, one of the other patients in Derosier's ward tried to pick up the mirror but found to his surprise that he could not lift it from the table. Neither could the nurse, a doctor who was called in, nor any number of other people who heard about the cursed piece of glass and tried to pry it away with various instruments. Finally, one nurse managed to loosen it with her fingernails. The mirror popped up and crashed to the floor, but did not break. Every attempt to make the mirror stick to the table again failed; even wetting the glass did not help. The "haunted" mirror was eventually broken and discarded. Whatever Jeffrey Derosier saw in it and what inspired him to pronounce the glass immovable will never be known.

Seney
Schoolcraft County

P.K. Small, "Jaws of Death" Ogre of Seney

Modern day rocker Ozzy Ozbourne may have figured he was pulling a daring new stunt when he bit the head off a live bat on stage. But Ozzy had nothing on P.K. Small, an itinerant logger who gagged the townfolk of the UP town of Seney back in the 1890s to early 1900s by chewing the noggins off any unfortunate creatures he could fit between his bone-crushing jaws. Once, he even snatched a child's pet crow, crunched its neck in his snaggled teeth and then gen-

erously offered the limp, decapitated body back to its horror-stricken young owner. Small then gulped down the head, beak and all, and probably belched in the boy's face.

Stunts like that earned him the nickname "Ogre of Seney." He was also known as "Snagjaw," and his looks justified either label. Brawny of frame and covered with a perpetual, malodorous layer of greasy sweat and dirt, Small scared people just by looking at them. His face was pocked with numerous scars from fights and lumber-camp accidents, and his nose, once bitten off by some enraged adversary, had been reattached by a frontier doctor who left a Frankensteinish, visible seam around it.

Granted, Seney was one of the wildest of the old lumber towns, with almost equal numbers of taverns and houses. Bloody brawls would often fill the streets from one end of town to the other. No-holds-barred mayhem was the norm. The local doctor was so overwhelmed with bleeding carcasses that on weekend nights he was forced to set up primitive triage centers at the fight scenes. Still, even in the midst of all this gore, P.K. Small managed to shock the most hardened of lumber thugs and earn his daily booze at the same time.

Small would ingest almost anything for a swaller o' whiskey. His recorded meals included horse manure (fresh or dried), live mice, live snakes, and the heads of innumerable frogs, toads, and barnyard fowl. The schoolchildren of Seney jumped rope to a sing-song verse that went, "P.K. Small eats them, feathers, guts and all," according to *Michigan Rogues, Desperados and Cut-Throats,* one of the best sources of information on Small. One of Small's most stomach-wrenching habits, though, was bobbing for the unidentifiable globules swimming in the potent mixture of saliva and tobacco juice that filled the brass spittoons found in every tavern.

Small was not above picking fights in order to pick the pockets of whomever was unlucky enough to end up in his smelly bear hug. And the results were usually not pretty. Gnawing off an opponent's ear or other body part was standard practice. Small eventually tried his hand at robbing a train but he and his inept companions were caught and sent to jail in Detroit. He leaves the historic record after that, but it's a safe bet Small kept making a living at what he did best, swallowing disgusting objects and helpless creatures to keep the refills coming.

Lumberjacks of the Seney area

Small was not the only person earning his keep this way around the early 1900s. In sideshow lingo, people who bit the heads off living things were called "gloaming geeks." According to author Robert Bogdan in his book, *Freak Show*, "Often this form of geek was a down-and-out alcoholic who performed in exchange for booze and a place to stay....Wild man and woman shows were the bottom rung of the freak show exhibits, and the geek show was the bottom of the bottom." Those who caught Small's performances would probably

agree with that assessment. But Small may have visited one of the hundreds of dime museums or circuses that featured weird human tricks and decided he could do that, too. At any rate, his cast iron stomach and pitiless "jaws of death" ensured that he would be remembered as the most vile of the nasty carousers on the streets of old Seney.

 ## A Whoop in the Night

In August 2003, Angela, her husband, and her daughter set out to explore the UP on their summer vacation. But while hunting for a good campground, they got a bit lost on the dirt roads inside the Seney National Wildlife Refuge. Finally, after dark, they found a decent spot to pitch their tents and settled in for the night.

Later Angela awoke, sensing something amiss. The silence, she realized, had awoken her. The insects and other night creatures had fallen dumb, leaving in their wake an absolute silence.

Ee-yoop.

The sound startled Angela. Her daughter, sleeping nearby, woke. She asked her mother what had made the eerie sound. Angela suggested a loon's call, but the explanation didn't satisfy her. She had heard loons before—the birds sounded nothing like the whooping cry. As Angela and her daughter huddled together, another whoop resounded through the forest, then faded away into the night. Angela and her daughter tried to get some rest.

The next morning Angela happened upon a mom-and-pop grocery store in Grand Marais. On the wall she noticed a plaster cast. When she asked the store owner about the cast, she was told it was of a Bigfoot track found in the area. The owner seemed uncomfortable discussing the issue, so Angela let it drop. But she has wondered ever since whether she might've heard a Bigfoot that night. Recordings of supposed Bigfoot screams sound similar to what Angela reported hearing.

Somerset Center
Hillsdale County
The Mexican Concrete Park

If it looks like wood and acts like wood, it's probably wood, to paraphrase an old saying. Unless, that is, the "wood" is in McCourtie Park in Somerset Center, in which case it is concrete! Trees, footbridges, twisty twigs, and logs…all may not be what they appear to be. Visitors need to look twice and give the bark a quick rap to decide whether landscape items are from Mother Nature or examples of the Mexican art of *el trabeio rustico*, fool-the-eye concrete.

So what is traditional Mexican folk sculpture doing in an early 20th Century-era Michigan Park? One-time Somerset resident, William H.L. McCourtie, earned a fortune in the oil and cement businesses and decided to use his favorite material to create an enduring—if slightly unnatural—park. He had seen examples of Mexican fool-the-eye concrete work, so in 1904, he hired several Mexican artisans to create a total of 17 faux-wood bridges and two trees (originally intended as chimneys for a berm structure) on his property. Once it was complete, he invited the whole community to come and enjoy the artwork at a big party once every year.

Eventually the township purchased the land and turned it into a public park, with a grand opening in 1987. The bridges had begun to deteriorate by then but the town began an immediate restoration project. Each bridge is different, but with their looping, intertwining branches they look as if they were woven by particularly clever elves. The trees stand as stark columns and the bane of local woodpeckers. The park is still open, off US Highway 12 near Jackson Road.

Bernardo Puzzuoli and Truus Jones

Standish

Arenac County

The Cussing Canoeist

Legislators love to pass new laws to make themselves feel useful. Sometimes these laws linger on the books for decades, forgotten like the bustle and the hitching post. For one Michigan man, however, an old law sprang up to bite him in the derriere.

In 1998, Timothy Boomer found himself convicted of cussing in front of children. Boomer had cussed out a rock that knocked him out of his canoe on the Rifle River. A nearby mother and her two small children heard Boomer's obscenities. But by an old state law, Michiganders cannot legally curse in front of women or children; however, in 2002, a Michigan appeals court overturned the conviction. With the ACLU's help, Boomer convinced the court that the First Amendment grants him the right to cuss out a rock no matter who else is present—even in Michigan.

Sterling Heights

Wayne County

Tiki Paradise

Bernardo Puzzuoli's "Polynesian" yard isn't quite as easy to spot from the street as it used to be. The city declared his place an "attractive nuisance" after a gawker slowing up to watch him move a giant sculpture caused a four-car pileup in front of the house at 3701 Metro Parkway. Puzzuoli responded by transferring his frontlawn decor to his amazingly designed backyard, a wondrous assortment of original and store-bought statues and fountains. The artworks are accented with plantings Puzzuoli trained to grow in arches and other designs by hand-bending pipes in the crotch of a tree and fastening them to the branches. It's a paradise any Surrealist would approve.

Tours of the private property now require permission, which in turn requires catching the ebullient Puzzuoli at home and in the right mood. *Strange Michigan* lucked out and managed to do both. Puzzuoli and his friend, Truus Jones, showed us around the place and then invited us to sit under one of the property's many fanciful trellises made up of grapevines, trumpet vines, and Virginia creeper. Sipping a cola at the shaded table and gazing at the wonders surrounding us, it was hard to remember we were just outside of urban Detroit.

The Polynesian Paradise takes its name from assorted tiki-like wood carvings enhancing Puzzuoli's sanctuary. One Tiki rests in a ceramic basin next to a statue of a man in a yellow sombrero riding a donkey. Puzzuoli has carved others to resemble fertility goddesses, inspired by a trip to Hawaii he made many years ago. The décor is nothing if not eclectic; bowling balls dangle from trees like a giant's wind chimes while a 3,000-pound concrete dolphin leaps nearby. A Puzzuoli sculpture dedicated to a disliked relative is dubbed, "Six-faced Tony."

Weeping fountains are also a favorite of Puzzuoli's. He created one called "the Crying Bear," and another features the wizened face of Steven Spielberg's *E.T.* crying like a baby.

But Puzzuoli, a former Arthur Murray dance instructor and cement contractor who emigrated from Italy in 1954, says the place is a mere shadow of its former self. "I used to have over 2,500 lawn ornaments. Some I gave away, some I buried," he told us. The highway in front of his house was widened twice, and each time his property shrank and he had to do away with a little more art. He had started the collection as a business when his late wife was diagnosed with cancer and he needed more money, he said. "But the neighbors didn't like the business."

And the neighbors may eventually win out entirely. He's planning to sell the property, and doesn't know whether a new owner will want to keep his homegrown paradise. The statues will be sold with the land, however. "They weigh too much to move," he said with an expressive flourish of his hands. He thinks the property will be put to commercial use, which would probably bring an unfortunate reality to the Joni Mitchell's "Big Yellow Taxi" lyric, "They paved Paradise, and put up a parking lot."

Tecumseh

Lenawee County

Henry Lee Lucas, the One-Eyed Terror of Tecumseh

Henry Lee Lucas used to brag that he'd killed 150 women. One news source said he claimed as many as 600. The exact number has never been determined, but it is known for sure that the killings started with his own mother, Viola, in the beautiful little southern Michigan town of Tecumseh in January 1960.

Mother and son were staying with Henry's sister at the time, and had begun an argument one evening at Bagshaw's Bar in downtown Tecumseh. They finally returned to the two-story house at 303 Pottawatamie Street, and Henry, 23, settled the argument in an upstairs bedroom by stabbing his mother in the main artery of her neck with a five-inch blade.

Henry had just been released from a prison term for burglary in Virginia, and he left town immediately after the murder. Authorities caught up with him outside Toledo, Ohio, and he was tried and convicted of second-degree murder. He was sentenced to 20 to 30 years, but only served 10. Soon after his 1970 release, Henry tried to drag a 16-year-old girl who was waiting for a bus in Palmyra, Michigan, into his car. She managed to wrestle away and report him, and he was given the maximum sentence of four years. This time he served them all, but evidently decided it was time to get out of the Wolverine State upon his next release in 1975.

That's when the multi-state bloodbath began. Henry meandered his way to Texas where he lived with a 15-year-old girl until he killed her. He also was blamed for killing two hitchhikers and an 80-year-old woman. His murders became progressively more gruesome; one of the hitchhikers died from having her head cut off while she was still alive. Texas lawmen finally caught up with him, and after confessing, Henry enjoyed a lengthy investigation period during which he was ferried around on private jets to every place he claimed to have dragged a body. He was given special food and even his own TV, probably the most positive attention he'd enjoyed in his entire life.

It was true his mother hadn't been exactly the nurturing type. Henry's father lost both legs in a railroad accident and was confined to bed. Enterprising Viola used the other half of the bed as a workplace for her prostitution business, and Henry claimed she forced him to watch her have relations with the johns while his father lay there, helpless.

His siblings weren't any comfort, either. One of Henry's brothers stabbed him in the eyeball, and Henry had to get a glass eye that always leaked so that he appeared to be perpetually weeping.

None of this made any difference to the Texas jury, which sentenced him to death. As it ended up, Henry became the only man to have his

death sentence reduced to life in prison by then-Texas governor George W. Bush, when doubts surfaced about his actual role in the murder of a hitchhiker known as "Orange Socks" because that's all she was wearing when found dead on the roadside. Of course, Henry still had to serve out six life sentences plus 210 years. He made it a few more years after his death reprieve, finally succumbing behind bars at the age of 64 in 2001. His mother, Viola Lucas, is buried in Tecumseh's Brookside Cemetery.

Legend of the Trails

Tecumseh is a small town in southeastern Michigan, and a large piece of the town is a park that used to be a sacred Indian burial ground. Now, there are walking trails through the area. No one in town will venture into the woods after dark because many people say that strange and vicious things happen there. A group of my friends went out there one night just goofing around and they heard low voices out in the woods. They made it as far as the bridge into the trails, when they saw an old man dressed like an early settler with a lantern, and he started to come after them. There are many, many stories involving those woods. One thing I do know; if the cops are too afraid to follow you in there in the dark, there has to be something sinister there.

—Peg

Junk Parts Dinosaur and Earth Caterpillar

When life hands you a big mound of dirt, make earth art. Such is the evident philosophy of the Tecumseh Trade Center, an indoor flea market that runs every first and third weekend on Clinton Highway in Tecumseh in southeastern Michigan. That's how a large earth berm ended up as a big earth worm. The company found itself with the dirt pile after digging a driveway. Then some mystery artist stuck a "face" on the berm for the fun of it, owner Raffaele Recchia told *Strange Michigan*, and people enjoyed it so much that the company decided to keep it. "We never did find out who put the face there," said Recchia. "We had planned to sell the topsoil but after it got the face we just never did." The dinosaur made from metal scrap standing just in front of the berm-worm is the artwork of sculptor Martin Kailimai of Belleville.

TRAVERSE COLANTHA WALKER
361604
BORN 4-29-1916
DIED 1-8-1932
WORLD'S CHAMPION COW
MILK 200,1149 LBS.
FAT 7,525.8 LBS.
NINE LACTATIONS
BRED, OWNED, DEVELOPED
BY TRAVERSE CITY HOSPITAL

Traverse City
Grand Traverse County

Queen of the Insane Asylum

It was an hour or so after dark on a moonless, starless night… probably the choicest of times to be fumbling around the old gravel roads of the former Northern Michigan Asylum in Traverse City. *Strange Michigan* was busily hunting, moreover, for a 73-year-old grave, having arrived in the city a bit longer past the witching hour than we'd planned. We admit that we were creeped out by the semi-abandoned grounds. We knew only that the grave was located near a barn, and that only a few barns were left on the massive acreage that once hosted orchards, gardens, and livestock all tended by asylum inmates as part of their "work therapy."

We looped again and again past crumbling buildings with darkened, boarded-over windows that looked custom-made for spirit observation posts. Stones crunched beneath our tires as we cruised Red Drive in search of the big grave marker. Beneath it, we knew, would lie the absolute queen of the asylum, the most popular of all the residents at the time of her death in January 1932. So beloved was she that a banquet was held in her honor when she died, and dignitaries came from all over to see her laid beneath the soil she had walked daily with her admirers.

The old roads, no more than overgrown paths now, were unlit, and we dangled a tiny flashlight out the car window to search the weeds for traces of old marble. Nothing appeared that resembled a gravestone, and we finally gave up. But as we headed for the main asylum grounds, something inspired us to drive one more round. Figuring we had nothing to lose, we scooped the loop from a different direction this time, and suddenly, there it was, lit up in the headlights like a granite banner…the grave of Traverse Colantha Walker, World Champion Cow. It was worth every minute of the search. We could almost hear her mooing in the fetid August air.

Calved in 1918 on the asylum grounds, Traverse Colantha was raised like all her kin as part of the farm program, but she soon proved herself a Holstein of Holsteins. Over the nine lactations of her life, she provided 200,114.9 pounds of milk and 7,525.8 pounds of fat, and became the spotted darling of all who knew her. She lived in an ornate, electric-fan-filled stall in a beautiful brick-floored barn, and her final headstone bested many markers of human graves in the cemeteries of Traverse City. Few funerals of the day could equal the feast held at her burial, either, although we are left to wonder whether the main entrée was pork chops from the farm's celebrated piggery or, disconcertingly, roast beef.

The asylum was closed in 1989 after having changed its name to Traverse City State Hospital, and now it is known as Grand Traverse Commons, a development in progress. A gourmet restaurant occupies the lower level of the architecturally wondrous Gothic main building, and other gentrification projects and condos are planned for various parts of the complex. Strangely, the turn to the old asylum's drive is still marked by an old stone pyramid on US Highway 31 and 11th Street.

Strange Michigan gave Traverse Colantha a mournful salute as we clicked our trusty flashlight off and sped away, knowing we had probably seen the one thing left in the whole giant place that had meant something to the psychiatric patients who lived their lives out here. Traverse Colantha was the world's best cow, and even in death she would always be one of their own.

Mastodon Mystery

Long, long ago in Michigan, strange creatures roamed the land. No, we don't mean Frenchmen. The creatures that roamed ancient Michigan were natives, and they left behind proof of their existence in the form of fossils. Now archaeologists may have found a different kind of evidence for the mastodon—a mysterious carving which may depict the elephant-like animal.

In 2007, marine archaeologists working in Grand Traverse Bay discovered a strange boulder submerged nearly 40 feet underwater. The rock measured just over three feet tall by five feet wide, but the markings on its surface attracted their attention far more than its size or composition. The markings seemed to be a petroglyph, a picture carved in rock, showing a mastodon with a spear in its side.

Mastodons survived until about 10,000 years ago in North America, and fossils of the beasts have turned up in southern Michigan. But none have surfaced in northern Michigan. If the carving really does depict a mastodon, then either mastodons ranged farther north than currently believed or the human who created the petroglyph had come from or traveled to southern regions of the state.

Michigan has a few other examples of genuine ancient rock art—the Sanilac Petroglyphs in the Thumb area, a carved rock near Mackinaw City, and the Burnt Bluff pictographs on the Garden Peninsula in the UP. Does the rock found in Grand Traverse Bay preserve ancient artwork on its surface, or did natural processes create lines that the human mind wants to interpret as pictures? One day the mystery may be resolved, but a greater mystery may not be: Where exactly is the mastodon rock? Archaeologists plan on keeping that secret to themselves, at least for now.

Wakefield

Gogebic County
The Leading Man Sculpture; One of the Silent Watchers

Twisting through Wakefield at the intersections of US Highway 2 and M-28 in Gogebic County, you'll come across a stylized statue of a Native American on the southwest shore of Sunday Lake. There's a visitor center and store with plenty of off-road parking for easy access to the solemn *Nee-Gaw-Nee-Gaw-Bow* or "Leading Man." The imposing figure is one of a multitude of Native American figures sculpted by Hungarian Peter Wolf Toth as memorials to the "Red Man's Trail of Tears." The figures are intended to "watch over the country" to keep such tragedies from recurring.

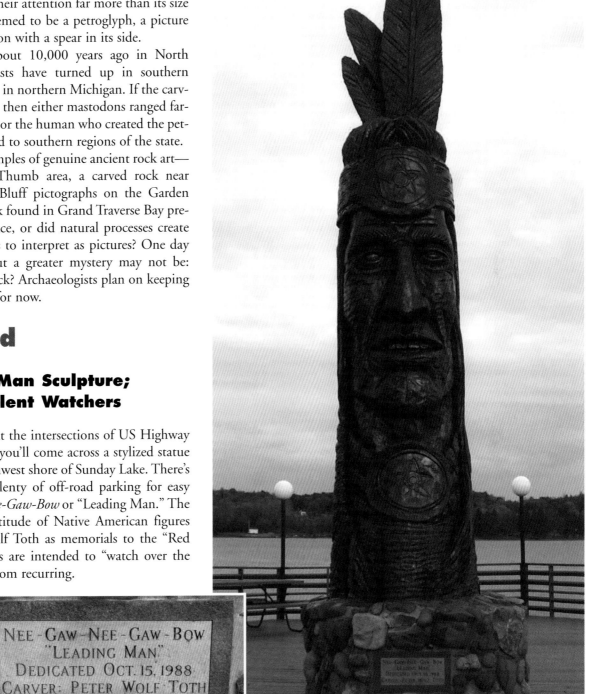

NEE-GAW-NEE-GAW-BOW
"LEADING MAN."
DEDICATED OCT. 15. 1988
CARVER: PETER WOLF TOTH

Walled Lake
Oakland County
A Jet-Pack in Every Driveway?

Back in the 1960s, people fully expected that everyone would be living the life of the Jetsons in the foreseeable future. Robot housemaids, spaceports in every home, and best of all, personal jet-packs! If that hasn't come true, it isn't because Michigan engineers didn't try. The first flight of a man in a "jet flying belt" took place April 7, 1969, in Niagara, New York…using a turbo-fan engine invented by a company from Walled Lake. The Williams Research Corporation came up with the two-foot-long engine that burned kerosene to power the jet belt. Military and rescue missions were the jet belt's primary intended uses. But although the test flight managed to soar about as high as a two-story building and raced at 30 MPH, the jet-powered belt project somehow never made it off the ground.

Williams also created a one-man, rocket-powered vehicle called the "Flying Pulpit," officially the Williams X-jet. It was about the size and shape of a standard speaker's pulpit and the person standing behind it could take off, hover, spin around, and fly at speeds of 60 MPH. An original prototype is on display at the Seattle Museum of Flight.

Perhaps the Williams Research Corporation was just a bit ahead of its time, however. With automatic vacuum cleaners and robotic pets now on the market, can personal rocket vehicles be far behind?

Indeed, the July 2007 issue of *Popular Mechanics* featured two new rocket belts for sale… price range around $200,000.

ranged from being fairly close to one another when viewed moving upgrade at one point (hands just in front of the rump), to an average of 31 inches between the outside of the handprints and 30 inches between the back side of the rump and the fingertips.

The distance between the slash marks and the hands also varied, with measurements of three inches, six inches, and seven inches. Space between the slash marks and rump also varied with one at a distance of just five inches. Interestingly, I measured the distance between each combined set of impressions in the soil at between 22 inches and 58 inches, rump to rump.

Waterford

Oakland County

Entity Unknown: Bighand, Not Bigfoot

In May 1969, while rock hounding in a heavily excavated rural sewer installation site at the west end of Woodhull Lake in Waterford, I encountered an extensive pattern of impressions that suggested the prior presence of some very unusual unknown entity. Handprints, combined with two other sets of unique depressions, were repeated over the course of 200 yards in both coarse gravels and sandy areas of the excavation site. No human footprints could be found anywhere within the excavated area due to the earlier final entry by heavy earth moving machinery used to cover over the completely installed sewer system. All construction had been achieved by the Oakland County Drain Commission to prep for the future residential development of the rural farmland.

Each set of impressions in the soil consisted of both a right and left handprint with each backed up by a compressed, elongated, triangular shape, which I viewed as a slash mark. Following the handprints and slash marks was a third set of impressions that consisted of four elliptical or oval depressions that I perceived as the entity's rump.

Each handprint measured at least eight inches in length while each slash mark was three inches long by one inch wide at the base, which paralleled the base of each hand. The area depressed by the entity's rump covered an area of almost one square foot, with two small ovals centered between and slightly behind two larger oval depressions. The overall area impacted by each set of impressions

Searching for the initial source of the track pattern, I noted that the entity entered the excavation of the hillside from the lakeside grassland. The rump slid partly downgrade before entering the roadcutlike excavation that paralleled the lakeshore in a north-south direction before turning westward toward Waterford, Michigan, while paralleling the Clinton River watershed. There, at the north end of the earth removal and near the mouth of the Clinton River, the entity's trail ceased.

Having preserved the above information on film and in the plaster of paris casts of one set of impressions has only facilitated my continued interest in attempting to discover the source of the tracks over the last 38 years. When I presented the information to a professional anthropologist at a local science center, the expert only noted that the entity was unmarried and suffering from arthritis—the entity had no visible wedding ring and obvious swollen joints. I found a brief mention of a similar case in an article in *Fate* magazine in the early '70s, which mentioned that a farmer in northern Minnesota or Wisconsin had encountered a similar set of impressions. That farmer and I both found evidence of an unknown entity—Bighand, not Bigfoot.

—*Norman A. Thomas, contributor*

Watersmeet
Gogebic County
An Investigation of the Paulding Light

Just over the Wisconsin/UP border near the tiny borough of Watersmeet lies one of Michigan's eeriest and most controversial features: the Paulding Light. While it falls loosely into a category of unexplained phenomena called ghost or spook lights, some people think there is an obvious explanation while others insist that the light behaves in ways too bizarre to understand. *Strange Michigan* presents two different looks at the light, one from seasoned Wisconsin investigator Todd Roll, and the other from an anonymous observer whose experience was passed on to us from a Michigan contributor.

Mundane reflections or otherworldly presence? Readers will have to decide that for themselves…or do a little personal research in Watersmeet some suitably dark evening.

Lights from the (Highway) Beyond

The Paulding or Dog Meadow Light can be seen nightly from Robbins Pond Road just south of Paulding, Michigan. According to the legends, it is either the lantern of a dead railroad worker, the spirits of a murdered couple involved in a love triangle, or the ghost of a mail carrier killed on his rounds. It is claimed the light will grow brighter and dimmer, grow and shrink in size, chase people, and cause electrical disturbances.

In the summer of 1991, a group of friends and I conducted an investigation of the Paulding Light. Before visiting the light we checked rail records to determine if a line had run through the area and found that there was a Chicago and Northwestern line that ran north from Watersmeet to Paulding and then west to a number of spurs. The past presence of a railroad suggested that perhaps the ghost of a worker could be walking the old rail line. Our spirits up, we traveled north to Robbins Pond Road to conduct an investigation. We brought along a tripod and a high-powered telescope to get a good look at the light.

After arriving at the viewpoint on Robbins Pond Road around 7:30 p.m., we quickly determined that the area had more than a three percent grade and a rail line through here was highly unlikely; however, the lights appear at a distance so perhaps a section of the old line could be seen from the view point.

The light appeared before we exited our cars. It moved along a power line cut and appeared to sway back and forth and change color from white to red. The light didn't appear to be moving any closer to us and was visible for about the same length of time before it would disappear.

After setting up the tripod and telescope we waited for the light to appear again. It did and through the scope we could see the headlights and tail lights of cars. At one point we saw a police car pull someone over through the scope. After looking through our telescope, several of the people there to witness the light agreed that it was car head and taillights. However, others there claimed that on different nights the light came much closer; bouncing off the roofs of cars and chasing people down the road. We did not witness this phenomenon during our time there. Other groups of investigators have repeated our experiment with similar results. Some have even found the section of Highway 45 north of Paulding from where the lights originate, going so far as to signal from the highway to those at the viewpoint. Further digging found that the light was not seen until after Highway 45 was moved to its present location. Despite stories that the light appeared well before the first car was invented no literature exists to substantiate this claim. And, if the stories of a $100,000 reward to anyone who can prove what the lights are from *Ripley's Believe It Or Not* are true, I will gladly accept their check.

—*Todd Roll, Wausau Paranormal Research Society, contributor*

"Classified Strange and Unusual"

My name is Lori and I'm 27 years old. My husband is usually very skeptical so when he admitted he saw "something," I had to find out what it was. I definitely classified it as "strange and unusual." We don't see these sorts of things in our area in Illinois.

We were vacationing on a short get-away weekend to northern Wisconsin. Friends who live in Land O'Lakes told us of these lights just over the border into the UP. The more they talked of it, the more I had to see it.

It was about 10:30 p.m. when we made it to Robbins Pond Road. We drove to the second or third hill and sat among 15-20 other vehicles, all with the lights out. I thought to myself, "We're all nuts!" All of a sudden, our friend said, "There it is!" Just above the treeline on the right side of the road, up in the sky was a

little, red, glowing light. It jumped up about ten feet and was gone. My husband was the only one who didn't see it. Then it came back two or three more times. We were trying to figure out the probability of it being the taillight of a car when suddenly it came "alive." It went upward and in small zigzags then exploded into a beautiful, bright white star and came closer to us.

It was unbelievable. We all just sat there with our mouths open. We talked about it all the next day after following Robbins Pond Road to see where the light was coming from—nowhere, was the best explanation. I had no record of the event, as the camera was in its case under my feet but I was too awe-struck to pull it out.

—Lori

Whitefish Point
The Edmund Fitzgerald's Regret

On the job one day in one of the first lighthouses on Lake Superior, keeper Robert Carlson stood counting ships in the harbor when he suddenly saw a vision of his father. He would later learn the vision occurred at the moment his father died in Bayfield.

The old station, where it is claimed lights wink on and off unexpectedly and spirits are sometimes seen, lies just 12 miles north of Paradise, on a stretch known as "Graveyard of the Lakes" for the more than 70 shipwrecks that have occurred off this bit of coastline. The most famous was the *Edmund Fitzgerald*, which sank enroute to Detroit in 1978 and lost 29 crew members to the deep waters of Lake Superior.

The 729-foot freighter was thought to be heading toward the shelter of Whitefish Point, but the lighthouse had gone dark that night after the storm brought down a power line. Today the Whitefish Point Light Station is open May through October along with its attached keepers dwelling as a museum. The old bell from the *Fitzgerald* is displayed in the museum as a memorial for those lost, and is rung 29 times, once for each lost sailor, every year on the anniversary of the shipwreck. So if a few old seamen come ashore to play with a light switch or two here and there, they can be forgiven. The lighthouse, through no fault of its own, literally let them all down that night.

Wolverine
Houghton County
The Stone Boats that Float

Most boats float on the water—at least passengers hope they do! But a trio of boats in the Keweenaw float in a different way. The best-known sails on a cement foundation, while its companion drifts in grass. A third boat has fallen into ruins. What makes these boats special? They're made of cement, mine rock, and sandstone from nearby Jacobsville. The boats, constructed in 1933-1934 by the Works Progress Administration, also have gun turrets, cannons, and other artillery. The little warships, their prows rising from the earth, look ready for battle.

The best-known boat resides in Wolverine, along US Highway 41 north of Calumet. A memorial behind the boat commemorates veterans, and a plaque display tells visitors about the many incarnations of the USS Kearsarge, a series of navy ships all bearing the same name as the town right next to Wolverine. The first USS Kearsarge fought during the Civil War. The ship took its name from Mount Kearsarge in New Hampshire; the Michigan town got its identity from the ship, thanks to an employee of the Calumet & Hecla Mining Company (based in Calumet) who served on the original USS Kearsarge.

All aboard the stone boats!

Stone boat

 ## Ypsilanti
Ghost of the Ladies' Library

Researchers that we are, if *Strange Michigan* suddenly found ourselves turned into ghosts, we'd haunt libraries. Especially if we had donated one to a city. Maryanne Starkweather, generous benefactor of Ypsilanti's Ladies' Library, has shown herself in the building's upper story many times since her death, and many workers claim to have heard her footsteps when no patrons were in the building, as well. It's currently used as a private residence, and we met the building's owner when we stopped by. He admitted feeling a ghostly but ladylike presence in the house from time to time.

The Ypsilanti Ladies' Library

Haunted Academia—
Freshman Ghosts Gone Wild!

Almost every campus roils with urban legends, many of which revolve around ghosts. Theaters, with their heavy curtains, dramatic atmosphere, and hordes of human visitors, are particular favorites for college haunts. Dormitories are probably the major site of young lives turned otherworldly, though, with whiffs of antique cherry tobacco from spectral pipes sometimes mingling with the aroma of microwave popcorn. Again, a mere sampling...

Michigan State University:

Michigan State's Fairchild Auditorium in East Lansing is rumored to be haunted by a young boy wandering around the stage and seats at will. He is accompanied by unidentifiable noises coming from the stage area. *Strange Michigan* spent some quiet, scary moments in the dark theater, waiting for the little boy to make his appearance but he was apparently playing hooky that day.

The school's Holmes Hall is also reported to have an extra "resident" on its sixth floor; a man who is seen entering the elevator, but is never found inside it or anywhere else. Mayo Hall pops with more activity, however, as it is home to the ghost of Mary Mayo for whom the building was named. According to campus legend, the dorm is equipped with a secret fourth floor "Red Room" that once was reserved for the bloody altar of a circle of devil worshippers.

Central Michigan University:

In a town named Mt. Pleasant, a student wouldn't expect to find anything spooky, much less haunted dormitories, on the town's well-known campus. But Warriner Hall residents claim to have seen the ghost of a young woman who was decapitated in an unfortunate accident with the old-fashioned floor-to-floor lift platforms called dumbwaiters. As one story goes, she was about to use the dumbwaiter shaft as a sort of telephone by sticking her head inside to shout upward at a friend on a higher floor when the dumbwaiter came crashing down with a guillotine effect. Other legends say the beheaded one was a careless cleaning lady. Whatever her origin, she makes herself known to students by flashing a blue light, often dropping some nearby object for effect and attention. Ghosts have egos, too!

Northern Michigan University:

An old janitor in the Forrest Roberts Theater on this Marquette campus doesn't threaten, he just likes to make his presence known. After dying of a heart attack there, he has shown his spectral body to numerous witnesses.

Warriner Hall, Mt. Pleasant

Naked Giants and Rustlers in the Sky: the Michigan Airships of 1897

Largely forgotten now, the strange "Airship of 1897" mystified Michiganders and people around the entire country. This was before Roswell, and before the flying saucer mania of the '50s and '60s, so it wasn't as if things from space were on people's minds. But suspiciously enough, the first Michigan airship newspaper reports appeared on April 1, 1897. The *Detroit Evening News* announced that a brilliant white light and "sharp crackling sound" appeared over Galesburg about ten the previous evening. Startled observers reported seeing a huge black object "tipped with flame" in the sky overhead, and one woman thought she heard voices coming from it. The *Grand Traverse Herald* also reported that residents spotted a "beautiful ball of fire" over Holland that same night that was visible for about an hour. Airships had already been seen over California, Nevada, Nebraska, Illinois, and other states as early as November 1896, so perhaps Michiganders were keeping an eye on the sky. The *Chicago Times Herald* wrote with readers' health in mind, "This is becoming alarming. Try bromides."

Things would become much more alarming. People likely consumed mass quantities of bromides to settle their panicky innards as the airship appearances intensified. One wag suggested the sightings were due to a bedbug climbing out onto a witness's eyelash and reflecting the setting sun. But the Saginaw *Courier-Herald* soon reported that the enigmatic sky machine had been spotted over that town and Bay City on April 16, and was observed both accelerating and slowing down. Two policemen spotted it over Saginaw, and claimed it was cigarshaped with a light that "illuminated the whole vessel." It sounded like a snare drum, they said, and had a basket hanging down.

As the sightings continued and the airship occasionally landed, witnesses began describing occupants of the vessel. Most said the "riders in the sky" were one or two men, a mysteriously mute woman, and an older, bearded man. In Missouri, a man claimed he saw a male and female disembark, both completely nude. On April 16, Saginaw's *Courier-Herald* claimed a naked giant stepped out of a landed ship near Howard a few days earlier. The immodest giant was said to stand over nine feet tall, and his speech was more like "bellowing." Supposedly he kicked a farmer who dared to get too close, and that incident dampened the crowd's enthusiasm.

The airshippers often asked locals for water, and ominously stated there were many more airships. There seemed to be a strange and recurring reference to the name "Wilson" in their conversations. Speculation grew. Some thought the whole thing was a blatant publicity stunt by those circus rascals, the Ringling Brothers. Others thought the vessel must be a government warship on its way to help the rebels in Cuba fight for independence from Spain. Still others figured the ship to be the secret effort of a Texas "flying club."

The airship continued to breeze on through Saginaw, Port Huron, Muskegon, and Newago County where it flew directly over a train as if racing it. A man in Maybee said he saw one of the riders take a swig from a "short-necked bottle." Sarsaparilla or moon juice? The *Marshall Daily Chronicle* reported that the airship had made a woman in Findlay, Ohio, go "stark mad." And the *South Haven Sentinel* claimed there were too many witnesses in that city to give all their names. A farmer in Gennessee County said he received a Canadian newspaper, dropped into his field as if from an overhead paperboy, as the airship passed overhead.

The airship reports were not always so innocent. In Kansas, witnesses claimed they saw the airship snatch a three-year-old heifer by dropping a slip noose over its neck and dragging it aboard. The cow's hide was discovered in the next county the following day, identified by its branding stamp. The head and legs were also found…a premonition of today's mysterious cattle mutilations? Hogs were said to have been pignapped from an Illinois farm, and the ship was also accused of filching chickens. And it seems the mysterious occupants were not above some riotous partying to accompany their farm animal barbecues.

On April 30, the *Muskegon Daily Chronicle* said the airship hovered about 200 feet over the town at 11:30 p.m. the night before, brightly lit and filled with noisy "revelers." Unfamiliar yet "entrancing" music emanated from the ship, and townspeople streamed from their homes in their pajamas to watch. They judged the ship to be about "300 feet long, tall about 40 feet, its breadth and depth about 90 feet." The biggest event of the evening came when the ship lowered an enormous grappling hook, snagged an unnamed townsman like some helpless salmon, and hauled him up to the airship to join the merriment. The man came back the next day on the 11:30 train from a neighboring town where he'd been dropped off, babbling nonsense about "aerial navigation."

The final known sighting of the airship over Michigan was April 26 over Sidnaw, reported by Marquette's *The Mining Journal*. But on April 15, a farmer north of Appleton, Wisconsin, found an unsigned letter attached to an iron rod in his field, purporting to be from the fliers of the airship. They explained the vehicle was named the *Pegasus*; it was powered by steam, assembled in Tennessee, and had flown up to 150 miles an hour and 2,500 feet above sea level in its many cross-country test flights. But where was the proof?

Blogger Aaron Sakulich opines that the whole thing was a big hoax. He notes that 10 years before the airships began appearing,

Jules Verne wrote a book, *Robur the Conqueror*, about a man who builds an airship and navigates the world. The concept, then, had already been planted in the public's mind. And newspaper reporters and editors of that day were not above creating sensational stories worthy of today's tabloids that they would print as fact in order to sell product. Also, some of the witnesses later admitted they had been joking, and a few even confessed to sending up kites or balloons with lamps or candles to befuddle their neighbors.

Others have pointed out that hot air balloon flight has been taking place since 1783, arguing that an airship would have been well within the range of technology at the time, and that it's doubtful so many witnesses and newspapers in all those states would have lied. In fact, many patents for airships were applied for in the last half of the nineteenth century.

As for Michigan's airship and its Gilligan-esque crew, they disappeared and were lost to history once the fabulous sightings ended. The "beautiful ball of fire" is still as much a mystery to us as it was to the awestruck Victorians who first laid eyeballs on it.

The Puzzling Ancient Garden Beds of Michigan

"The Prairie People, *Yam-ko-desh*, made them," the Potawatomi of southern Michigan told white settlers who asked about the strange formations that once blanketed this region. The Prairie People were from very long ago, before the Potawatomi came, according to the tribal legends, but their spirits still guarded the huge geometric designs they had once laid out in raised mounds of earth. The settlers should be careful not to destroy the ancient places, they warned. Of course, today not one of the ancient "garden beds" remains. But as late as 1956, at least one Michigan archaeologist was warned about the *Yam-ko-desh* by a Native American he asked to guide him to one of the old mound sites, according to an article that year in *The Detroit News*. Luckily, a few early travelers and surveyors preserved diagrams so that we can know what they looked like. But no one understands for sure why the puzzling formations were built in the first place.

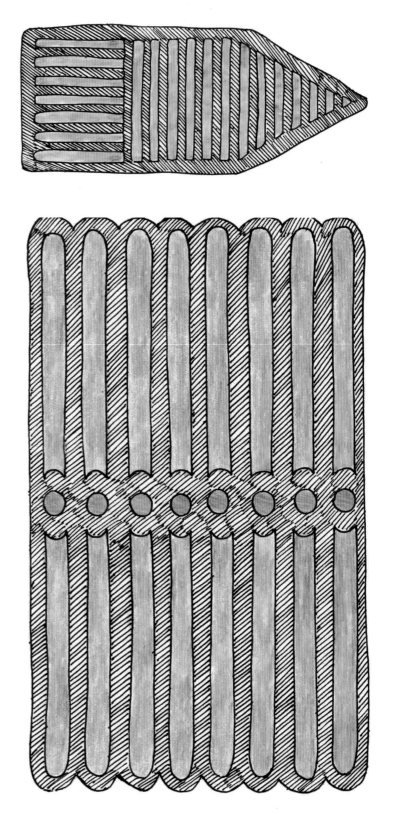

They were dubbed "garden beds" because they looked almost exactly like the formal gardens of the grand old estates of Europe. Laid out in precisely straight or circular paths, most of the designs consisted of berms about 18 inches high, some with deep furrows in between. Some looked like spoked wheels, others resembled modern "log cabin" quilt patterns with rectangles set in opposition to one another. Spread throughout the river valleys of the Grand, the St. Joseph, and the Kalamazoo, some measured hundreds of feet long and wide, and together they covered hundreds of acres. Luckily they had been dug into tough prairie sod, which preserved the outlines of the ancient structures almost perfectly and showed the great precision of measurement involved in their layout and construction.

By counting the rings in trees that had grown up on some of the sites, early archaeologists figured the garden beds were there a minimum of 100 years before the first French voyagers arrived in the 1600s. And they could have been in place much earlier than that. During the time that the mounds were in use, their creators probably kept them free from plant overgrowth so that the outlines would remain sharp.

Exactly who built them, however, has been a matter of great debate for centuries. Scholars have suggested one of the local indigenous tribes such as the Potawatomi, Miami, Mascouten, Sauk, Fox, or Chippewa was responsible. Others argued it could have been a combination of any of the above. However, most now agree that the beds were made by the mysterious, prehistoric Hopewell culture. Presumably, these were the "Prairie People" of Potawatomi legend.

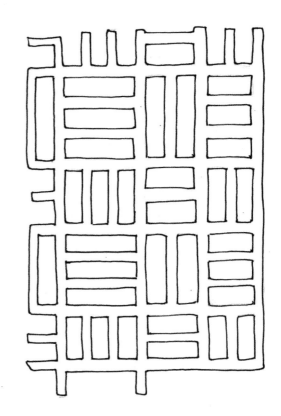

The symmetrical earth mounds made by ancient Indians reminded Europeans of formal gardens

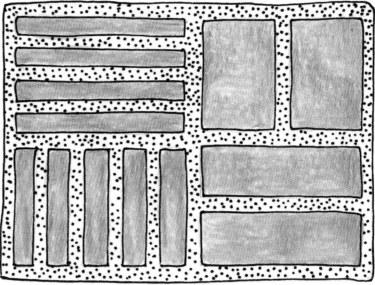

The Hopewell, mainly based in the Ohio River valley (along with an earlier people called the Adena), lived from around 500 BC to 400 AD. And what we know about these groups has evolved along with our own technological tools for dating and interpreting artifacts and remains. For instance, until the 1950s most archaeologists believed they were a very tall race, with men generally standing close to seven feet tall. It is now accepted that most of this prehistoric population was closer to what we would consider average height, however.

It is true, though, that some of the skeletons removed from ancient Michigan mounds and dated back to this period were so large that they probably seemed like giants to the smaller-boned tribes from the east who eventually replaced them as well as to white settlers. In 1870, an ancient "ridge" excavated near Detroit revealed the bones of a man who stood seven and a half feet tall in life. He was accompanied by several beautifully worked white quartz lance heads, each seven inches long and evenly serrated, a copper necklace, and copper needle in the grave, among other items.

Evidently the people who lived in southern Michigan at the time the garden beds were made were gifted craftsmen. Many of their burial mounds were filled with exquisite objects such as hand-carved pipes, wolf masks, polished stone tablets and jewelry, all probably added to the graves as funerary gifts to honor the deceased. The elegant garden beds would have been well within the capacity of such artistically talented people. Some believe that the precise layouts of the garden beds also prove the Hopewell possessed sophisticated mathematical knowledge.

During the 1800s, the beauty and antiquity of many of the Hopewell structures and objects found in Michigan and other states (such as Wisconsin's famed animal effigy mounds) led to the belief that the Hopewell were a "lost race" from some other, seafaring people. Supporting this rather racist argument was the fact that, based on seashells and other exotic grave goods including copper artifacts found in their mounds, the Hopewell evidently traded widely. Michigan copper has also been found in other artifacts from the ancient Old World, begging the question of who the long-ago exporters/importers may have been.

Building on the copper connection, many claimed the Hopewell were actually far-flung Celts, Phoenicians, Vikings, or even refugees from the doomed continent of Atlantis. Another popular idea was that they were a remnant population of Mexican Aztecs who had migrated northward. And one of the most frequently repeated theories was that these early Americans were none other than one or more

of the Lost Tribes of Israel, who were exiled in 722-721 B.C. and supposedly made it to the New World. These notions have now been widely rejected, at least by the vast majority of accredited archaeologists.

But regardless of where the Hopewell people originated, what purpose did their complex, raised structures serve? Because the "ditches" running alongside the raised areas reminded pioneers of irrigation channels, it was first assumed that the beds were used for raising plants. But why go to such painstaking care to plant their crops in elaborate geometric designs when simple rows in large fields would have been so much easier? Besides, other structures called "corn hills" have been proven to be the remains of these peoples' very efficient agricultural sites.

Some ridiculous theories have been proposed for uses of the garden beds. One of the silliest was that the ridges served as "speed bumps" to slow down stampeding herds of buffalo during the annual hunt. It's hard to imagine that any type of formal landscaping would have withstood many seasons of buffalo trampling.

Others think the key to the garden beds lies in the mystic realm. A few researchers have suggested that the Hopewell people were aware of ley lines, the invisible paths that some say mark a grid of geomagnetic energy around the globe, and that perhaps these berm structures had something to do with this perceived power source. Some also have observed that other Hopewell structures, especially earthen circular or horseshoe-shaped mounds and enclosures that were believed to have been used for ceremonial purposes, are aligned along the same latitudes and longitudes, suggesting advanced geographical knowledge. And while opinions still vary, most archaeologists now believe that the garden beds, whether used for plantings or not, were at least related to some type of ceremonial purpose.

Eventually, the Hopewell people either left the area or perhaps were simply absorbed into other Native populations. At any rate, they stopped building mounds and making copper artifacts. Some think that they may have died out from disease or been obliterated by an alliance of the Algonquian-speaking people who wished to live there.

Unfortunately, almost all traces of their beautiful earthworks have been destroyed so that the only way we can study them is from the journals and drawings of early pioneers. And that means we will probably never know why they were made, or where the spirits of those "Prairie People" finally ended up when the last garden bed was plowed under.

Whatzits of the Water

Michigan is unique in that it is made up of two major peninsulas, both surrounded on three sides by the Great Lakes. The interior spaces are also well supplied with rivers and smaller bodies of water. With such a generously watery habitat, it's small wonder that the state has earned a longtime rep for harboring lake monsters.

The Ojibwe who called the peninsulas home long before the French trappers and fur traders first arrived were wary of a marine creature they called *Michipeshu*, the great horned water lynx. This strange being cruised Lake Superior, stealthily roiling the waves and smashing unwary travelers from their canoes with its whiplike tail. *Michipeshu* was a manifestation of the evil spirit, *Matchi Manitou*, who could also appear as a merman or water serpent. The fearful name, *Michipeshu*, was never uttered by the Ojibwe except in winter when ice covered every lake and stream and the people felt safer from its depredations.

Ancient pictographs of both the horned lynx and the water snake are carved into rocks around the shores of Lake Superior. Their original purpose isn't clear, but some think they may mark the spots where these creatures were seen, to serve as a warning. Shamanic ceremonial purposes are also very likely, and some sources say the images are records meant to preserve the old knowledge for future generations. But people who travel the lakes and rivers around Michigan might do well to remember those forms and keep an eye out…just in case *Michipeshu* and the sea serpent still lurk. After all, a six-humped water monster was reported spotted by two women on the Paint River, near Crystal Falls in the Upper Peninsula, in 1922. And according to modern accounts, it has a few cousins around the state. Some say they are just cases of mistaken identity and are only giant sturgeons or oversized catfish. Others remember the legends and always keep one hand on the motorboat engine's throttle.

Giant deer statue, St. Ignace

Many thanks to the investigators, authors and artists who lent their professional talents to this volume of *Strange Michigan*:

Randy L. Braun resides in Madison, Wisconsin, and owns a summer home in Michigan. He's had a diversified career in government and corporate employment. Randy is married to Berniece and they have eight grandchildren.

Nicole Bray, based in the Grand Haven area, is a paranormal researcher and founder and president of the West Michigan Ghost Hunter Society. She is also cohost of WPARANORMAL.com Paranormal Radio talk show.

Jennifer Cupples is an investigator from northern Michigan. She says, "Growing up in Hazel Park, Michigan, an area known as 'Hazel Swamps' began my interest in paranormal experiences. Since then, I have traveled the world and become a backpacker and mountaineer.

Crossing the Continental Divide in Montana, climbing to the top of Mt. Sinai, and exploring the Himalayas in India led me to many adventures and sightings. The Wilderness Paranormal Club is an avocation of my lifetime interest in the strange andunusual. Contact me at 231-539-8886 or e-mail at genafir@voyager.net. A cup of tea is always on. I do intuitive readings, lectures, presentations, and presentations as a storyteller and facilitator."

Nathan Godfrey is an illustrator, painter and filmmaker with a bachelor's degree from the School of the Art Institute, Chicago. His historical and folklore illustrations have appeared in *Strange Wisconsin: More Badger State Weirdness*, on the *History Channel* series *Monster Quest*, and in *Werewolves* and *Lake and Sea Monsters* (Chelsea House). He is the son of author Linda Godfrey.

B.M. Nunnelly, a self-taught writer and artist and a 40-year-old native of western Kentucky, has actively chased down reports of Kentucky enigmas for over 20 years, conducting on site field research and interviewing witnesses to the unexplained. He also claims personal firsthand encounters with a wide variety of Bluegrass mysteries such as Bigfoot, black panthers, aquatic unknowns, Thunderbirds, UFOs, and ghosts. In 2005, he co-founded www.kentuckybigfoot.com, and authored his first screenplay, *The Spottsville Monster, a True Story*. In 2006, he was a contributing writer to Chad Ament's *Cryptozoology and the Investigation of Lesser-known Mystery Animals*. Due out in 2007 is his *Mysterious Kentucky*, a regional study of Kentucky phenomena with co-author Jan Thompson. Upcoming projects include *Bigfoot in KY, Gravediggers and Dogmen*, and the novelization of the Spottsville events of 1975. Contact: artslave_66@hotmail.com

Kristy Robinett is a wife to a very supportive and tolerant husband and a mom to four beautiful children. She works as a spiritual intuitive, life coach, paranormal investigator, author, and radio host of ParaWomenRadio. Visit her at www.tangledwishes.com.

Holmdene Hall, Grand Rapids

Legs Inn, Cross Village

Todd Roll has been on the trail of the weird since he read his first children's book on sea monsters back in 1972. His quest for the unknown has led him to the Rhodope Mountains of Bulgaria, where he jumped from a moving train to avoid the police, to boating across Loch Ness, investigating vampires in Highgate Cemetery, and tracking the wilds of Wisconsin in search of ghosts, ancient cities, and Manwolves. A reference librarian and founding member of the Wausau Paranormal Research Society, Todd has written several articles on ghost stories from around the Badger State, and has been a contributor to *Weird Hauntings*, published by Barnes & Noble. Todd lives in Wisconsin with his beautiful wife, Kat, energetic son Max and his insane border collie mix, Pip.

Michael Schwab has had a fascination with all things that go bump in the night from an early age. He lives in rural Wisconsin, down some twisting, turning roads where he is said to be hiding the Bray Road Beast in a shed out back of his property. Some might say it is synchronicity that he ended up living there; Michael seems to think it was something much weirder. He lives with his lovely wife, Sandra, also an artist, three goblins, and a dog named Igor. He has more than 45 published book covers under his belt, and numerous illustrations and photos published on Web sites and in books. Michael creates his art from colored pencils, scratchboard, pen and ink, and Photoshop, sometimes all at once. Visit his site at www.manyhorses.com.

Joseph Stewart, as a Michigan-based UFOlogist, has been an investigator for the Aerial Phenomena Research Organization (APRO). He has served the Mutual UFO Network (MUFON) as an investigator, state section director, assistant state director, and a special investigator for the Transcription Project (alien abduction research). He is also a cryptozoologist, paranormal researcher and founder of the Ghost Research Center. His organization runs a Web site dedicated to the investigations of the paranormal at www.theparanormalnomad.org.

Cheri L. R. Taylor holds an MFA in writing from Vermont College and is currently working as a Writer in Residence with the Inside Out Literary Arts Project conducting poetry workshops in the Detroit Public Schools. She has four chapbooks of poetry and has been published in *Rattle, Awakenings Review, The Café Review, Reintegration Today, Clean Sheets, Current Magazine, Ellipsis, Third Wednesday* and others. Her newest book, *Wolf Maiden Moon*, was just released from Pudding House Press. Cheri received a 2007 RARE Foundation Everyday Heroes Award. Director of the Blushing Sky Writer's Playground, an organization dedicated to all things creative, Cheri has presented workshops for the Washtenaw County Intermediate School District, University of Detroit Mercy College, the Vermont College of Fine Arts in Writing, and others. Contact: Cherrion@aol.com.

Christmas, Michigan

Alleged haunted building in Gay, Michigan

Troy Therrien holds a bachelor's degree in studio art from the University of Wisconsin-Green Bay. A large part of his undergraduate work was focused on character development under the direction of professor Steve Wadzinski. Troy currently lives in Wisconsin and does illustration, design, and writes and produces his own original music. "It's exciting to develop creatures based on eye-witness accounts...all the while thinking those things could really be out there." Contact: omega_therion@excite.com

Norman A. Thomas has had a lifetime of experience in creative 2D and 3D artistry in metals, clay and wood, and paint and paper, as well as geologic studies and research. In addition, he has a variety of business endeavors which are culminating with a current Web site, http://EarthenArtsGallery.com/, and multiple educational responsibilities ranging from personal to public and university-level coursework.

Index

Antler's Restaurant

Daggett

Holy Cross Cemetery, Grand Rapids

Houghton Ice Festival

Legs Inn, Cross Village

Lakenenland, Marquette

Art by Tim Péwé

"Hobbit house" of Charlevoix

Strange Michigan Art & Photo Credits

VIII lower right, Janet Marcuccio; 10 Seamus Norgaard; 14 John Hager; 17 B.M. Nunnelly; 22 (partial) *Scan This Book*, Art Direction Book Company 2002; 26 *Kalamazoo Gazette* and Comstock Township Library; 28 Jennifer Cupples; 30 upper Ralph Haugen, lower Monica Haugen; 36-37 Menz's Teufel Scrapbook, Labadie Collection, University of Michigan; 42 United States Environmental Protection Agency Great Lakes National Program Office; 44 Don Simonelli; 52 right Rick Griswold; 53-54 Rick Griswold; 55 Georgia Donovan; 57 Rick Griswold; 60-61 left, Mike Molenar collection; 62 Glenn Arntzen; 63 left Donna L. Pulkowski, right Nate Godfrey; 64-65 Timothy J. Péwé collection; 66-67 Walter P. Shiel; 77 Joe Koberstein; 85 Kalkaska Genealogical Society; 89-91 U.S. Air Force; 97 United States Environmental Protection Agency Great Lakes National Program Office; 98-99 left Haunted Theater, Mackinac Island; 99 right United States Environmental Protection Agency Great Lakes National Program Office; 101 left Jerry Bielicki; 104 Walter P. Shiel; 106-107 Walter P. Shiel; 109 Walter P. Shiel; 110 Marquette County Historical Museum; 117 B.M. Nunnelly; 121 Felicia Lanham; 122 United States Environmental Protection Agency Great Lakes National Program Office; 124-125 Northville Historical Society; 130 Don Fritch; 135 bottom Jennifer Cupples; 137 left *Animals*, Dover Publications 1979; 141-142 Ritch Branstrom collection; 143 Troy Therrien; 144 Dawn Wendzel; 155 Robert F. Dorr collection; 156 right Seney Historical Museum; 157 Seney Historical Museum; 167-168 Norman A. Thomas; 184 Michael Schwab.

Lakenenland, Marquette

Holmdene Hall, Grand Rapids